D0971203

ARE WE WINNING?

27 Nov 2010

Maureen & Wayne --
    Go Giants! 2010 World
Series Champions!

ARE WE WINNING?

Fathers and Sons in the
New Golden Age of Baseball

Will Leitch

HYPERION

New York

SUSTAINABLE FORESTRY INITIATIVE   Certified Fiber Sourcing
www.sfiprogram.org

THIS LABEL APPLIES TO TEXT STOCK

We try to produce the most beautiful books possible, and
we are also extremely concerned about the impact of our
manufacturing process on the forests of the world and the
environment as a whole. Accordingly, we've made sure that all
of the paper we use has been certified as coming from forests
that are managed to ensure the protection of the people
and wildlife dependent upon them.

To my dad,
and his dad,
and dads everywhere.

ARE WE WINNING?

Dear Bryan,

It's worth noting that, from the get-go, before we've met, before I even have *any* assurance that you will someday exist, I'm a little concerned that I'm not going to have anything to talk to you about. We are, by nature, by design, at a distance from each other. To everyone else on Earth, I'm just a regular fellow walking around, trying to figure out what's what, trying to make sense of a chaotic, confusing, anarchic planet.

To you, though, I am Dad, an omnipotent, oppressive presence, someone to pattern yourself after, someone to secretly resent, someone to advise you, someone to doggedly resist. Every step you take in life will somehow be guided by me. I apologize in advance. That's just the way it is. I don't make the rules.

It'll be difficult for us to find common ground. We're both guys, and talking is not our strong suit, not to each other: Heart-to-hearts with your father, I'm afraid, are not in the Leitch family DNA. That's not the way it works here. Sorry.

But that's OK, because we'll communicate and bond the way fathers and sons have throughout the generations. We'll talk about baseball.

Baseball's the one language, you see, I know I'll be able to use with you. When everything is blocked, when you want to punch me in the face, when you are suffering but can't say it, when you're joyous but are too embarrassed to show me just how much . . . we'll be able to talk about baseball. It's what I talked about with my dad, what he talked about with his dad, what millions of dads and kids have talked about for a century. I think this is why baseball exists. I think this is why it was given to us.

By the time you see this, baseball will be dramatically different than it is now, just like it's different now than when my father was my age, and so on. But it's the same, really. Ninety feet between each base, three outs, nine innings, no clock. It's important that you want to talk about baseball with me. I'm not sure I'm going to be able to talk about anything else, not for a while. The game is the one constant we're always going to have. You might be able to tell by all the Cardinals wallpaper in your room, I'm sort of counting on it.

In September 2008, your grandfather and I, along with my friend Mike, a recent father himself, went to Wrigley Field in Chicago to watch our beloved St. Louis Cardinals play the hated Chicago Cubs. This book is about that game, and about baseball, and about dads, and about how, deep down, those three sacraments are all pretty much the same thing.

I don't know how good a dad I'm going to be, if you do end up existing. I've lived a selfish life, driven by my own ambitions and fears and insecurities and a whole score of demons and gumdrops that have nothing to do with you. I've been waiting a long time. I'm writing this to see if I can do it.

But mostly: I just want you to know what baseball was like in 2008, and how important it was, and can still be.

Don't worry, though! This won't just be some endless self-indulgent dirge. First: It has to end. It's a book! Second: To make it easier on you, and keep you playing along, I've ended each chapter with notes on Things You Have Learned. Think of this like a workbook, the kind you'll have in school, except with less space to doodle in the margins.

So anyway, let's go on in. Now that I've given you the primer on What This All Means, and Why This Is Important, I'd like you to forget all of it. Because we are solid Leitch men, and we will never discuss it again.

Best,
Your Dad

P.S. In case you are never born, please give this book to your sister.

MORNING

In which your narrator tries
not to slap a three-year-old.

"UNCLE WILL! UNCLE WILL! WAKE UP!"

I'm in a guest room. It's one of those guest rooms that young couples who are expecting large families, but haven't gotten there yet, have for their old friends visiting from out of town who are too cheap to spring for a hotel. Someday there will be a child here. Right now, there's a thirty-two-year-old nursing a hangover. There's a dresser, a mattress, a clock, and some piece of Ikea art on the wall. No one cares much about this room. It's a room to be named later.

I arrived at Mike's early the evening before. He wasn't home from the newspaper yet, so it was me, his wife Joan, the other leg of our college triumvirate, and their son, Jack. Jack is three years old, which means he's just starting to develop a personality that doesn't make his parents want to put him through a wall half the time. The suburban parents don't quite know what to do with their single friend from halfway across the country, so Joan asked if I wanted to accompany her and Jack for a walk.

They live in the Chicago suburb of Lisle, in a clean, safe, empty neighborhood with a collection of early thirtysomethings raising small children, finally taking life seriously, following in the footsteps of their parents, hesitantly. In *A Heartbreaking Work of Staggering Genius*, Dave Eggers writes about how graduates of the University of Illinois, like Mike and Joan, inevitably end up living in Chicago proper before upgrading to the suburbs when grown-up life beckons. "So few make it out of the state," Eggers wrote. "To most, Chicago was Oz, anything beyond it was China, the moon." The University of Illinois has sort of a thirty-year round-trip shuttle bus. You grow up in the Chicago suburbs, you head downstate for four years of college, you come back up to Chicago to live in the city until you become the oldest guy at the bar and/or start having baby fever, and then you move to the suburbs and put your children through the exact same thing. In a weird way, it's kind of a well-rounded life; you've pretty much covered all your bases. This is what Mike and Joan have done. They seem happy with it. I suspect they're right. They sure as hell pay less for their home than I do for my apartment in New York, and they can move around in there without knocking over a shelf too.

Joan pulled Jack behind her in a wagon while I resisted the temptation to light a cigarette. The family park was just a couple of blocks away, as much as this twisting cul-de-sac land had "blocks," and a few children ran screaming past us while their parents watched, more bored than nervous. I noticed that the playground joys of my youth are a lot safer than they once were. The teeter-totter, which was mostly used for sadistic Jump Off So You Can Free Fall The Child On The Other End To The Ground games when I was young, has been kid-proofed. You sit on one end, and your opposite sits diagonal to you. Neither one of you even approaches the ground. The merry-go-round, the contraption responsible for 35 percent of my bodily scars, has a governor to make sure it doesn't go too fast. Joan, humoring my line of inquiry, pointed out that a kid last week still found a way to break his leg on the slide, which might as well have been made of foam. Do what you want, but kids will always find a way to hurt themselves.

On the way back, Jack asked me, whom he'd taken to calling "Uncle Will," to pull him on the wagon. I eyed Joan for approval, and she nodded, glad to have a few minutes off. I pulled him faster than I probably should have, and he screamed in joy. So did I. Back at the house, sweating, I asked Joan if I went too fast. "You can't go fast enough for him," she said. "I wish I had the energy of either one of you."

Jack is a fun kid. Before he went to bed last night, I showed him my iPhone, and an application called "Koi Pond," which provides a serene fake-fish-tank environment where you can touch the screen and splash the fish around. It's meant to be soothing. He enjoyed this for about fifteen seconds before asking "what else?" Like all boys, he preferred the game where you get to shoot zombies.

"What's a zombie?" he asked.

"Well, they're the walking undead," I cheerily replied.

"The walking undead!" He liked the sound of that. So do I. Joan sighed with condescension and then put Jack to bed. Then I stayed up late with Mike and got drunk and remembered a long-past miserable time fondly because what else can you do really?

And now Jack is screaming. "Uncle Will! Uncle Will! Wake up! Can I play with the zombies? Wake up!" The room is hazy, but I'm not ready to wake up yet. *Come on, kid: I didn't start shaking you at 4 A.M. and demanding we get out the wagon again.* My eyes start to come into focus, and I see Jack a few feet away from me, jumping on the bed, yelling "Zombie! Zombie! Uncle Will!"

Then I see what he is wearing. It is a Chicago Cubs T-shirt jersey. It is the jersey of Jim Edmonds. Jim Edmonds had specifically signed with the Cubs that season, for the sole purpose of sticking it in the face of his former team, who had traded him because he'd grown too old. The Cubs had embraced their former rival, and now he had helped lead the team to within one win of the National League Central Division title. That one win could come today. It could come against that former team. The St. Louis Cardinals. *My* St. Louis Cardinals. At Wrigley Field. Today. For the division title. This is why I was in town, after all.

It's all a bit much for 7 A.M. I extend my arm out, grip Jack's head, and lightly toss him off the bed. He lands with a weak thud.

Confused, he pulls himself back up, looks at me, and starts laughing. "Uncle Will! Zombies! Uncle Will!"

I pull the covers back over my head and wait for him to go away.

MIKE IS A MANAGING EDITOR of a suburban Chicago newspaper, which, these days, pretty much means he's in charge of the Web site. We met in college. We were both social introverts studying journalism, obsessed with grunge rock, unattainable women, and baseball. On baseball and grunge, the years have clearly proven me the winner. My Cardinals have won a World Series while his Cubs have floundered and broken hearts; I doubt even Eddie Vedder would claim that Mike's Pearl Jam was ever a better band than my Nirvana. As for women, he married Joan, whom I had halfheartedly dated before he swooped in and saved both their lives. He had a son, lives near his parents, and covers city politics and crime. I moved a thousand miles away and started a sports blog that made fun of professional athletes for having their pictures taken while drinking with college students. He's a month older than me, but lives in a universe decades older, where he wipes up spittle, worries about his 401(k), and takes his child to playgrounds that have met city safety specifications.

He's pouring coffee and trying to feed Jack, who's still babbling about zombies. The kitchen is in a quiet suburban enclave but is louder than the most chaotic New York City block. Electronics whirring, kid screaming, the television blaring—everything seems teetering on the precipice of combustion. His face, slack, betrays none of this. He pours the coffee with one hand and spoons some orange gloop into his son's mouth. Neither endeavor is proving particularly successful, but he doesn't seem to notice.

A friend of mine in Brooklyn, Jason, is older than me, with an eight-year-old son. Jason loves the Mets and is desperate for his son to share his obsession. His son has learned this, and discovered that if there's a product with the Mets logo on it, his father will buy it for him. Jack might not understand this key parental manipulation tactic, but he will soon: His room is covered with Cubs memorabilia, from Cubs bibs to Cubs onesies to Cubs teddy bears to Cubs sippy cups. I have tried to explain to Mike that he is poisoning his son's mind, that he is subscribing him to a life of misery, but Mike never listens. On his own bedroom wall, he has a picture of Vedder (a Cubs fan) playing catch with former Cubs first baseman Mark Grace. I'm always surprised Joan lets that stay up there.

"Who's pitching today again?" Mike says. I am surprised by the question. The Cubs have had one of the most dominant seasons in their history. It is the one hundredth anniversary of the Cubs' last World Series title, and the whole season, pretty much from Opening Day on, has felt like a coronation. There was never any doubt that the Cubs were the best team in the National League. The fuzzy Cubbies, the lovable losers—this year, they were dominant. Every day was a celebration for the Cubs in 2008. Guys like Mike had been waiting for a season like this since they were babies. It was perfect. One hundred years. World Championship. 2008. Billy Goat. Bartman. All that nonsense, *gone,* with one season. That's the plan. This is the year. I imagined Mike was spending every waking moment immersed in all Cubs minutiae. After all, I was doing the same thing for the Cardinals, and we weren't even contenders anymore, not after a dreadful stretch in late August and early September. That hadn't slowed me down. Watching and thinking about the Cardinals was better than watching and thinking about life. I assumed Mike was the same way. And he didn't know who was starting?

"Ted Lilly," I say, masking annoyance. "Cardinals can't hit left-handers. So you should be good."

Jack is finally working on the orange gloop, and Mike's sipping his coffee and flipping aimlessly through the paper. He turns to Jack. "The Cubbies are going to win their division today," he says. "Do you know what that means?"

"Zombies!" Jack says.

Mike smiles. "It means we're going to beat Uncle Will's Cardinals. Daddy's going to the game with Uncle Will. We don't like the Cardinals, do we?" Jack giggles while the goop drips onto the table, and Mike dabs it up without missing a beat. I look down and stare at the koi pond fish on my phone. They really are quite soothing.

My phone rings. A picture pops up on my phone, the same one that pops up every time the 217 area code number dials in. It's of a middle-aged man, wearing Oakley sunglasses, drinking a Natural Light, sporting a dirty gray tanktop. He's sitting behind the wheel of a truck. The picture makes him look like he's driving down a private road that only he's allowed to be on. It's iconic. It should be in the Smithsonian.

This is the picture:

"I'm in Rantoul." My father has a gruff, abrupt, you're-lucky-I'm-talking-*this*-much voice. He talks like he's under a court order; he'll talk, sure, but he doesn't have to like it.

"I'll be at Union Station in an hour-and-a-half," I tell him. "I'll be the guy wearing a Cardinals jersey who kind of looks like you." He hangs up before I hear his response.

Mike turns to Jack. "That was Will's dad on the phone," he says. "He's going to the game today. He likes the Cardinals too. So Will's dad is very sad."

I interrupt. "My dad is a zombie, Jack. A Cardinals zombie."

Jack screams again, spewing gloop everywhere. This tickles him, and he keeps spitting it in all directions. Mike lets him know this is unacceptable and wipes it up.

"You know how to get to the train station?" he asks. I nod. "You know," he says, "I wouldn't wear that jersey. You're in Chicago." I am wearing a Rick Ankiel 66 jersey. It is my most prized possession.

"I have GPS," I tell him. "And I think the jersey will be just fine. Won't it, Jack?"

"Zombies!" The walking undead.

WEARING A CARDINALS JERSEY does not get me accosted by Cubs fans. It gets me accosted by panhandlers. I have to admire the strategy of the Chicago Union Station panhandlers. The best of them is pulling a suitcase behind him, talking into a cellphone, saying things like "This'll never work, man. I'm stuck here. Why would some stranger help me out? *I* wouldn't help me out. Shit!" before telling whoever's next to him, "Man, I lost my wallet, and I just need twelve bucks to get home." The suitcase and cellphone seem to be working for him. He spotted my Ankiel jersey and tried it with me, and I probably would have fallen for it had I not seen him run the con on half the station.

The robot lady voice informs me that Train 58, the *City of New Orleans,* has arrived. I didn't need the help. I could have heard my dad from the parking garage.

He is surrounded by four people, a family, it seems, carting an unnatural amount of luggage. Each of them is dragging two suitcases behind them, and Dad's carrying three bags; I have no idea how they would have handled everything had they not run into him. But of course they did. Dad talks to everybody. I can't tell what he's talking about, but the family is laughing so hard the mother drops one of the suitcases. He's wearing a white Cardinals jersey that has maybe one button attached; maybe they're talking about his navel, since they can see it. Amazingly, he is also swigging what I am sure is a stiff Bloody Mary from a plastic thermos. I had no idea my father had so many hands. It is a cluster of activity—warm, chaotic, random. It is pure Bryan Leitch.

"Yo!" he says when he sees me. He is wearing sunglasses. "Go Birds!" He gives me a high five.

Mike has taken the Metra to the station. He's just around the corner. We're in parking garage five. Dad's Bloody Mary is eating through the plastic. Dad says good-bye to his friends. I bet they tell everyone they meet in Chicago about the very nice man they met on the train. The big city's a crazy place.

MY FATHER TURNS SIXTY years old this year, and save for trips to visit his children on opposite coasts and his time in the military, he has rarely left his home state of Illinois, or his hometown of Mattoon. He is not a simple man, but he is a basic one: He cares about his family, his job, his dogs, and his St. Louis Cardinals, not necessarily in that order. And despite living just two hundred miles south on Highway 57, he has never visited Wrigley Field. His answer has a fierce ideological purity: "That place is crawling with Cubs fans. Why would I want to go there?"

I am the one who talked him into this. "Come on, Dad, it'll be fun," I said. "Cardinals-Cubs! Wrigley Field! I'll even buy the tickets." How was I supposed to know this would be the game where the Cubs might clinch the division? That he'd be arriving at Wrigley Field just in time for a party to celebrate the destruction of all he believes in, all he values, all that matters? Am I overstating this? I fear that I am not.

He looks nervous. Dad doesn't like traffic. I look nervous too. I don't like my dad in traffic. Not Mike, though. He's not a surburban dad anymore. He's three years old. He's looking out the window, a goofy kid eager to go outside and roll around in the grass.

We pull into the parking garage. Thirty goddamned dollars. Freaking Wrigley. We are here.

"So, who needs a beer?" my dad says. Me. Me. I need one.

KNOWLEDGE YOU NOW HAVE

1. Back in 2008, there was something called an "iPhone," and it was considered the height of modern technology. Unlike what's wrapped around your wrist right now, it was unable to beam you to China when you typed in a personalized PIN code.

2. A Bloody Mary will remain cold in a thermos throughout a four-hour train ride.

3. The reason your father is so much older than your friends' parents is that he found himself much more interesting in his early thirties than he really was.

PREGAME

In which your narrator
uses a urinal trough.

IN JULY 1993, MICHAEL JORDAN, WHO HAD JUST WON HIS THIRD
NBA championship with the Chicago Bulls and had solidified himself as the most famous athlete on the planet, had a conversation
with Bulls owner Jerry Reinsdorf. They were at a White Sox game,
and Reinsdorf, who also owned the Sox, was surprised by a request
from His Airness: Jordan wanted to know if he could play a few
minor-league games for the team's Kannapolis, North Carolina, affiliate, a Class A team.

Now, you see this every so often, celebrities who have excelled
in other fields deciding that the one thing they *really* wanted to buy
with their fame, the one thing they truly wanted to do as a kid but
just weren't allowed to do, was to play professional baseball. Garth
Brooks has an annual midlife crisis and shows up to take some
swings at the spring training of whatever team might need some
positive publicity. Billy Crystal—whose obsession with the late fifties/
early sixties New York Yankees provided him with boomer cred he
probably wouldn't have earned otherwise—actually batted against
Pittsburgh's Paul Maholm in spring training a couple of years ago,
and, all told, it *was* kind of impressive that he hit a foul ball. If I had
a billion dollars and worldwide fame, I'd do the same thing.

But this was different. This was Michael Jordan, Air Jordan,
the most exciting, most amazing, most marketable athlete of his

generation, asking his team's owner if he could take a few swings with a minor-league team, just for fun. It was just a casual conversation; Reinsdorf told Jordan he'd find out what he could do for him, and everyone went along his respective way. Except, in Reinsdorf's telling, the conversation later took on an awful subtext: At that moment in July 1993, as they spoke, Jordan's father, James Jordan, was being murdered by two carjackers in Lumberton, North Carolina. Michael would learn about his father's death that evening. Three months later, he would retire from basketball, and seven months later, he announced he was going to be a baseball player, signing up with the Birmingham Barons, the White Sox's AA affiliate. It would be Jordan, future Red Sox manager Terry Francona, and twenty-four twentysomethings, whose net worth neared what Jordan would drop on one hole of golf, riding around the country in a bus. "This is something my father always wanted me to do," he told a jaw-dropped gaggle of reporters. "He actually advised me to try it two years ago."

It's worth noting that the Reinsdorf story is highly suspect. The central fact doesn't check out: Reinsdorf, who gave that anecdote in an interview with MLB.com on the fifteenth anniversary of Jordan's brief foray into baseball, clearly isn't remembering everything correctly. The Kannapolis Intimidators didn't actually exist until 2001; the franchise itself wasn't founded until 1995, when they were the Piedmont Boll Weevils and an affiliate of the Philadelphia Phillies. (The White Sox made them their farm team, and changed their name and location, before the 2001 season.) But that's beside the point: In Jordan's mind, basketball was something he was uniquely gifted at and preternaturally intelligent about dominating. But it was a job. His heart was always in baseball. Because that's where his dad's was.

The beauty of this, and the reason Jordan's quest was as admirable and perfect as it was quixotic, is that Jordan was horrible. Here, it's worth noting that "horrible" is relative. Jordan hit three homers, stole 30 bases, drove in 51 runs and struck out 114 times in 127 games. His batting average was a nasty .202, and one of his teammates, a jerk who hopefully never made the big leagues himself, snarked that Jordan couldn't have hit a curveball with an "ironing board." And obviously a world that was used to seeing Jordan dominating everything in sight wasn't ready to see him flailing at sliders in the dirt—he faced the first real criticism of his career. (*Sports Illustrated* put Jordan on its cover with the line "Bag It, Michael," inspiring a grudge from Jordan that lasts to this day. The reporter of the piece, who didn't write the cover line, was Steve Wulf, who once told me that after he left the magazine, the *SI* brass called Jordan's representatives and pleaded for him to reconsider, "now that Wulf was gone." No dice.) But again: It's relative. I'd like to see Garth Brooks or Billy Crystal steal thirty bases.

Jordan plugged ahead, and if the baseball strike hadn't have been looming the next season—Jordan, who had been a union representative in the NBA, promised he'd honor any strike by the baseball union, though he certainly would have helped goose attendance as a replacement player—he might have kept going, following through on his dream. I remember being a little disappointed that he gave up; it was kind of an honor that one of the world's most famous people was secretly obsessed with the same sport I was. (It was like learning that you and the President share the same favorite film.) There would have been something lasting, epic, about the world's greatest basketball player walking away from the game he ruled to ride around the country, hearing the crack of the bat, still trying to solve the breaking ball. That sounds like a happy life to me.

That's not what happened, of course. Jordan came back to basketball, won three more titles, and retired again. (Let's all be generous and ignore what happened in Washington.) It all worked out fine. But history has pronounced Jordan's baseball sojourn as a failure, an embarrassment. This is a shame. I think Jordan's baseball career is the most recognizable, profound trait in a guy who, in the end, was so consumed by megalomania and feigned immortality that he was more a brand name than a recognizable human being. Baseball was the sport that reminded him of his father. It was the sport they both cared about the most. In this context, it's almost cruel that he could dunk better than he could hit a curveball. I bet he would have been happier if he had been playing baseball. I know his dad would have been.

I REMEMBER the first time my father looked old to me. I mean, he always looked "old"; he was my father, I was a kid, and as far as I knew he had been on Earth forever, like Richard Alpert in *Lost*, forever roaming the Earth and absorbing wisdom, gathering different strategies and techniques to inform me I was doing something wrong. I was eleven years old, and we were walking from the old Clarion Hotel—the one with the revolving restaurant that made me feel like I was in outer space—to the old Busch Stadium before a Cardinals game.

I was just growing old enough to start realizing my own limitations, which is the first step toward dying, I think. I was telling my father that I wanted to be a baseball broadcaster, like my hero Jack Buck. My dad laughed at me.

"Most kids want to be professional baseball players. You want to *talk* about people playing baseball?"

As a youth league baseball player, I was an above average catcher but too small to bat higher than eighth in the order, and my arm was too weak to throw out any base runner able to avoid falling down. If I were to become the quality of baseball player able to make it to the big leagues, I'd certainly need to be the best player in Mattoon, Illinois, and I was a far cry from that. This seemed obvious to me, and I was surprised it didn't seem obvious to my dad.

"Dad, let's face it," I said, trying to sound knowing and world-wise, like the adults talked when they were in the other room drinking margaritas while we kids were playing Nintendo and pretending we couldn't hear them. "I'm never going to be a major leaguer. It's just realistic."

Dad had been an above average baseball player as a kid and had even played for some of the same coaches who were currently coaching me. He was better in his day than I was, but not by a lot. Every dad thinks his kid is going pro, because he didn't.

After my "realistic" soliloquy, my father, then just 37 years old, a little older than I am now, looked a lot like Grandpa right then: tired, slower, a little vacant.

We didn't say anything else until we reached the stadium, and now that I think about it, it seems like we played a lot less catch after that, a lot less than we used to.

ACROSS THE STREET from Wrigley Field, at a bar called Vine's on Clark ("Magnificent! One word describes every sensation you will feel upon entering our restaurant! Magnificent!" the establishment's Web site begrudgingly admits), my father, Mike, and I are discussing the inherent inferiority of the Chicago Cubs to the St. Louis Cardinals. Actually, my father and I are discussing it, while Mike limply attempts to *debate* it.

The word I've always used to describe Cubs fans is *cute*. I do this in the most dismissive, mean way possible, equating Cubs fans' optimism that their team will finally win that World Series with a three-year-old child who believes his teddy bear really does listen to him, and understands. *Aw, that's cute. You really think you have a chance. Adorable.*

Circumstances would imply that this would have become increasingly difficult in recent years; the Cubs have transmogrified from the reliable doormats of the National League into a powerhouse with whom all must reckon. There's a reason, after all, we're sitting outside Wrigley Field waiting to see if they can clinch the division rather than us. Worse, they've actually done it while remaining somewhat likable. Manager Lou Piniella is alternately one of baseball's vivid originals and a staple straight from the *Saturday Evening Post,* the irascible, sardonic ancient mariner who's seen it all, kid. Derrek Lee is a stoic, likable veteran; Ryan Theriot is the metaphorical collector of scrap every team needs; and starter Ryan Dempster is the kind of wacked-out goofball that baseball consistently provides. (He once claimed his late-career resurgence was because he was a ninja. "You have to [learn] how to throw a throwing star and nunchucks and all those kinds of things. Obviously you've got to do martial arts and learn how to be really quiet, which is a tough task for me because I talk a lot. It's pretty cool. I wear the outfit around the house and try to sneak up on people.")

Truth be told, though, it's no more difficult to make fun of Cubs fans this year than any other year, because they are, and shall eternally be, the Cubs. The notion of the Cubs actually winning the World Series—which might be the only achievement in sports that would earn instant nonstop front-page coverage across the globe, from *Time* to the *Taipei Times,* assuming magazines and newspapers will still exist when that happens—is beyond normal human (and presumably Vulcan) capacity for logical thought. A world in which the Cubs are world champions is a world that cannot be understood. It is a world that can never exist.

You see, most people probably think of the Cubs as lovable losers who just can't ever push the rock up the hill. But to us Cardinals fans, their ineptitude is a sign that the universe remains in its natural order. The Cubs reaching the World Series would be the equivalent of the mountains crumbling and the earth opening up and swallowing us whole: It would be obvious that the end was nigh.

There was a time where our galaxy was in peril. It wasn't that long ago. It is my favorite Cubs memory.

October 2003. I was at my apartment in the Inwood neighborhood of Manhattan, listening to Game Six of the National League

Championship Series between the Cubs and the Florida Marlins on the radio, because I was an idiot for moving to New York and didn't have cable. The Cubs were up 3–0. Bottom of the seventh. Six outs away from the End of Days. My phone rang. It was my father. I knew what he wanted.

"Jesus, it looks like they're really going to do this."

"I know."

"I don't really know what to do with myself now. I don't know if I'm ready to live in a world where the Cubs have made the World Series."

"I know."

There was real, palpable terror. We sat silent, my father's breath hanging there. I thought of noble deaths, the storied warrior finding one last moment of grace and honor in his last moments on earth. How could I go? What would be fitting? How could I be William Wallace?

"Dad?"

"Yeah?"

"I've been listening to the game on the radio. But you know what? I think I should go to the bar downstairs and watch the end. I mean, I've hated them for so long, I feel like their history is kind of my history. In a weird way, I feel like I owe it to them. I should watch them do this. They've earned it, I think."

Dad's breath continued. Was that disappointment? Resignation? Respect? Wait . . . He is still breathing, right?

"You go ahead. I'm going to bed."

I put on some pants and went to the bar downstairs. The top of the eighth began. I ordered a cool, icy Budweiser, brewed in St. Louis, Missouri, and settled in, resigned to my fate: Salute the enemy, pray Earth does not career off its axis. I wasn't ready; I hadn't accepted what was happening.

Then Steve Bartman happened. We'll talk more about him later.

But that's my favorite Cubs fan memory. I will never doubt the fates again.

It is to Mike's credit that he takes all this in stride; he pretty much always has, because I am louder than he is and more obnoxious. He is mild-mannered, sober-minded, a Serious Journalist who has patience that I do not. He has the patience and serenity of someone who has cared deeply about the Chicago Cubs his entire life: He's hopeful but knows better, has learned that once it all goes down, no matter what, they're still playing baseball out there, and watching that is better than doing just about anything else. And hey, if the Cubs somehow pull it off one year and blow up Earth . . . he can say he earned it. And smile for about a hundred years.

"More places to drink here than outside Busch, right, Mr. Leitch?" Mike will never stop referring to my father as if he is his science teacher.

He's right about this, of course; the preponderance of bars outside Wrigley Field has helped contribute to Cubs fans' reputation as people who are there more for the beer than the baseball. (As if the two are mutually exclusive.) Outside Busch Stadium, there is a big hole in the ground that was supposed to feature countless local business, hankering to suckle from the St. Louis' Company Town Team's teat: It remains, four years after the stadium opened, a hole in the ground. There are a few bars in the area, but they're not places you'd ever dare step foot in any time of the year other than the few hours before and after a game. Busch may have a superior franchise with a winning history and (insert official Saint Louis Cardinals Baseball Corporation trademark here!) The Best Fans In Baseball. But it isn't in the middle of rows of upwardly mobile white people. Wrigley is.

"Bah," my dad says, sucking down his third Bud Light in about an hour. "The Bud always tastes better in St. Louis. They brew it there. I think they brew it in the outfield. That's why we don't have any of that weird ivy shit on our walls. The beer kills it. Thank God."

The main topic of our conversation was the one hundredth year of Chicago Cubs baseball since they last won the World Series. They beat the Detroit Tigers in five games back in 1908, in a Series best known for something called Merkle's Boner, the name given to the play in which a poor soul named Fred Merkle cost his New York Giants the pennant (which the Cubs won) by not touching second base after a single that brought in the winning run. Historians have attempted to vindicate Merkle for years, to little avail, mostly because "Boner" is a much funnier word today than it was a hundred years ago.

The Cubs, led by player/manager Frank Chance, walked off Bennett Field in Detroit on October 14, 1908, world champions. 1908 is an absurd number of years ago. It was the last time that would ever happen. Until this year. This was clearly supposed to be the year.

It has felt like the Cubs' year since Spring Training. The rest of the National League Central was clearly inferior: The Reds and the Pirates were toast by May; the Astros' late run was falling short; the Brewers' acquisition of CC Sabathia was only bringing them close enough to fight for the wild card with the Mets; and our beloved Cardinals, after some inspiring early season ball, were running out of steam. The Cubs, however, just motored through everybody, en route to the second-best record in baseball. They would end up winning ninety-seven games, their most since 1945, when they last reached the World Series. This was their year. It was in the air. It was everywhere you looked.

What was strange about this was that the sense of doom I would have expected was nowhere to be found. Cubs fans are not like Red Sox fans were before 2004, seeing tragedy around every corner, hiding under the bed until the boogeyman goes away, unable to truly invest in the communal joy a winning baseball team can provide. Cubs fans are unique in their ability to expect the worst but embrace possibility. This is almost inhuman. Eventually, after a hundred years of repeatedly slamming his genitals in a car door, a normal person will zip up and take the bus.

This year was unique in that not only were Cubs fans optimistic, they were serene, calm, Zen-like, as if they were watching a film of which they already knew the ending. This was the one hundredth year since the last World Series win, the Cubs had one of the best teams in their history, they had Old Salt in the dugout. The stars were aligning. *Obviously* this was happening. It was merely a matter of absorbing everything going on around you while you watched it. Mike explains it as "simply being a witness to history," and I think he's fucking insane.

"You are asking to be smote down by the gods," I tell him, puffing on a cigarette and settling up our bill. "You are sitting there telling me that you just *know* your team is going to win the World Series. That it's your 'time.' The Cubs! You are begging to be kicked in the face. And you will deserve it!"

Mike smiles and takes a drag from my cigarette, something his wife is going to be angry to read right here. "Sometimes you just know," he says, coughing. "Every single person here knows it. Look at everybody. It just feels right. We knew it had to happen sometime. Of course it would happen this year, the one hundredth year. How could it not?"

Mike does not say this smugly, or tauntingly, or even with much gusto. He says it like Biff came back from the future and gave him the *Sports Almanac* from 2015. He does not look cocky. He looks re- lieved. It's unnerving. It makes me fear he's right.

Dad has no such fear. "You've gotta be shitting me." He looks at me. "He's gotta be shitting us, right?"

He has to be. Of course, the team that's playing in there today to clinch the division isn't us. It's them. And it's time for us to go watch it.

––––––––

NO ONE remembers this—and why would they—but Wrigley Field was not built for the Cubs. A man named Charles Weeghman owned the Chicago Whales (known, in the hip parlance of the time, as the Chi-Feds) of the Federal League, which Weeghman had helped found. The team won the final Federal League title in 1915, behind manager Joe Tinker, and then, after an antitrust suit filed by the Federal League against the American and National Leagues failed, the league folded. Weeghman bought the Cubs—"serving to partly complete the conditions of the treaty of peace signed here," breathlessly wrote the *New York Times* the next day—and named the stadium "Weeghman Field." William Wrigley took the place over in 1919 and called it Cubs Park until 1926, when he pulled a Weegham and named it after himself.

The great Bill Veeck planted the ivy on the walls and, amusingly, once tried to plant elm trees in the bleachers. The building felt as old as it really was until 1988, when they installed lights, the last major-league park to do so. One of the main reasons? Major League Baseball, because of their postseason television contracts, threatened to make the Cubs move potential playoff games to Busch Stadium if they didn't install the lights. This would have been something to see.

Wrigley Field is, quite a coincidence, in the middle of the Wrigleyville area of Chicago, which, as this alum of the University of Illinois can tell you, is where recent college grads in the Land of Lincoln move right after they graduate, so that they may drink beer and have a series of initially thrilling sexual experiences that provide diminishing returns but are still worth the trouble.

This to me has always been one of Wrigley's charms: Like no other stadium, it's in the middle of a thriving, vibrant neighborhood. (Or at least a neighborhood full of affluent, spoiled young white people, which is what "thriving, vibrant" is often secret code for.) It, like other stadiums of its time, was built around, and with respect for, where people live and eat and sleep and shit and dream and die every day. Its builders didn't raze the place, creating empty lots next door and a parking garage where the old Johnson chop shop used to be. The stadium, like everything else, had to fit in. It worked around us. Instead of the other way around. That's why Wrigley and Fenway Park look so different than every other stadium. Not just because they're old, but because they were built during a time when a baseball team and its stadium were just another part of the latticework . . . not the whole damn town. The charm of Wrigley's nooks and crannies is what lay outside their walls, why they had to exist in the first place. Not much in our country exists from a time when we were all in this together, when we all thought one way and figured that was the only way to be. I'm glad it's not like that anymore. But I'm glad Wrigley is around to prove it actually once was.

This is what I'm thinking, anyway, while urinating about fifteen feet from my father, who, lemme tell you, is absolutely *fascinated* by Wrigley's bathroom troughs. It's difficult to find a place in America that hasn't switched over to the modern convenience of personalized toilets, so, hey, thanks, Wrigley. As I wash my hands— and my dad breezily coasts straight from the trough to the exit—my father calls out behind him, "I ain't seen that many peckers since Langley."

My father is not wide-eyed at finally visiting one of America's historic landmarks. He's got a ball game to watch.

Because one person can only buy two beers at a time at Wrigley, we stagger our way to our seats, in Section 131, about thirty rows behind the Cardinals dugout. I bought the tickets through StubHub months earlier, thinking the Cardinals and Cubs might be battling it out for a playoff spot. I should have waited a few months for the world's economy to collapse: They cost me about $250 apiece. Had I known, I probably could have bought them for canned goods, gold teeth, and automatic weapons. Alas.

Mike, who has been going to Wrigley since he was his son's age, comments that these are probably the best seats he's ever had, which says something about the problems with procuring great seats at Wrigley, even during the lean years.

He also decides it's time to tell me a story that will "make you appreciate how special this is for the Cubs."

"They've invited Leo. Finally." Leo is Leo Hildebrand, and he is 104 years old, which makes him one of the few human beings unfortunate enough to have lived so long that he saw the Cubs' last World Series title. He is a lifelong Cubs fan and was ecstatic to watch this 2008 Cubs team, which, if Mike's Stepford Wife–like confidence is to be believed, every damned Cubs fan is convinced is The One. The *Chicago Sun-Times* ran a story on Hildebrand's family's attempts to talk the Cubs into letting him throw out the first pitch before one of the key September games. As his sixty-nine-year-old daughter put it: "He can't wait much longer." I don't want to be out of bounds here, but I hope that's not something my daughter someday says about me. I want Future Daughter to say, "Dad's indestructible. I fully expect him to live another one hundred and forty-eight years."

The Cubs were initially hesitant—a tone-deaf Cubs spokesperson told the paper, "Due to the large number of requests and suggestions, and given the limited opportunities, it's difficult to accommodate everyone"—but once the story hit the paper, they could fight public opinion no longer. Thus: Trotting out to the pitcher's mound, as the team attempts to clinch its second consecutive National League Central title, wearing a Cubs jersey with "104" on the back, is Leo Hildebrand.

"That's him," Mike says.

"Oh, really?" I say. "I could have sworn that was Derrek Lee."

Mike is beaming. "This is what Cubs baseball is all about," he says. "Understanding that fans are what's important. It's why the whole Cubs Lovable Loser thing is just an outsider's thing. Here we appreciate our fans." Dad's belch is perfectly timed.

Leo "throws" his pitch, to a Cubs batboy standing about five feet away from him, and exits the field to a smattering of oddly limp applause. The crowd goes silent as the public address announcer cranks up. Wrigley Field does not feel particularly quaint or ancient when decibels are attacking your hair.

"Now, Cubs fans, if you'll direct your attention to the Cubs dugout . . . a hometown boy from Lake Forest, he's become one of Hollywood's biggest stars thanks to films like *Swingers, Wedding Crashers,* and *The Break-Up* . . . and he's one of the biggest Cubs fans around! Here to throw out today's first pitch and sing Harry's song at the seventh inning stretch . . . Mr.! Vince! Vaughn!"

The crowd explodes. I look at Mike and don't say a word.

YOUR LINEUPS TODAY:

ST. LOUIS CARDINALS	CHICAGO CUBS
SS Cesar Izturis	LF Alfonso Soriano
CF Ryan Ludwick	SS Ryan Theriot
1B Albert Pujols	1B Derrek Lee
2B Felipe Lopez	3B Aramis Ramirez
3B Troy Glaus	CF Jim Edmonds
RF Adam Kennedy	C Geovany Soto
LF Brian Barton	2B Mark DeRosa
P Joel Pineiro	RF Kosuke Fukudome
C Jason LaRue	P Ted Lilly

VINCE'S THROW goes farther than Leo's did but, honestly, not by much.

WE STAND FOR the national anthem. I'm sure they also play the national anthem before basketball, football, and hockey games, but I don't remember a single version. I always remember the national

anthem before baseball games. Maybe it's the whole national pastime thing, maybe it's all the moments in baseball lore that seem
inextricably linked to key points in our nation's history, maybe it's
just that you're supposed to take off your cap. It somehow means
more in baseball.

Someone named Rocco DeLuca has the singing honors, and
though everyone agrees it's one of the worst versions of "The Star-
Spangled Banner" we've ever heard—this man sings like someone
is chasing him—everyone applauds anyway, because that's what you
do at the end of "The Star-Spangled Banner" as long as Roseanne
isn't grabbing her crotch and spitting at you.

The Cubs sprint onto the field, and they're being chased by
women in their mid-fifties. Each player takes his position as each
woman stands next to him, looking proud and nervous and pleas-
antly bewildered to be there. None of us can figure what all this is
about.

The public address announcer chimes in again. "Today, the Cubs
are proud to welcome the Susan G. Komen for the Cure Foundation.
Before the game, the Cubs presented a check to the Susan G. Komen
Foundation and their efforts to defeat breast cancer. At each position
with each of your Chicago Cubs is a breast cancer survivor, and we
salute these women and will continue to fight for a cure."

Five years ago, my mother, my father's wife, was diagnosed with
breast cancer. It devastated our family. Breast cancer threatened the
soul of everything we knew and cared about. My mother underwent
grueling chemotherapy, lost all her hair, and cried every night for
about a year. Just thinking about it makes me want to run down the
street smashing car windows with a crowbar. We still haven't recov-
ered. Even though she's OK now, the cancer is in remission now,
she's as healthy and as in-shape as she has ever been in her life
now . . . we'll never be the same as a family again. Everything's a
little more focused now, more real, brighter and dimmer, more vital
and more scary. It's the biggest thing that's ever happened to any of

us. Cancer is the death shit, evil parasitic little nuggets of monster. Nobody takes breast cancer more seriously than the Leitches.

My dad leans over to me. "Doesn't it seem like the Cubs should be *for* breast cancer?" he says between sips of oversized Old Style. "I bet they're secretly rooting for breast cancer. I mean, they're the *Cubs*."

"Without a goddamned doubt," I say, and next thing you know, Ted Lilly's ready to throw the first pitch.

KNOWLEDGE YOU NOW HAVE

1. There was once something likable about Michael Jordan.
2. It is important to your father that your sister consider him indestructible.
3. Cancer fucking sucks.

TOP OF THE FIRST INNING

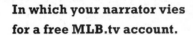

**In which your narrator vies
for a free MLB.tv account.**

*When I was thirteen years old, I was playing baseball with my
buddies. I had two strikes on me when I hit a line drive into the
gap in right field. As I rounded first base, I felt a pinch in my groin
area. By the time I reached second base, I was somewhat in
pain. Feeling embarrassed, I told my friends that I heard my
mother calling—this was a lie—and that I would be right back.
I limped home. The pain was getting intense. I confided in my
father about the pain; surely, he would understand. I told him
that I was playing ball, and the next thing I knew, my testicles
were hurting. My father looked at me for a second and said in
his very authoritative voice, "It sounds like you pulled your groin.
But don't worry. It's not a big deal. A lot of guys do that." I looked
at my father in shock and immediately blurted out, "Honest,
Dad, I didn't touch anything!"*

— JAMES SWEENEY, Clarks Green, Pennsylvania

IN 1961, THE TOTAL ATTENDANCE IN MAJOR LEAGUE BASEBALL
was 18,894,518 souls. When Roger Maris hit his sixty-first homer on
October 1, 1961, in Yankee Stadium, which held 58,000 seats, 23,154
were there, most of whom were gathered in right field, hoping to
catch Maris's homer and collect the $5,000 reward. That season,

673,057 fans visited Wrigley Field (an average of 8,303 a game), 597,287 visited Griffith Stadium in Washington, D.C. (7,374 a game), and 590,039 went to Shibe Park in Philadelphia (7,282 a game). These games were not broadcast on television, and if you wanted to listen to them on the radio, you had to live within the limited range of the AM station or reside on a very tall hill.

When you look at pictures from Maris's sixty-first homer game, what's immediately most striking is how many empty seats there are. If you believe Billy Crystal, Bob Costas, and every baby boomer prone to waxing rhapsodic about the Golden Age Of Major League Baseball, that game was the final resolution of the central question of the age: Mickey Mantle, Roger Maris, or Babe Ruth and his asterisk? They've made films about that game. Its importance has been considered vital not just to baseball history but world history. It's a stand-in for some innocent age, back when everybody drank Ovaltine, worked out in oil fields to support their nuclear family in the off-season, and spent their evening drinking bourbon with sportswriters and, presumably, astronauts.

And there was nobody there. Hardly anyone was watching.

The lowest noted attendance of any Major League Baseball game since 2002 was an April 22 game at Tropicana Field between the Tampa Bay Rays and the Toronto Blue Jays. Tampa Bay's James Shields outpitched Jesse Litsch in a 6–4 victory thanks to home runs from Eric Hinske and rookie Evan Longoria, playing only his second week in the majors. There were 8,269 fans there. That's more than the average attendance of the Griffith Park Senators and the Shibe Park Phillies. That number, of course, does not include the hundreds of thousands of people watching the game at home on television, or on their computers through MLB.tv. Even considering the small number of Rays and Blue Jays fans that could be classified as loyalist enough to never miss a game on television, you're looking at a minimum—and I'm being conservative here—of ten to fifteen times more people watching that dull game on a Tuesday evening inside a dome on an eighty-degree day in St. Petersburg, Florida, than watched what is supposedly one of the most important days in baseball history.

So much of the discussion of baseball is steeped in the notion that somehow baseball has lost its mojo, that what was once The National Pastime has Lost Its Way. Expansion, free agency, exorbitant contracts, the designated hitter, steroids, sabermetrics, interleague play—they're all supposedly symptoms of the central illness of baseball, the loss of the game's pastoral beauty, the idea that Things Just Aren't What They Used To Be.

Which is true. And thank God for that.

IN NOVEMBER 2000, Bob Bowman had never worked in professional sports. A Brewers fan, Bowman was former president of ITT Corporation (whose Web site breathlessly reports it is "one of the world's largest and pre-eminent conglomerates," though it takes a bit of research to discover that this "conglomerate" specializes in "water and fluids management"), had founded howtoguru.com, a "sports instructional site," and served as CEO of consumer technology retailer Outpost.com. In November 2000, the dot-com boom was collapsing—personally, I was laid off by three different dot-coms in 2000—and everyone was pretty much convinced that you were never going to make money off the Web. In sports, no one had any idea what to do. ESPN was futzing around with their old ESPNet Sportszone site, something called Sportsline USA had an unusually high market share, and you couldn't watch any sports highlights on the Web unless you were willing to dial up and wait around for a couple of hours.

No sports league had anything resembling a useful Web site, but, as you might suspect, crusty old Major League Baseball was the worst of them all. Months before Bowman was approached by Major League Baseball, the URL mlb.com directed you to a Philadelphia law firm. Bowman was skeptical: The last place you'd expect to see the Web revolution would be at MajorLeagueBaseball.com. He told me in an interview that he mostly just thought "it would be fun to watch Brewers games for my job."

MLB Advanced Media started in 2000 with a $75 million investment pooled from the thirty clubs; that's roughly the salary of a slap-hitting middle infielder on each team. Bowman spent much of his early budgets buying up server space. At the time, market analysts were skeptical that American homes had the broadband capacity for massive streaming of live video. Bowman looked in a different direction: the office. "We essentially have baseball games from 1 P.M. every day until long past midnight," he says. So the focus needed to be on the fan who could pop in throughout the day. The idea: The old broadcast model was leaving money on the table. The league generates so much content—2,500 games a season—that no one TV network (or three) could possibly broadcast it all. Fans were being underserved.

"In 2002, the first year we tried streaming live games, we did a total of thirty," Bowman says. "And it was anything but a success. It was difficult to watch." The quality improved as Bowman grew the infrastructure, and he began to expand his original vision, "to get the games immediately available on every possible device," he says. "If it takes a plug or a battery, we should have baseball on it."

MLB Advanced Media bought up a ton of server space to stream video—to the point that they now rent out their video servers to other companies; the majority of the time you're watching something live online, whether it's a concert, a press conference, or the NCAA Tournament, it's running off MLB.tv servers—with the understanding that if you gave people the *opportunity* to watch baseball anytime they wanted to, they would take advantage of that opportunity. They have.

MLB Advanced Media has turned online video into such a cash cow that it's a major reason why analysts believe baseball is about to pass the NFL in total revenue. In 2007, Major League Baseball hauled in around $6.7 billion, just even with NFL's $6.7 billion. Its biggest growth engine was MLB Advanced Media, which brought in $450 million (up from $236 million in 2005). Continuing at its current pace, MLB should catch up with the NFL next year. "The growth has exceeded our wildest expectations," says MLB president Bob DuPuy. "No one in the game believed that the Internet would be as pervasive a commercial vehicle for us in such a short amount of time."

Think about that: Major League Baseball has a chance to pass the NFL in total revenue. This is entirely against the accepted notion of what Americans value and obsess about in sports. We baseball dorks have been complaining for years that ESPN and other networks have nearly turned into all-NFL, all-the-time gladiatorial exhibitions masquerading as athletic metaphor for America. And lookie there: Baseball's about to catch up.

What changed in the last fifty years? You want to know what baseball's golden age is? It's right now. It's this very second. There are more people watching baseball right now than at any other time in human history. Mickey Mantle is a relic. And he never drank Ovaltine anyway, not really.

HERE ARE THE AVERAGE attendance figures for Wrigley Field—which has essentially had the same capacity for seventy years—during the Cubs' contending seasons (I shall note, with a smug titter, how few there are):

    1945 (98–56): 13,637
    1969 (92–70): 20,679
    1984 (98–65): 26,020
    1989 (93–69): 30,765
    1998 (90–63): 32,385
    2003 (88–74): 33,248
    2008 (97–64): 40,739

———

CONSIDERING THE CUBS are attempting to clinch the National League Central today, it's no surprise that this game is a sellout, like almost every other Cubs game this season. They'd probably sell out this game at Busch as well—the Cardinals-Cubs ticket is always a hot one—but clearly the stakes are considerably higher for the blue team than the red one. The Cardinals are, sad to say, twelve-and-a-half games behind the Cubs, at 80–73 after a recent downward swing pushed them out of the NL Central race. They're technically still alive in the wild-card chase, five-and-a-half behind the Phillies, but there are three other teams in between them, and let's face it, gang, there's no hope. (Shame they couldn't sneak into the NL West: They'd be in first place.)

One of the many amusements of an extended, 162-game baseball season is the havoc it wreaks with any plans a team had initially. The lineup the Cardinals are fielding today would have given manager Tony La Russa a heart attack in Spring Training, had he known this would be his best crunch-time, pennant-chase option. It's all twisted, weird, and flaccid.

The Cardinals are:

- Playing Ryan Ludwick in center field. This is a position he has not played since 2002 with the Texas Rangers. Ryan Ludwick is an excellent corner outfielder but has the foot speed of a mollusk.
- Batting Felipe Lopez cleanup. The Washington Nationals, one of the worst teams in baseball, released Lopez one hundred games into the season, mostly because he's a noted malcontent, easily distracted, notoriously birdbrained in the field, and batting .234 with only two homers. The Nationals—who were so desperate for talent that they brought in Elijah Dukes (who once text-messaged

his girlfriend a picture of a gun with the phrase "you dead, dawg") and Odalis Perez (who, hilariously, once shut down his charity that gave tickets to underprivileged children because the team demoted him from the starting rotation)—were in no position to get rid of *anybody*. And they dropped Felipe Lopez for nothing. Today, he is our cleanup hitter and the primary lineup protection for Albert Pujols.

- Playing Adam Kennedy in right field. Before this season, Kennedy, a second baseman who was named MVP of the 2002 American League Championship Series with the Los Angeles Angels of Anaheim, had played one game in the outfield. This year, because La Russa was bored or something, he has been playing him in the outfield. It's also possible La Russa is just annoyed with Kennedy for suggesting the Cardinals trade him (an odd pronouncement, just a week before today's game, for a guy hitting .260) and has put him in the outfield to punish him with public humiliation.

- Batting Cesar Izturis first. Cesar Izturis is an outstanding fielder but swings that bat like he still has his infield glove on.

Injuries are a part of this (ordinarily Rick Ankiel would be playing center field), but regardless: This is not the lineup of a team in any position to contend for the postseason. This is not the lineup of a team that instills much hope that it will avoid causing my father to watch the Cubs clinch the National Central right in front of him in his first trip to Wrigley Field.

"How in the hell did these guys win eighty games?" Dad says.

Mike shakes his head. "Aw . . . how *cute.*"

I expected more guff from Dad when I asked him, back in

June, if he wanted to come to this game. After all, Wrigley has all those Cubs fans. The conversation was quick and simple, somehow.

> WILL: Hey, Dad, you wanna go to Wrigley Field
> in September? For that Cardinals series?
> DAD: Are you going?
> WILL: Yes.
> DAD: Sure, let's do it.

If I'd had any idea it would be that easy, I would have done it years ago.

At last count, I have been to twenty-six baseball stadiums, and other than St. Louis, I've never been treated better, as a Cardinals fan, anywhere than I've been treated at Wrigley Field. Dad had been concerned about this, announcing that he'd be wearing his Cardinals 24 Rick Ankiel jersey, "and I just dare anyone to give me any shit about it." He needn't have worried. Even though our nice seats have the two of us as the only splash of red in Section 131—there are plenty of swaths of red in other parts of the park, just so you know— the good vibes at Wrigley have turned us, and our team, simply into fellow travelers on the road to history. Today the Cubs are clinching the National League Central during the one hundredth season since they won the World Series, and no one is going to keep it from happening, least of all a couple of Leitch boys from downstate wearing "ANKIEL" on their backs.

I LEARN LATER that someone named Maria Kanellis, a "WWE Diva," is announcing the lineups on Fox's national telecast of the game, and it's probably for the best that none of us know this at the time.

Maria Kenellis, according to about thirty-five seconds of Web searching (aka "Thanks, Wikipedia!"), is "Maria Frances Louise Kanellis (born February 25, 1982), an American professional wrestler and model of Greek heritage, currently signed to World Wrestling Entertainment (WWE) performing on its SmackDown brand. Kanellis was a contestant on the reality show *Outback Jack* in 2004. In the same year, she placed fifth in the *Raw* Diva Search, but was later hired by WWE as a backstage interviewer. Kanellis began competing in the ring as a wrestler in 2005. It was not until 2007, however, that she received her greatest push in the company, as the on-screen love interest of Santino Marella. As a result, she received more airtime and began winning more matches than she had previously. She also posed for the April 2008 cover of *Playboy* magazine, "which was incorporated into a storyline on *Raw*."

So that sums up everything you might possibly want to know about Maria Kenellis, except: She is a Cubs fan. A rather serious one, it seems. According to an interview she did with WWE.com, she claims that the thing that would make the Ottawa, Illinois, native happiest would be the Cubs winning the World Series. She's twenty-seven. She's young. She takes chairs to the head occasionally.

I remember a talk I had with my father back when I left for college in August 1993. My father did not tell me to be wary of drugs and alcohol, to study hard so I could have a life he never could, to use a condom, to call my mother. He told me not to date a Cubs fan.

"There's going to be a lot of Chicago people up there, and a lot of Cubs fans," he said. "You can fool around with a Cubs fan if you want, but don't you dare bring one home."

Maria Kenellis, by all objective measures, is an attractive woman. (This checks out with multiple sources.) But I have to tell you: She is in no way arousing. She actually kind of makes me ill. Maria Kenellis is freaking hideous, man.

———

THE CROWD SETTLES IN. Ted Lilly finishes up his warm-up tosses. Cesar Izturis readies in the box. Mike is bobbing up and down on his feet; the air is one of quiet anticipation. The abstract is becoming concrete. A guy standing behind us asks my father to move so that he might take a picture of Ted Lilly's first pitch, and when someone is desperate for a snapshot of Ted Lilly, clearly something momentous is occurring. We are awash in Cubs sentiment. At this moment, I'd do anything to see Izturis knock Lilly's first pitch over the wall and shut the sonuvabitches up.

Lilly kicks and fires . . . and Izturis hits the first pitch about fifty feet in the air and five feet behind him. Geovany Soto, if just to be polite, throws his mask off and makes an easy catch, and Wrigley Field is already in a collective tango.

"Goddammit, Izturis," Dad says, and I mark an "FO" in my scorebook and we are off and rolling.

BLEACHER TICKETS at Busch Stadium, the old, ugly, metal, Astroturf, multipurpose Busch Stadium, used to cost $6. My father and I would go every Sunday the Cardinals were at home. This was not a planned event. The surprise of it was what mattered. Dad would wake me up at 8 A.M., like he did every weekend, baseball or otherwise, for some new chore—wood-splitting, weed-eating, trash-burning. (One of the highlights of growing up in Central Illinois was that you were expected to burn your trash. This was back before Al Gore told us it was bad to incinerate Styrofoam. There is no better chore for a twelve-year-old kid than burning trash. "Hey, Will, take this big bag of random crap and set it on fire." Yes, please!) When the Cardinals were in St. Louis, Dad would tell me that if I finished my chores in time, we'd go to The Ball Game. It was a one-hour, forty-five-minute trip to Busch from Mattoon, and we'd wait in line an hour before the game to get bleacher tickets. They were never sold out. We saw about ten games a year, for a total of $120, plus gas.

When Mark McGwire came to town in the late nineties, the bleacher seats stopped being the point of easiest entry at Busch Stadium and became the most desired seats in town. Today, two bleacher tickets on StubHub for a September Cardinals-Cubs series at Busch run $275 apiece. That's more than twice what it cost for the both of us for a whole season.

But in the late eighties, the Cardinals were terrible. They made the World Series twice in the aughts, and the playoffs nearly every season. Much of that was made possible by the expanded fanbase and extra revenue. Would I have made the trade-off? Would I rather have a cheaper, more interactive fan experience? Or would I rather have a winning team?

There's no question in my mind: Go Cardinals. Raise those prices. We'll pay them. You do your job, and we'll do ours.

RYAN LUDWICK is having an amazing season, one no one could have foreseen. He was in the minor leagues just last season, a twenty-seven-year-old still trying to overcome his Failed Prospect status from his years in Oakland. He was mostly a curiosity, one of the few odd ducks (Rickey Henderson is another) who hits right-handed and throws left-handed. This is basic baseball wiring done backwards. We were just hoping he could fill in left field occasionally and allow Chris Duncan to sit against left-handed pitchers.

We have gotten a tad more than that. Ludwick comes into today's game hitting .294 with 34 home runs and 104 RBIs, all career highs by a multiple of at least three. This has been disorienting. Watching a baseball team all season—as both my father and I inevitably do, every day, every pitch, every game recorded, in case the real world rudely steps in the way for an hour or two—exponentially both increases and diminishes the value, importance, and staying power of each game. When someone nondescript and relatively unaccomplished—say, Nick Stavinoha—knocks in a couple of runs, we see him both as a better hitter than he is in the short term (as he was in that particular at bat, or that particular game) and as an anomaly in the long term, just one guy getting one hit at one time. Baseball is a game that rewards perspective, but when you watch a baseball game every day, the same team in the same uniform in different situations, perspective is the one thing you don't have. This is why sabermetricians and old-timey scout types are always fighting: Either you're too far away to see what's happening, or you're too close. You become less of an expert the more it seems like you are one.

Which is a fancy way of saying it took us forever to realize that Ryan Ludwick was great. He wasn't a full-time starter until May, and we didn't embrace him as the best-hitting outfielder in the National League (which he was) until August, at the earliest. We started with surprise, then amusement, then bewilderment, then denial, and it's only now that we're really accepting it: Ryan Ludwick is awesome. He's a symptom of the constant churn of baseball, a guy who was once the hottest prospect in the game and faced such a relentless string of injuries for so many years that by the time he was ready to play, everyone had forgotten why they considered him a prospect in the first place. The Cardinals fans, forever terrified they're going to waste the prime of our Ted Williams, Albert Pujols (there is a general notion that the 2006 World Series Championship was a bit of a fluke, and that Albert deserves more, in a Michael Jordan–type way), spent most of the year screaming for "lineup protection" for Pujols, a big bat like Matt Holliday or Manny Ramirez to "protect" Albert. Ludwick has been better than both of those guys, all year. But we didn't notice.

You know the old adage about how, if you put a frog in a pot of boiling water, he'll jump out, but if you put him in a pot of lukewarm water and increase the temperature by five degrees every hour, he'll eventually boil to death? Well, that's absolutely not true: As James

Fallows of the *Atlantic Monthly* has reported, the curator of reptiles and amphibians at the National Museum of Natural History points out that frogs are not stupid. They would jump out, because boiling water is extremely hot and painful. Fallows suggests an alternate metaphor, of a man who owns a cat becoming so accustomed to the smell that he does not realize until a visitor comes by that the whole house reeks of feline urine. That one's much better. Cardinals fans just realized that Ryan Ludwick makes Busch Stadium smell like cat piss. That's what I'm trying to say.

A month before this game, during my last trip to Busch Stadium, I bought a Ryan Ludwick T-shirt. Now we believe. And he rewards us with a shot into left field that just soars over the glove of leaping left fielder buffoon Alfonso Soriano and nicks the bottom of the ivy. Ludwick cruises into second base easily. We are in business, and the loudest people in Section 131.

WITHIN NINETY SECONDS of Ludwick's double, while Albert Pujols flares his nostrils at the plate, I am watching a highlight of it on my iPhone. (Soriano looks uniquely ungraceful even on a two-inch-by-three-inch screen.) I'm a subscriber to the MLB At Bat application, which allows you access to MLB.com's Gameday service (real-time score updates with full box scores and stats) and provides almost immediate replays of important events in the game. The Gameday function actually updates faster than the famous manual scoreboard in center field at Wrigley Field.

The idea behind the application, Bob Bowman told me, was to cater even more intensely to the obsessive fan. "Even the most stat-oriented fan likes to have the context of what happened," he said. "You can not only see the score, you can see everything that went into it, immediately. And as impressive as it might seem to have game highlights on your phone within a minute, it's just the first step. Eventually you're going to be able to watch a game, live, on your phone, no matter where you are." He smiled. "I suspect this will make weddings, church, and even funerals more tolerable."

I paid $4.99 for the application. I would have paid $50. Dad leans over to me. "You gonna watch the game, or you gonna fart around with your phone?"

I've set Dad up with an MLB.tv subscription on his home computer, but he's never been able to figure out how to use it. He's never been able to find the "T" on the keyboard.

ALBERT PUJOLS takes the first two pitches outside the strike zone, and it's pretty obvious that Lilly wants to walk him with first base open. Of all that can be said about Pujols's greatness—and trust me, you're going to be reading a lot of it in this here book—he has one definite weakness that keeps him from the otherworldly (and, of course, enhanced) brilliance of Barry Bonds: He is not as selfishly patient. That is to say: Barry Bonds was perfectly happy to sit there with his bat on his shoulder all day until you gave him the pitch he wanted. If it wasn't *exactly* where he wanted it, he would politely demur and trot over to first base. What Bonds was doing—walking—was ultimately helping his team, but I'm not sure that's why he was doing it: I think he figured, hell, I'll just walk, and if they lose, hey it's not my fault.

Pujols is incapable of doing this. When he doesn't have an outstanding hitter behind him—like, for example, RIGHT NOW, thank you, Felipe Lopez—Pujols feels compelled to *make* something happen, even if it means refusing the walk owed to him and swinging at pitches outside the strike zone. Which he does, pulling a low and outside changeup on 2–0—the quintessential hitter's count—limply to shortstop Ryan Theriot. I know Pujols feels like he is helping. I know he is being a "gamer." But I'd be a lot happier seeing him on first base right now.

Lilly takes Lopez to a 1–2 count, and broadcaster Josh Lewin, noticing that the crowd is rising to its feet, points out that "it's not a frat party out there." Wrigley Field is the only baseball stadium in which the announcer would feel the need to remind people that it is not, in fact, a bunch of drunk dudes doing Jäger bombs. Yes, I'm saying that because I am bitter. I am saying that because Felipe Lopez, Great Pujols Protector, Grand Striker Of Terror In The Hearts Of Lanky Left-Handers Everywhere, takes a curveball right down the middle for strike three.

I had been dreaming of a ten-run first inning for the Cardinals, followed by three hours of Old Styles, remembrances of times past, and Mike suffering repeated Leitch family wedgies. Alas.

I turn to my father, but he's already gone. "Beer line," Mike says. "He said he had to go now before the Cubs fans realize they're batting." I do hope he grabbed me one.

KNOWLEDGE YOU NOW HAVE

1. At one point in human history, people legitimately felt they could make money off the Internet.
2. Setting big piles of trash on fire is truly the greatest of all possible chores.
3. There was a reason your father spent hours holding frogs underneath boiling water.

BOTTOM OF THE FIRST INNING

**In which your narrator encourages
you to recycle your bottles and cans.**

*My mom died when we were little, leaving us three little girls,
ages seven, ten, and thirteen, and my dad, who was a crazy Yankees fan. Dad was so lost; he didn't know what to do with our
bangs so he cut them off. We looked ridiculous. Baseball was
where we all came together. Sitting on that old couch, watching
Bernie Williams and John Wetteland dominate for the Yankees,
was where we learned a common language. I'm in college now,
halfway across the country from Dad, we don't get to speak as
often as we used to. Still, during the playoff games that start so
late, too late for him to stay up for, I call him, the phone ringing
and ringing. He picks up, sleepy but hanging in. "You watching?"
he asks. "Yeah, Dad, let's go Mo," I say. It is our language. I hope
neither of us ever forgets.*

— JEANNIE CAMBRIA, Evanston, Illinois

MY FATHER DRINKS AND DRIVES.

That sounds worse than it is. Those of you from the coasts might
not understand this, but in the Midwest, particularly in Central Illinois, where there's little more than unnamed roads, cornfields, and
chubby cows, beers are permanently fused to your hand. When I
go home, there isn't a moment past 5 P.M. that I don't have a beer.

(In New York, I barely drink beer. Home, though, they just tap a vein when you enter city limits.) It's just part of the fabric; you go to a friend or neighbor's home, and you immediately head for their fridge and pop open a Budweiser. People aren't drinking to get drunk, not necessarily. You just drink because that's what you do.

Beer is everywhere. At a post-service "mixer" at my mother's Catholic church, they had a keg. On the Fourth of July, we all had a Bud in one hand and a lighter to set off the illegal explosives in the other. While visiting my cousin, there was a car accident outside his house. We were both drinking beer, and we sauntered outside, curious, beers still in hand. I was downing an MGD when I went up to the responding police officer. I was a little surprised he didn't ask me for a sip. When teaching me to drive, my father once told me, half-jokingly (I think), "You gotta learn to drive with your knees so you can open your beer." (My mother smacked him on the head after he said this. Then, from the backseat, she opened a beer for herself.) I feel less comfortable with my father driving without a beer in his hand than when he does. It's just part of the driving process. My parents live outside of Mattoon city limits, and it takes us fifteen to twenty minutes just to go to the supermarket. That's one or two beers, right there.

It's not like my father is an alcoholic or anything; I've never seen him drunk, ever, and I've seen that man consume many beers in my lifetime. It's just: When you're driving for hours through the middle of nowhere, drinking is just a way to get by. When you have to pee, you pull over to the side of the road. My father was pulled over once by a Mattoon cop; Dad got out of the car with his beer in hand. He did receive a ticket . . . for speeding. It's not encouraged, mind you. Just accepted. Don't abuse the privilege, and we'll all be fine.

Every year since I moved to New York, I go back home for a weekend of Cardinals series at Busch. Making it to Busch is less a pilgrimage than a yearly doctor's appointment, a way to make sure everything's still working, see if anything weird happens when I turn my head and cough.

A few years ago, in 2002, the year Darryl Kile died and Jack Buck died and no one knew what the hell to do, I flew back for a series with the Padres. Dad and I drove the hour-45 from Mattoon to St. Louis, I-57 to I-70, with a couple beers on the way there, had three or four of the industrial-sized monsters at the game, talked about our lives without talking about them in the way that men do. Then Ryan Klesko grounded out to second, and the Cardinals had a victory.

It was time to drive home, but once we hopped in the car and crossed back into Illinois, we realized with alarm that we were woefully short on beer. There were only four Natural Lights left in the cooler. This simply wouldn't do. We had made it to Vandalia, about halfway there, when we both finished up our stash. We were rapidly approaching midnight, the drop-dead time when gas stations and supermarkets stop selling beer. We pulled off the interstate and into Vandalia . . . but we were too late. They'd already locked up the freezers. Bastards.

This left us only one option: a bar. One of the highlights of rural Midwestern bars is the To Go option. Essentially, you can sit in a bar, usually sparsely populated, and drink all night. Then, when you're ready to leave, you slap another seven bucks on the table and get a twelve-pack to take home. I can't believe there are bars in this country that *don't* do this.

One downside: You often have interlopers popping in, with no intention of actually drinking at your bar, soaking in your atmosphere, joining in the conversation. They come in, grab the twelve-pack, and bolt, like the bar is some kind of drive-through. When I've been at a bar and seen this, I sneer at the hops tourists and insult them when they leave. Dad and I didn't want to be like these guys—we were proud to know the code—but with no beer back at home, we had little choice.

Another obstacle: We were in Central Illinois, and the only bars you'll find open there past midnight sneak up on you. You'll be on a deserted road, and all of a sudden you'll see a sign that says "Dietrich—Pop: 1423," and they'll have one bar, which looks like a trailer home, with a Hamm's sign and a couple pickup trucks out front. After that, there will be nothing for thirty miles.

But we were undaunted. "I think I know a place in Sigel," Dad said. This was not a comforting statement. Sigel is essentially a suburb of Effingham, which is essentially a suburb of Mattoon, which has fifteen thousand people. Sigel has a population of 150. It is possible that they all have the last name, "Sigel." The town has one stop sign, about forty houses, a post office, and a bar. The types of people who populate Sigel's one bar at 1 A.M. guzzle motor oil, devour lit cigars, and have food stuck in their beards from 1983.

We were hardly dressed the part. As is expected at Busch Stadium, we were decked out in all bright Cardinal red T-shirts and white shorts. Dad had binoculars around his neck. I was carrying a score book. We had a sneaking suspicion that Sigel's finest wouldn't take too kindly to our popping in for package liquor. There would be nothing left of us but a pair of Oakleys and a few strands of hair.

But we needed that beer.

We arrived in Sigel. The exterior of the "bar" was not comforting. First off, it was called "BAR." It had a sign on the door for "Chicken Fried Steak." There was a huge crack in the glass of the front window. A flag waved out front with "Don't Tread on Me" blazoned across it. There were four vehicles out there too: three pickup trucks and a Harley. One truck had a bumper sticker: "I Got Your Jihad Right Here." We were clearly toast.

We climbed out of the car. Dad looked at me and tried to make a joke.

"You got your fighting clothes on?"

I looked back at him. "Dad, I have a picture of J. D. Drew on my chest. What do you think?"

I made Dad go first. He pushed the door open, ringing an awful, awful bell. I cringed. Here we go.

There were four people sitting at the bar, big dudes, and a bartender, even bigger. They all darted their heads toward the door. We had clearly interrupted something, and we were about to pay. Why hadn't we kept the car running outside? How quickly could we escape? Being beaten to death by bikers in Sigel, Illinois, with my father, while searching for beer and wearing a T-shirt emblazoned with the image of a lethargic fundamentalist Christian . . . well, it wasn't the most honorable way to die, though it made some sense, really, when you thought about it.

They registered our faces, blinked, and then turned their heads directly back toward the television. They were entranced. The room was silent, except for the TV.

They were watching *Mr. Holland's Opus.*

More specific, they were watching the end of *Mr. Holland's Opus,* when Richard Dreyfuss's character sums up his entire career during a rousing concert as an entire town weeps. The music rises, the crowd swells, everyone's crying. Mr. Holland sure did touch a lot of lives.

Dad and I stood at the front door. I looked at him. He looked at me.

We waited until the film ended, tiptoed to the bar, asked for a twelve-pack of Natural from the moist-eyed bartender, and drank all the way home.

ALFONSO SORIANO is one of those players who drives baseball fans crazy, not least of which the ones who actually root for him. In any other sport, fans appreciate the ease and fluidity of a natural athlete, someone who is able to do the logistically improbable without exerting any visible effort. This is not what we admire in baseball players. Baseball is a game that, if you really wanted to, could go a full nine innings without you breaking a legitimate sweat; half of the game involves sitting down, and for the other half you stand up and then

stand around. Because of this, we expect our professional athletes to *hustle*. (I remember an ESPN.com poll that once asked fans:
"What is the worst crime a baseball player can commit: Gambling
on His Games, Using Steroids, Using Illegal Drugs, or Not Hustling?"
It wasn't even close: "Not Hustling" won about eight times over.) We
know they don't *have* to work hard to play baseball, but we like to
think we would, if we had the chance. So we ask that, for our hard-
earned entertainment dollar, they at least pretend to.

This is not Alfonso Soriano's strength. Alfonso Soriano is preternaturally blessed; fast, smooth, quick-wrist-crazy strong, a guy who
will toss his bat at a low inside breaking ball and just flip it over the
wall. It's frustrating for opposing fans because it shouldn't be that
easy; it's frustrating for Cubs fans because if it *is* that easy, shit, why
isn't he doing that all the time? And in the outfield, Soriano carries
himself like he is casually shagging butterflies on a lovely spring day,
and hey, if he misses one . . . there will always be more butterflies,
right?

Cardinals pitcher Joel Pineiro, on a 1–2 pitch to lead off the bottom of the first, throws a lame curveball that is saved from the dirt
only by Soriano's flippant *oh why not, I've been at the plate long
enough already* check swing. The ball travels about twenty feet, to
where Pineiro grabs it and flips it to first for the first out of the inning.
Dad returns with beers for me, Mike, and himself. It's probably his
years of experience, but somehow my father flaunts any alcohol
rule wherever he's at. Two beers per person? Not for Bryan Leitch!
Frantically waving for the bartender's attention at a crowded club?
Not for Bryan Leitch! "Sir, you can't have an open container in your
vehicle." Not for Bryan Leitch! Mike takes a big swig. "At least Soriano turned in the direction of first base that time," he says. "He's
making progress."

I check my phone and point it out to Mike. At the same time this
game is going on, the Milwaukee Brewers are facing the Cincinnati
Reds. If the Brewers lose, because the Cubs' magic number is one,

Chicago will clinch the National League Central regardless of what happens in this game. To Dad and me, this is the ideal scenario: The Brewers lose today, and so do the Cubs. If the Cubs are inevitably going to win the division anyway—and they are—let's make it so they have to do it in the most depressing way possible: looking at that old scoreboard after losing on their home field to the Cardinals. I wonder if they'll even have the audacity to celebrate in public. Anyway, Reds first baseman Joey Votto has an RBI single off Sabathia in the first, and the Brewers are down 1–0. The Reds are doing their part. Now we must do ours.

A man next to us is wearing a Cubs T-shirt and a (blue) Cardinals hat. On the way out of our row, he bumps into my father, who bumps into me and spills my beer all over the cement below. (I've never seen my father spill a beer.) The man apologizes, and I say, "Naw, it's cool, man, Weird Guy With Cubs T-Shirt And Cardinals Hat," though his uniform is not cool, man, not cool at all. I wipe off my jeans and look to my left. Dad's already gone, up out the other side of the row, off for more beer. No son of his is going to be empty-handed.

THE FIRST TIME I ever had a beer with my father, I had just turned twenty-one years old. Both my parents were drinkers, though my mother took a year-long break from booze when I was twelve because she was in nursing school and needed to concentrate. I was impressed with her seriousness, and her organization: The night after her first day on the job in the emergency room at the hospital, she drank three beers, as if nothing had changed, as if the last year hadn't happened. Even today, my mother, sprung into a fitness craze in the wake of her breast cancer, still can knock down beers with the most grizzled barfly, though now she always makes sure to know the caloric content beforehand.

Despite all this, I didn't drink alcohol in high school, which, in Mattoon, marked me as an eccentric at best, a frightening zealot at worst, like one of those crazy Catholic guys who whip themselves so that they do not even think of sin. I'm not sure why I didn't drink in high school: Everyone else on the baseball team did, and I certainly had lots of opportunities. Maybe it was as simple as: Mom and Dad told me not to. It is not in my nature to rebel against authority—at best, I'm an *Authority, may I have a polite word, and if you hear me out, I will adhere to your judgment* person. It's probably a personality flaw.

Anyway, when I was twenty-one, I traveled the forty-five miles home for Christmas break of my senior year at the University of Illinois with a specific purpose in mind: I was going to tell my parents that I planned on asking my girlfriend to marry me. They had met her and enjoyed her, and even though twenty-one is a stupidly young age to be engaged, well, my parents were even younger and stupider when they got engaged, so they were more supportive than they probably should have been. I told my mom first, and she cried and gave me a family heirloom, the same ring Dad had given her, the same one his father, my grandfather, had given his mother, my grandmother. Dad called from work and asked if I wanted to meet him for lunch at Gunnar Buc's, a greasy spoon watering hole with a robot bucking bronco and old video poker machines that didn't give you money even if you won. I drove over. We sat at the bar, and my father ordered me a beer.

At this point, I'd drank many, many times—I am not so much a drip that I did not destroy myself as thoroughly as possible in college— but I'd never had a beer with Dad. I didn't think much about it when he ordered me one, though. We're all so stupid at twenty-one.

We were halfway through the beer when I told Dad I was going to ask the girl to marry me. We'd never discussed women before— my sexual education consisted of my mother sitting me in front of a *Nova* episode about Human Reproduction and handing me a book while my father found a lawn, somewhere far, far away, to mow— and, all told, my father was still a Parent to me, a distant figure I admired and feared, someone at the center of my life but ostensibly on the periphery, someone I tried not to disappoint with the chaotic, jumbled, collegiate issues I thought were important at the time. I told Dad very little back then. It felt like a leap to even mention it, but telling your father you were asking someone to marry you seemed like something you were supposed to do. Which is how we'd ended up here. Not that either of us were doing backflips about it.

Dad looked down at his beer and reflexively went into Dad Mode. "You don't even have a job! How you going to have a wife if you don't have a *job*?" He drew out the syllable in "job," so it sounded like "jaaaaaaaaaahhhhhbbbb," as if the soft vowel sound underscored his imperative. "You're a college kid. You don't know shit. You better get yourself a job before you start thinking about getting married. Don't you forget that. That's what's important: You have to support a family now." This went on for about ten minutes, some fatherly haranguing about responsibility, about what it meant to be a husband, a father, a man. It meant nothing to me. I was callow and omniscient. My dad didn't understand me. He was a dad. If he understood me, and my desire to go to Los Angeles and just *write, man, write,* he wouldn't be my dad. It wasn't even upsetting. This was the way it was going to be. This was what we had both expected.

We finished our beers, and we each ordered another. He paid, because he's the dad. He had talked himself out; I had no answers to the questions he was asking and could not pretend I did.

Then Dad paused. "You know, I think your grandpa would just about shit a brick if he knew I was sitting here having a beer with you." My grandfather, named William Franklin Leitch, like me, worked on the railroad and at Howell Asphalt road paving, smoked three packs of unfiltered Pall Malls a day, and sired eight children. He was a quiet, taciturn military man who, when he came home from work, lacked the energy or the patience to deal with a massive brood of screaming, wild kids. He would go into his "office"—really just a desk in his bedroom—drink whiskey, smoke, and read the paper. From all accounts, he was a kind man, but damned if he was gonna let you know it. When he was dying, my mother, newly a nurse, took care of him. He showed his affection and appreciation for her care by twisting and yanking her arm hair. "It was the same as if he'd given me flowers," my mom once told me. When my grandfather met my mother for the first time, he sat across the table at a Mexican restaurant drinking and smoking. Mom says she doesn't remember him saying a word. She knew that meant he liked her. She didn't know why she knew that, but she did.

"You never had a beer with Grandpa?" I asked, legitimately curious. What *else* was there to do with Grandpa?

"Drink in front of my dad?" he said. "Bill Leitch wouldn't have stood for it."

We finished that beer, and two others. My dad was never The Dad after that. He was my drinking buddy. I got myself a job before I graduated. (Don't you forget it.) The marriage didn't happen, though. For the best. The transaction was well worth it.

WITH TWO OUTS, Cubs first baseman Derrek Lee steps to the plate. In 2005, when the Cardinals were still ruling the division, when the Cubs were still reeling from 2003 (when Lee, amusingly enough, played for the tormenting world champion Marlins), Lee had the best year of his career, hitting forty-six home runs, batting .335 and leading the National League in slugging percentage. Because the Cubs were under .500 that season, back to their natural place in the universe, Lee was their lone source of bragging rights against the first-place Cardinals: *Albert Pujols is supposedly the best baseball player in the world; why all of a sudden is our first baseman having a better season?* Cardinals fans tried to laugh this off, but we do not take well to ruffians casting aspersions on The Great Pujols. Lee's injury-riddled 2006 season, along with our own World Championship, felt like karma.

Coming into the game, Lee was 5-for-7 lifetime against Pineiro. It's always strange when one hitter dominates a pitcher so thoroughly. You see this every once in a while in baseball, one guy just owning another guy for no reason other than some sort of mental Jenga where one piece happens to fit in *just* right. Old-time Cardinals left-hander Tony Fossas—who looked suspiciously like Luigi from *Super Mario Bros.*, minus the mustache, and whose nickname was, fittingly, "The Mechanic"—had a lifetime ERA of 3.90 and never started a game in his life. And he struck out Barry Bonds nearly every time he faced him. No rhyme or reason for it: There was just something in Barry Bonds's wiring that made him incapable of hitting off Tony Fossas. Having watched Fossas pitch for the Cardinals, I can only assume few other hitters were wired that way.

Derrek Lee smashes a 1–1 ninety-one-mile-per-hour fastball straight to center field, over Ludwick's head and to the base of the ivy. He trots into second base like he knew this was going to happen, like there was never a doubt in his mind. He's now 6-for-8 lifetime. For the first time today, and hopefully the last, Wrigley is vibrating with noise. The old place can bring it, all these years later.

Lee's still no Pujols. Not even freaking close.

IN NOVEMBER 2000, ten months after I'd moved to New York City flittering with dreams of media stardom, I moved back home. The move was to be temporary: I'd been laid off from my job, was running out of money, and needed to nurse my wounds. I was twenty-five years old. I had no idea what I was doing.

I also owed about $5,000 in rent back in New York that I could not repay. I had never borrowed money from my parents before, but I had no choice. There was no nest egg to fall back on. I had no magic benefactor. I had been living check-to-check for quite some time, which is fine when you're sure each of those checks will come, but disastrous when they stop. Home was the only place I had to turn.

I had been staying with a cousin, and I made the wretched, murderous drive to my parents' place for the dreaded conversation. I was a grown man, without a "jaaaaaaaahhhhbbb," and I had failed. This was my reckoning, and I deserved this.

They were not home. I waited, and waited, and waited, and they never showed. Tired, I left them a note, explaining what I needed, what I'd done, and how awful it had become, and returned the next morning. My mother was waiting: "We got your note." She looked so sad. My parents had always known I was flaky, and perhaps had my head in the clouds more than was good for me. But it had never come to this before. For the first time, she was seriously questioning everything she thought she knew about her son. *Oh my,* her eyes said . . . *he might really be a screwup.* "Let me talk to your father."

The next weekend, after they had given me the money, with no conversation whatsoever, just a check, I, feeling worthless, decided to visit old friends in St. Louis, where I'd lived three years before. I drove a beaten-up old 1986 Chevy Caprice, my deceased great uncle's former car, the green mile. About an hour into the drive, I noticed more smoke than there should have been shooting out the exhaust pipe. I pulled into a gas station, lifted the hood, and realized that the car had overheated. It was fried. There was only one number to call. Again.

Dad arrived two hours later, having left work. We sat out in the cold for two hours, picking the car apart, putting this here, placing that there. At one point, the wrench Dad was using slipped out of his hand and cut his left thumb. The blood oozed out, quiet, trying not to be noticed. The gash opened up further a few minutes later, and a large patch of skin was noticeably dangling. Dad didn't pause in the slightest. He just kept working, as the oil and the grime and the soot mixed in, turning his thumb purple. He just kept working.

The car was continuing to leak, and it was obvious this problem would not be fixed tonight. Dad would have to take the next day off of work and drive all the way back, just to help his failure son fix a car he shouldn't have taken off with in the first place. We had an hour to drive home in his truck, just the two of us. We had yet to discuss, one-on-one, the money I had borrowed just two days before.

Dad walked inside the gas station and bought a six-pack of Natural Light. We hopped in the truck and were silent, motionless, for about fifteen minutes. He then handed me a beer.

"So . . . did you hear about the Cardinals thinking about trading Tatis?" And so it was. He didn't yell, he didn't scold, he didn't even grimace. We just talked about what we'd always talked about, until I was ready, no longer too ashamed, to discuss the matter at hand.

"Dad . . . I screwed up. I'm sorry." I told him how I felt what had happened over the last few months was in fact some sort of karmic punishment, my proper comeuppance for a cocky kid the dot-com boom had fooled into thinking he was important. He didn't say a word. He just handed me another beer and listened, or didn't, I don't know, and it doesn't matter. About five minutes in, I stopped. I didn't need to say anything more, and he didn't need to hear it. We'd already had our conversation. The beer was enough; it was his tacit acknowledgment: *I don't think you're a fuckup. But don't do this again.* And I didn't.

"We'll get back to the car tomorrow," he said as he dropped me off at my cousin's place.

"Bring your work gloves."

ON A 1–0 PITCH, Cubs third baseman Aramis Ramirez—an annual all-star criminally given away by the Pirates (along with Kenny Lofton!) for Matt Bruback and Jose Hernandez—hits a grooved Pineiro fastball to deep right. The crowd gasps, but Ramirez swung under it, and it lands harmlessly in the glove of inexplicable right fielder Adam Kennedy. The inning is over.

As the crowd shuffles around, I see the man with the Cubs T-shirt and the blue Cardinals hat. Right behind him is Dad, carrying, again, three beers. He's smiling: Our stash should be set for the next few innings now.

"Here ya go!" he says.

Don't mind if I do.

KNOWLEDGE YOU NOW HAVE

1. Making jokes about drunk driving is fun as long as you ask no follow-up questions.
2. There was a point in your father's life that he owned work gloves and didn't pay the nice Latino man to do everything.
3. There is a reason your sister's name is Sigel.

TOP OF THE SECOND INNING

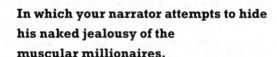

In which your narrator attempts to hide his naked jealousy of the muscular millionaires.

My father passed away on July 12, 1993, of brain cancer. I was thirteen at the time and a benchwarmer for my team. The coach let me start because he knew my father's situation and wanted him to see me play. I started in left field. My first at bat wasn't pretty; I got plunked first pitch. My dad started feeling ill from the chemo and was getting ready to leave. I told him I was up to bat first the next inning, and he stuck around to watch me hit. Anyway, it was bottom of the seventh and it was a tie game. I worked the count to 3 and 0. The third base coach signaled to take the pitch. The pitcher laid it right down the pipe. I have never hit a ball so far. My father passed away two days later. I have never played organized baseball since.

— JASON BARRICK, Lemoyne, Pennsylvania

DURING THE BROADCAST THAT I'LL WATCH LATER, FOX MISSES Troy Glaus's strikeout to lead off the top of the second inning, to provide us with some newsreel trivia. Here are events that happened in 1908, the last year the Cubs won the World Series:

- Theodore Roosevelt is President.
- Ford Model T is introduced.

- Jack Johnson is heavyweight champ.
- Mother's Day celebrated for the first time.
- Boy Scouts of America founded.
- Average cost of home: $4,500
- Average MLB player salary: $2,500

Just out of curiosity, I found some other, less TV-friendly 1908 trivia (via Wikipedia, which I'm 100 percent certain is where FOX got their facts too):

- New York City passes the Sullivan Ordinance, making it illegal for women to smoke in public.
- Japanese immigration to the United States is forbidden.
- At Fort Myer, Virginia, Thomas Selfridge becomes the first person to die in an airplane crash.
- Western bandits Butch Cassidy and The Sundance Kid are supposedly killed in Bolivia, after being surrounded by a large group of soldiers.
- An earthquake and tsunami destroys Messina, Sicily and Calabria, killing over 70,000 people.

I don't think a single one of those is worse than the Cubs winning the World Series.

AFTER A QUICK TWO OUTS, Cardinals left fielder Brian Barton steps to the plate. I am going to do my best not to cast aspersions on St. Louis baseball fans here, The Greatest Baseball Fans on Earth, but I will say that players like Barton—black dudes with dreads and leisurely lopes in their step—have not always been near the top of the team's merchandise sales charts. Brian Barton is an exception. This is because Brian Barton is a genius.

Brian Barton, the guy batting .283 and stuck on the major-league roster because he was a Rule V pickup (the obscure baseball rule that allows teams to pick up players not on other teams' forty-man rosters, as long as they stay on the active roster all season), is smarter than you, than me, and just about everyone else we know. In college, he studied aerospace engineering (to be fair, it was at the University of Miami) and interned at Boeing while walking onto the baseball team. For his summer break, he visited Ethiopia to "better understand my African heritage." (He actually took time to learn the language before he left.) With just one semester left until he earned his degree, he took a siesta to play professional baseball. The guy who grew up in Compton and is obsessed with Sam Cooke, Cuba Gooding Sr., and "all kinds of old soul and R&B" was undrafted out of college because of what Cardinals general manager John Mozeliak called a fear that "his commitment was to his education and not likely to the game of baseball." This concern is understandable. Baseball players are not encouraged to have outside interests. They are expected to care only about baseball. I like baseball a lot more than I liked going to class too.

Brian Barton is exactly the type of guy you would think too smart, too worldly, too *serious* to play baseball. And in baseball, that's why no one ever thought he was very good. Thinking them wrong makes a wonderful story. It's brains over brawn. It's substance over style. It's also lazy thinking: Brian Barton is not a very good baseball player.

In an interview with Baseball Prospectus, Barton talked about his trip to Ethiopia.

> I travel for the culture; I travel for what it is to learn about different people's cultures and about different people in general. I like to learn about different ways of life. I know that a lot of people travel for the thrill and excitement, and for the tourist

attractions. I think that what I get from traveling is deeper than that. I feel a connection, and I try to get a connection when I travel, and I think that is what makes it more rewarding. I think that's why I have such an appreciation for it when I am there. And I think that when I talk about it with people, what they expect, and what they hear from me, might be two different things, because they expect me to describe it this way: 'I did this or I did that.' But when they actually hear, and they actually see, the passion in my telling of the story, they realize that I got something even more out of it.

This is not how baseball players think. This is not how most humans think. Brian Barton, theoretically speaking, should be my favorite player: thoughtful, intellectually curious, legitimately fascinating, fantastic taste in music. In real life, I would desperately try to become his friend. We would go on long walks and discuss Marvin Gaye and NASA and injera bread.

But this is baseball. I am not looking for friends. When the Cardinals traded him to the Braves in April 2009, my only frustration was that they didn't receive more from Atlanta than journeyman reliever Blaine Boyer. We kept Barton on our roster all season for *Blaine freaking Boyer*?

Barton played one game for the Braves in 2009 and spent the entire season in the minor leagues. At last check, he was out of baseball. Who cares if you are smart, if you cannot hit?

THIS IS TO SAY: I don't want to know athletes. Not only do I find it impossible to appreciate them as human beings—*stop studying, Barton, start hitting*—but even if I value them as athletes, I know as purveyors of individual thought they're inevitably going to disappoint me.

It'd be difficult to find many human beings who have provided me more sincere joy in this world than Albert Pujols. Watching him play baseball on a daily basis is like watching Picasso paint, or Bob Dylan write a song, or Phil Spector kill someone. It is a distinct genius that comes along once in a generation: I feel like I'm witnessing something historic every day. Even when he pops out to the shortstop, it's special, it's unique, it's an occurrence I feel uniquely fortunate to be around to watch. The confluence of cosmic circumstances had to converge at the exact right moment—Pujols's touched-by-Zeus skill, his preternatural work ethic and focus, the benificence of the universe not having him hit by a bus, or struck down by SIDS, or slam his shoulder in a car door—for any of this to even be a possible. It feels like a miracle.

But none of that has to do with Albert Pujols the person. From all accounts, Pujols is a dashing, noble, humble man of the community, a loving family man, a true leader. But those are only that: accounts. I cannot know what's in Albert Pujols's heart. He could secretly harbor a foot fetish, or leave the seat up, or drive slowly in the fast lane with his blinker flashing the wrong way. He could stiff his waiter on tips; he could send countless invitations to play Zombie Bite on Facebook; he could kill homeless men for sport. I have no idea, and neither do you. None of that has anything to do with his ability to launch home runs deep into the Busch Stadium night. The only interaction we have with our athletes is watching what they do on the field. More than that, I do not want to know.

When I was around twelve years old, the Leitch family went to Cincinnati for a three-game series between the Reds and the Cardinals. We stayed in the same hotel as the Cardinals. (Dad claims this was a coincidence, but I am skeptical.) When in the elevator heading down for dinner—I highly recommend Jeff Ruby's Steakhouse—Dad suddenly jumped out before the doors closed. I tried to follow, but Mom stopped me. When we reached the lobby, we saw Dad walking ahead of us. I rushed to catch up with him, and he put his fingers to his lips, then pointed five feet forward. Ahead, it was Ozzie Smith and his son Osborne Jr., then a small child, later a contestant on *American Idol,* a popular television program in which sad people try to become happy by letting a British man belittle them. Dad had ridden in the elevator with them. Ozzie shook his hand. We followed them long enough to absorb, but short enough that the police weren't called.

Later that night, after the kids and Mom were put to bed, Dad drank at the hotel bar, surely relieved to have a few precious seconds to himself. There, he ran into Dave Parker, a portly outfielder for the Reds. Dad had no real opinion about Parker, other than *Holy shit, there's a baseball player, just a couple stools away.* Dad asked if he could buy him a beer. Parker turned to him and said, "Leave me the fuck alone, man." Dad finished his own beer and went up to bed.

Now, it's easy to sympathize with Parker here. The man just wanted to drink his beer in peace and be left alone, and some guy in a Cardinals hat, drinking alone as well, starts bothering him. It can't be easy to be that much in the public eye, particularly if you're a black guy playing baseball in *Cincinnati.* He didn't have to be rude about it, sure. But baseball players are people too, and Dad surely wouldn't like it if people were interrupting him at the bar all the time either.

Still. Dave Parker could have saved the president from an assassin's bullet and discovered a cure for cancer in a pill that tastes like chocolate, and my dad would hate him. We have few moments to interact with athletes. If they disappoint us in that short time, we never forget it. It's not fair. It just is. It's best for us not to know them at all.

Baseball is a sacred gift, handed to us by the cosmos in ninety-foot intervals, and those who are able to play it at the highest level have been granted the ultimate blessing, a key to the eternal kingdom. If I had been given that sort of talent, I like to think that I'd spend every day just running around in circles, giggling: *I get to play baseball tonight! And they pay me for it! Weeee!!!!* I suspect many of you feel the same way. But we weren't given that talent. Others were. And those others have had dramatically different life experiences than we have, segregated at an early age as "special," coddled, protected, soothed, pampered, piano prodigies that can jump. This has made them different than us. This has made them slightly insane; this is not how normal people live and breathe and walk around the planet.

You have to wonder sometimes: *Do they really understand what it is they are?*

FOR A STORY for *New York* magazine, I spent a week of March 2009 in Tampa, Florida, staying at a hotel within walking distance of George M. Steinbrenner Field, Spring Training home of the New York Yankees. The virtues of Spring Training—the "renewal," the "smell of freshly cut grass," the "nine pitchers whose names you've never heard"—have been well documented and chronicled by more talented writers than I, and besides, this was not an assignment for dreamy-eyed spiritualists: I was there to Talk To Athletes. I had all the vital questions: *What would the Yankees be like this year? How will the Yankees play? Will they win lots of games? Will they outscore their opponents? Are you confident that this team will be a success? Just how awesome are you, anyway?*

I spent five days sitting in a cramped press box—my seat actually faced a *wall*—watching men in baggy clothes leisurely lope around in the sun, and then, afterward, I stuck a recorder in their faces and asked them variations on the above questions. I honestly could think of nothing else to ask them. When you are interviewing a naked person, I've found it's not the ideal circumstance to pick his brain on philosophy, the arts, and the sacred gift handed to us by the cosmos in ninety-foot intervals. My questions were so stupid that I wanted to ask them in a funny accent, like one of those "comedy" reporters they trudge out on Super Bowl Media Day.

I just wasn't curious about what they had to say. They were not mean, they were not dismissive, they weren't even all that dumb. It was just that their status as living humans standing in front of me in a towel darned near destroyed everything I valued about what they did on the field. The act of playing baseball is instinctual and reactive; the act of discussing that act of playing baseball is reductive and diminishing. Mark Teixeira could be the world's most loquacious poet, and anything he had to say about his on-field exploits (or his gimpy ankle, or his excitement about joining a new team, or How Much Damned Fun Everybody In This Clubhouse Has) couldn't even approach the actual experience of being out there, playing the game, or the actual experience of watching him do it. It's not an activity that benefits from psychoanalysis or reflection. It is a game in which contemplation and self-criticism are antithetical to success. Baseball is a game you either play or you rhapsodize about and obsess over. These activities are mutually exclusive. The people who play baseball, and the people closest to it, are the ones most likely to lose touch with it, the ones most likely to miss the point of it all. What they are doing is different than what we are doing.

And lemme tell you: Mark Teixeira is not the world's most loquacious poet. And, all told, I'm a pretty lousy sports reporter.

Once my big Are The Yankees Going To Be Good This Year? story ran, I returned to the locker room of the new Yankee Stadium, the behemoth that the team (and New York taxpayers) spent $1.6 billion on only to realize they'd turned their sacred Bronx ground into a home run–producing pinball machine. Everything in Yankee Stadium is State Of The Art, which is to say, it's all going to seem extremely old in five years, when they'll be stuck with it. (My favorite edifice example of this is Assembly Hall in Champaign, Illinois, built in 1963 as a big white ugly spaceship, with the idea that in the future, we would all play basketball in zero gravity.)

All lockers in the Yankee Stadium clubhouse have built-in computers, though they're PCs, which means they'll have to replace them every season even though the majority of players surely have never used them. (I suspect "typing into your locker" is not a necessity they've ever considered.) Each computer has a background image, chosen by the player, ostensibly as a form of self-expression, or at least as much self-expression as New York Yankees players are allowed to have. Teixeira has a picture of his family. Derek Jeter has the Yankees logo. (He's never touched it.) Mariano Rivera has a big frightening cross. But most of the computers have what you would expect professional athletes to have on their lockers: pictures of women in various states of undress. Johnny Damon's model is particularly buxom.

Obviously, there's nothing wrong with this. If you've ever taken your car into the repair shop, you know that when groups of men work together in a somewhat confined space, one of the few reasonable responses is to publicly display pictures of attractive women. That's precisely the point: This is a job. These are men who wake up, go to work, shower, and go home. They're traveling salesmen, on the road half the year, living out of a Gucci suitcase, just doing the best they can at their job so they can keep it. Like the rest of us. The same goes for the reporters, and the broadcasters, and the coaches, and the traveling staff, and the hundreds of people it requires to keep the traveling road show that is a professional baseball team up and running. To all of them, it's just their job. It is something dramatically different for the rest of us. It is something more.

JIM EDMONDS is creeping in from center field; He wants to be ready to back up the catcher's throw if Barton tries to steal. Edmonds was known as a defensive wizard with the Anaheim Angels, and an above-average hitter, but he wasn't a superstar until the Angels traded him to the Cardinals before the 2000 season. Cardinals fans—spurred on by Mark McGwire, who extolled the virtues of America's Best Baseball Fans (trademark!)—took to him instantly. He was both effortless and dramatic, a fantastic player who took great joy in making routine plays look spectacular: Jimmy Edmonds loved to play to the crowd, and we loved being played to. He had his best year in 2004, hitting 42 homers and driving in 111 runs for the best Cardinals team of my lifetime. The Cardinals won 105 games and outlasted the Houston Astros in a vastly underrated National League Championship Series, a series few were watching, thanks to the histrionics going on in the Red Sox–Yankees ALCS. (Thanks to rainouts, several games of the Cardinals-Astros series were stuck on Fox's tiny cable offshoot F/X, preempting numerous reshowings of the Patrick Swayze actioner *Road House*.) Edmonds put down roots in St. Louis, opening up a "high-class nightclub" named Fifteen, after his uniform number. As amazing as The Great Pujols was, you saw as many, if not more, Edmonds jerseys in the stands. He blossomed with us, and we loved him for it.

After the disappointing 2007 season, though, it was clear Edmonds didn't have much left: He had trouble covering ground in center field anymore, he was slowed by concussions, and his batting average fell to .252 in a mere 117 games. Edmonds wasn't much of an asset to the team anymore, particularly considering the emergence of Rick Ankiel, the former phenom pitcher who, after years in the psychological wilderness, had bizarrely morphed into a power-hitting center fielder with range that clearly outpaced Edmonds, now thirty-eight years old and fading. Edmonds demanded that he keep the starting spot in center, so the Cardinals, wanting to open a spot for Ankiel, traded Edmonds to the San Diego Padres. We were sad to see him go, but we understood. Besides, no one wanted to watch an elderly Edmonds stumble through the outfield grounds he once ruled. We wanted to remember Edmonds for who he was, not for who he had become. He was certain to remain beloved by Cardinals fans for generations, and we knew, when he came back to Busch Stadium as a Padre, we'd give him a standing ovation out of appreciation for all he had done for us. He had earned it, and so had we.

The Padres had been hoping they had received the 2004 Edmonds, and when it became obvious that they hadn't—he hit .178 in twenty-six games and couldn't patrol the vast expanse of Petco Park's center field—they released him, showing him far more disrespect than the Cardinals ever had. It looked as if Edmonds was finished. We wondered if he'd honor the old tradition of signing for one day with the team with which he had become famous, so he could retire. He should end his career with the Cardinals, with us, with the people who loved him.

That's not what happened. Edmonds, apparently still seething from the trade to the Padres that set all this in motion, called the Chicago Cubs. A few teams showed interest in him, but no: He wanted the Cubs. He made it clear why, telling reporters that he felt the best way to extract revenge against the organization that had "wronged" him was to try to help their hated rivals win the World Series. The Cubs eagerly grabbed him, hoping some of his Cardinals mojo would rub off.

Edmonds was delighted. "I've always admired [Wrigley Field], and this team, and wanted to see what it was like on this side one time," he said. Later, he would blow off interview requests from St. Louis reporters and television stations, saying, "You had your chance." He was angry with the Cardinals. And he took it out on all of us by doing the one thing Cardinals fandom rules prohibit: crossing over to the Cubs and acting like it was the greatest place to be in the world.

This didn't seem strange, or even potentially damaging, to Edmonds, as a human being. The fans are the supporting character in his story, after all. The rest of us knew better. *St. Louis Post-Dispatch* columnist Bernie Miklasz, as smart and reasoned a sports columnist as you'll find, wrote, "The reality that Jimmy will be teammates with Carlos Zambrano—who plunked him twice in a raucous game at Wrigley back in 2004—makes no sense." He even quoted me in the story, and if you'll forgive me, I'm going to quote myself:

"I don't think Jim understands what this means," Leitch said. "By signing with the Cubs, he may be thinking he's getting back at Cardinals management. But the fans who loved him, we're the ones who will feel this. The fan base is forever."

"Can we really give Edmonds a standing ovation when he's wearing a Cubs uniform? Can we really do that? I'm not sure we can," Leitch said. "Any other uniform, sure. It's easy. But that uniform? And if we do give him a standing ovation, he'd better strike out and sit down."

It wasn't just Cardinals fans: Cubs fans were furious too. One of my favorite Cubs blogs, Hire Jim Essian, said this:

> I don't care if Jim Edmonds lets my mom borrow his mascara before she walks into work. I don't care if he puts on the best damn burlesque show in Chicago. I don't care if this shithead hits a walkoff home run for the Cubs in Game Seven of the World Series. I don't care if, late one night, I stagger out of a Wrigleyville bar into traffic, and Jim Edmonds pushes me out of the way, saving my life. I am going to HATE this bastard.

So, yeah: Passions running high on both sides. But Jim Edmonds didn't know about any of that, or he didn't care. He just wanted to get back at Cardinals management. He equated fans with management. He acted like we were all the same thing. But we're not. We'll be around a lot longer than management. He had betrayed us. He didn't seem to understand what that meant, or why that was so much worse. Baseball is a job to him, and the Cubs just another employer. It's an occupation, a different name on the checks, to Jim Edmonds, and every other athlete. But not to us. It's so much more. He couldn't understand that. You'd almost feel bad for him, if you didn't find yourself hating him all of a sudden.

So scoot back, Jim. Barton's not running. Plus, if you're a little closer to the bleachers out there, someone might throw an object at you.

IN MY LIFETIME, the St. Louis Cardinals have had:

THREE OWNERS
"Gussie" Busch 1975–89
Anheuser-Busch Co. 1989–96
Bill DeWitt Jr. 1996–2010

SEVEN GENERAL MANAGERS
Bing Devine 1975–78
John Claiborne 1978–80
Whitey Herzog 1980–82
Joe McDonald 1982–84
Dal Maxvill 1984–94
Walt Jocketty 1994–2007
John Mozeliak 2007–10

EIGHT MANAGERS
Red Schoendienst, 1975–76, 1980, 1990
Vern Rapp, 1977–78
Jack Krol, 1978, 1980
Ken Boyer, 1978–80
Whitey Herzog, 1980–90
Joe Torre, 1990–95
Mike Jorgensen, 1995
Tony La Russa, 1996–2010

All sixteen of these men (and the corporation now owned by some company in Belgium) have, at one point, been considered the "organization," the "franchise," the "St. Louis Cardinals." They have been the people making the decisions in the name of the Cardinals for thirty-five years, they have been the ones with their names on the letterhead. They are all noble men, working in good faith to win championships, sustain the brand, and make as much money as humanly possible. There is nothing wrong with any of those things.

But they are not the St. Louis Cardinals. They are just the museum curators, the people we keep around to mind the store and keep the trains running on time. They are only temporary stewards, professional baseball men for whom the Cardinals are an employer, not a passion. (Perhaps exceptions are made for Schoendienst, Herzog, and particularly La Russa, who might be the only person who handles Cardinals losses worse than I do.) These men can go somewhere else: Jocketty can head to Cincinnati, Torre can become a legend in New York. We have no such options. We're not going anywhere.

When you break it down, what exactly *is* a sports franchise? Is it a succession of ownership? An institutional philosophy? A corporate machine? Pretty red uniforms? All of these can be changed, and will be changed: In ten years, even La Russa will be gone from the Cardinals, Mozeliak could move on or be fired, heck, the team might be sold. When you look at all those people listed up there—and remember too that the Cardinals have been one of baseball's more *stable* franchises—you realize that they're all, really, just temps. When people talk about The Cardinals, they're not talking about them. They're talking about *us*.

That's the one constant. That's the single continuous line from 1975 to 2010, or 1949 to 1975, or 1918 to 1949. Me. My father. The fans of the team. We are the one aspect that never changes, the only people who have that devotion, that link to history. My grandfather loved the Cardinals, so my dad loved the Cardinals, so I loved the Cardinals, so my children will love the Cardinals. That's all these franchises, these teams, these uniforms are. They can change the colors, they can change the stadiums, they can change the managers, but they can't change that. We're the only link from old Cardinals to new Cardinals, the grip that keeps the whole illusion together, that keeps it all from bursting and floating apart. Without us, the Cardinals really are just twenty-five millionaires running around wearing funny shirts and pants. With us, they are eternal, immortal. This is not something they can understand. But this is all that matters.

And this is how I justify calling Edmonds a motherfucker under my breath when he catches Joel Pineiro's fly ball to end the top of the second inning. I hope Dad didn't hear that. He doesn't like it when I curse.

KNOWLEDGE YOU NOW HAVE

1. If a Leitch male attempts to buy a man a drink and is refused, he will never forgive the offense.
2. An engineering degree does not help you become a better baseball player. But you still have to go to college, kid.
3. Your father has seen other men's penises and therefore assures you that the Leitch men endowment is nothing you should be all that ashamed about. Please stop crying.

BOTTOM OF THE SECOND INNING

In which your narrator natters on about college.

*My dad, Jack, played minor-league ball in the Phillies' organiza-
tion. He often encouraged me to play softball as a child, and that
failed horribly: I was one of those rail-thin, arty type girls with no
interest in hit-ball-with-bat. Regardless, years later I was spending a very dull summer at home from college with my then-
boyfriend, and we had taken to hitting-ball-with-bat to pass
time. My dad came out to join us one day to pitch. I tried to talk
my dad out of it, insisting I would probably hit him in the face.
Well: He pitched the ball, and I hit him in the face.*

— ANDREA HANGST, Chicago, Illinois

ON A 2-0 PITCH TO LEAD OFF—JOEL PINEIRO IS NOT THE TYPE
of pitcher who can afford to fall behind to *anyone*—Jim Edmonds
smashes a deep fly ball to left field. Brian Barton, calculating the
torque of the parabolas, sprints to the ivy, but the ball hits the top of
the wall and skitters past him. I miss most of this. I'm still watching
Edmonds.

When Edmonds hits a ball solidly to the opposite field, particularly one he thinks will leave the park, he does this little hop, a not-
so-muted *oh, look at what I just did* before the obligatory celebration
around the base paths. When Edmonds was a Cardinal, this was an

alpha male assertion of dominance: Jim Edmonds was informing the unfortunate pitcher that his penis was considerably larger than the pitcher's own. The hop was Edmonds's signature: It showed up the pitcher without showing up the pitcher. The definitive Edmonds hop came after his home run off the Houston Astros' Dan Miceli to win Game 6 of the 2004 National League Championship Series. The hop was a subtle admiration by Jim Edmonds's of his own awesomeness. When Jim Edmonds played in St. Louis, I loved the hop. Now that he's just done the hop after hitting a 2–0 meatball from Joel Pineiro, I want to dig out his trachea with a pencil. It's minor solace that the thirty-eight-year-old Edmonds of September 20, 2008, can't quite push the ball over the wall.

As everyone leaps to their feet around us, Mike knows well enough to stay quiet. I notice him tap his foot a little bit, do an understated hop of his own, and look vacantly onto the field. This makes me feel bad. This is a special moment for Mike, the opportunity to watch his blighted Cubs clinch a division title, from the best seats at Wrigley Field he's ever had, and he's too polite to make a show of himself around two Cardinals fans who bought him the tickets and asked him to come along. Mike should savor this. Mike should be going crazy. Mike shouldn't hold anything back.

Then again, he's a Cubs fan, so he should sit down.

MIKE'S TOP FOUR CUBS MEMORIES, NO. 4, BY MIKE

1987: The Cubs signed Andre Dawson during Spring Training after he presented the team with a blank contract and told then-GM Dallas Green to fill in the blanks. This guy wanted to play for the Cubs so badly, he would have played for nothing. Even as a twelve-year-old I understood the value and lure of money. This gesture made me think the Cubs and this man were something special to follow. I immediately ended my allegiance to the White Sox.

I'm not sure how it works in today's world of Twitter, Facebook, and every bong party photographed and loaded to the Web within seconds, but in the mid-nineties, working at a college newspaper was a bizarre confluence of the trivial and the temporarily substantial. My first day at the University of Illinois, I trekked to the offices of the *Daily Illini* and put my name on a signup sheet for freshmen who wanted to join the staff. I wanted to be a film critic, like fellow Central Illinoisian Roger Ebert, and just because I thought there was a chance I could sneak into Illini games free, I mentioned I'd be up for writing sports stories as well. A week later, I'd "covered" an intramural Greek basketball game and "reviewed" Woody Allen's *Manhattan Murder Mystery,* and I stayed up all night waiting for the paper to be delivered to my dorm. I paced the lobby of the Florida Avenue Residence Halls, watching every drunk coed stumble in, thinking this was the one . . . no, this one . . . no, this one . . . *no, this one.* By the time the paper finally arrived, and I tore it apart looking for my byline, I was hooked. I skipped most of my classes, earning the old Gentleman's C, and spent every waking hour at the newspaper, hanging out with the same people, drinking at the same bars, my own little version of a Princeton eating club. It was like the Skull and Bones Society, but with a few heterosexuals.

It was at the *Daily Illini* that I met Mike. We started at the paper at the same time and did the delicate dance of burgeoning friendship that every male knows intimately: We drank a lot of beer and played a lot of Sega hockey without learning a whit about each other, and not thinking to ask. As the years went on, a few biographical details lazily emerged. Mike was the only child of a suburban Chicago family, he had wanted to work for a newspaper since he was a toddler, he had a reporter's eye for arcania and thirst for dull detail, and he was a Cubs fan. College boys being college boys, the contrast of our baseball teams provided our only real attempts at meaningful conversation, disguised as jocular conflict. My father knew him as "your long-haired Cubs fan friend" up until . . . well, as far as I know, up until today.

College newspapers are the perfect place to pretend you're a grown-up without having to face any of the real adult concerns we're all now stuck with. One of the peculiarities of the *Daily Illini* was that, because of the *Champaign News-Gazette*'s anachronistic decision to publish in the afternoons—you know, when Dad comes home from work to slug a martini and fire up his pipe—we were the only morning newspaper for the entire Champaign-Urbana area, which had a population of about 210,275 cheery souls. This meant that we covered city politics in a way most college papers don't, sitting through council meetings, rifling through the county sheriff's police reports, filing intricate four-part series on arcane zoning issues. Also, because Champaign was only an hour-and-a-half from the state capital of Springfield, we covered state politics too; our senior year, Mike wrote a story on page A14 about an unknown state senator named Barack Hussein Obama, who told Mike, "I'm curious about the culture of Springfield." For many people, real, live adults, in the Champaign-Urbana area, we were the first source for news, what they read with their morning coffee, bagel, and Adderall. We took this responsibility seriously: The "City/State" editor was a more valued position than the "Campus" editor.

This was a job perfect for Mike, who ate up the world of filibusters and transit service municipality allocations and school board members. He'd grown up worshiping great Chicago newspaper legends like Mike Royko, Clarence Page, and John Kass. On Lower Wacker Drive in Chicago, the famous Billy Goat Tavern—immortalized not just by the notorious Billy Goat curse (which is supposedly the reason the Cubs haven't won a World Series is so long; Billy Goat owner Sam Sianis cursed the team when he was denied a ticket to Wrigley for his pet goat, perhaps because goats probably shouldn't be allowed in baseball stadiums), but also John Belushi's old "Cheezborger, Cheezborger, Cheezborger. No Coke. Pepsi" sketch, actually written by Chicagoan Bill Murray—sat strategically between the *Chicago Tribune* and *Chicago Sun-Times* offices, and served as the unofficial center of Midwestern political journalism. It was a shrine to the days of the ink-stained wretch, and specifically to Royko, whose picture graces every open area of wall space to this day. It's a living monument to the romantic, bygone, fedora days of men spending the day destroying one another for scoops and then heading out to slug whiskey and smoke cigars together until ole Sianis threw 'em out into the street. Mike was a reporter's reporter. All he wanted was to be one of those guys: caustic, grizzled skeptics hiding poets' hearts. Champaign-Urbana was a pit stop for Mike. Four years there, then back to a suburban paper, working his way up to the city beat, to the Billy Goat, to that gorgeous big-shouldered soul of America's last great city. That was the plan. Newspapers would thrive forever.

It wasn't until a trip up to Chicago, my first visit to the Billy Goat, before a drunken passing out of about eleven people on the floor of Mike's parents' living room (I have no idea how anyone ever survives college), that I even knew Mike was an only child. Most only children—and, hey, who's up for some blind, blanket social stereotyping? Me! Me!—particularly those from wealthy families, can't help but be a little spoiled, mollycoddled by baby boomer parents who wanted to be their kids' best friend rather than their disciplinarian. Mike wasn't like this at all. Once we'd been friends long enough to ask personal questions without being *damned gaywads about it,* I expressed my surprise to Mike that he wasn't a pampered snot. "They'd kick my ass at the Billy Goat if I came in there like that," he said. "Besides, I don't think Cubs fans are allowed to be spoiled brats." I think 38,000 frat boys at Wrigley Field at two in the afternoon would beg to differ. But I'm not sure they're real Cubs fans, *real* Chicagoans. But Mike is.

You can probably guess where it comes from. Mike writes again:

I'm a Cubs fan because of my father—and Andre Dawson. I can't remember any specific play by Hawk or game Dad and I watched together that would explain my loyalty. I just know these two men—one a fan who never let a losing season discourage him, one a member of that last class of baseball heroes who didn't burst the sports superhero mythology—are directly responsible for my summer pastime, and pretty much everything.

AFTER EDMONDS'S HIT, Tim McCarver says, "Wrigley Field is the perfect park for Jim Edmonds's stroke," and, not for the first time, I want to slap Tim McCarver. Pineiro then walks rookie catcher Geovony Soto on four pitches, and you have to appreciate that sort of pitch economy. If you're wild and reeling, hey, why waste time?

Pineiro throws two *more* balls, to Mark DeRosa and the crowd senses some beauty brewing. Pineiro is one of those pitchers who can't strike anybody out, doesn't throw hard, and can give up too many home runs. The only reason he's in the major leagues, the only reason he's pitching in *the game in which the Cubs can clinch the division*, is because his sinker ball induces ground balls.

Cardinals pitching coach Dave Duncan—who has two sons in the majors, Chris, a Cardinals outfielder, and Shelley, a Yankees first baseman, each of whom are about a foot taller than their father (something that would make me wonder about the Duncan family milkman)—is obsessed with "pitching to contact," which runs in the face of common baseball wisdom that the best pitchers are strikeout pitchers. Duncan, like most geniuses, is a control freak with a God complex; he believes he can mold anyone into an effective pitcher, strikeouts be damned, as long as the player gives himself over to him and allows Duncan to shape him in his image. Oftentimes, this works: Duncan did wonders with Jeff Suppan, Braden Looper, Dennis Eckersley, the late Darryl Kile. Sometimes, though, Duncan fools himself into thinking he can fix *anyone,* and you end up with Kip Wells, Mike Maroth, and, today, Pineiro, who came into the game with a 5.15 ERA and a total lack of confidence in himself, and from any Cardinals fan who dared watch him pitch at any point this season. A fundamental fact about pitch-to-contact hurlers? Hitters usually *hit the ball,* and this year, Joel Pineiro has been hit often, in many different directions. And now he's down 2–0 to Mark DeRosa with two runners on, nobody out, in a game neither my father nor I are mentally prepared to lose. Mark DeRosa is not a large man, but his nostrils are flaring and he might be swinging an ox.

Mike leans over to me, and his face does not change expression. "Big pitch here."

Pineiro throws a hanging, but low, breaking ball, and DeRosa obligingly beats it straight into the ground. It is, to be kind, one of the more perfectly placed double-play balls in baseball history. If aliens were to land on Earth, and you needed a physical example of the perfect double-play ball—and, of course, this is *exactly* how aliens should be introduced to Earth's culture—this is what you would show them. Joel Pineiro, with his 5.15 ERA, his ridiculous facial hair, his dipshit smirky smile, his two-year, $13 million contract, gave us the ground ball we needed. This game will not grow out of control. This will remain sedate and safe and not a problem.

Second baseman Felipe Lopez picks the ball up on an easy hop. The play here is so obvious that the lady accountant from your beer league softball team, the one who comes to the plate with the bat upside down and runs to third base when she makes contact, knows what to do: Flip to the shortstop for the force-out, then back over to first for the alien-approved tailor-made double play.

But Felipe Lopez is, to put it mildly, a flake, an all-star talent who never seemed to take the time to learn the intricacies of the lovely game he's playing. When he came out of high school in 1998, *Baseball America* called him the best defensive shortstop in the country, and he was named Florida's player of the year. The Toronto Blue Jays chose him in the first round of that year's draft but traded him three years later, quietly citing "personality quirks." His talent exploded in Cincinnati, earning him a spot on the 2005 All-Star Game, but the Reds tired of him quickly and traded him to Washington, where the amazing defensive shortstop led the majors in errors. The problem was never skill. The problem was his brain: He just stopped paying attention sometimes. The game was so easy to him that part of him simply couldn't help but make it hard. In a pinch, you could always count on him making the wrong decision. The Nationals finally became fed up with it and cut him outright. Which is how he ended up here, in Wrigley Field, fielding a double-play ball that you would show to aliens.

All Felipe Lopez has to do is flip the ball to Cesar Izturis as soon as it lands in his glove, a routine, rote, *obvious* play that anyone at this level of professional baseball has done scores upon scores of times. But this is not what Felipe Lopez does. No, Felipe Lopez becomes distracted by the Geovony Soto–sized blur passing in front of him and decides he wants to touch that blur, that he must tag that blur, because hey: *There's a guy right there! Let's touch him!* Soto's too far away to touch, so faraway, so close, so Felipe Lopez readjusts and finally—finally!—flips the ball to Izturis. At this point, Felipe Lopez's hesitation, the split-split-split second, forces Izturis's throw to Albert Pujols at first base to be a split-split-split-split second late to beat De-Rosa. He is safe. So instead of a runner at third base with two outs, there are runners at first and third with one out, and an inning that was nearly closed has turned into a valid, beeping opportunity. Because of one split-split-split second. Because Felipe Lopez was distracted by the Geovany Soto–sized object. Because the Washington Nationals had seen this many, many times, and the Cardinals had not.

Baseball is full of infinitesimal moments like this one, plays that don't seem to mean much but ultimately mean everything. One inch here, one half-second hesitation there, one slight whisper of wind— each adding up to turn the universe inside out. These moments are what baseball is: specks of sand that build up until you suddenly realize you're neck-deep in the desert with vultures circling. One little head bob, one tiny step forward, and it's all different now, the entire course of history altered forever. When these moments break right for you, you're spending a warm September afternoon on sacred baseball ground, trying to win the National League Central.

When they don't, you just try not to look around you, hoping that you're the only one who senses the coming storm, pretending that if you act as if it isn't there, it won't be. But it is. It's right there. You just saw it. And so did everybody else.

MIKE'S TOP FOUR CUBS MEMORIES, NO. 3, BY MIKE

Mark Grace vs. Frank DiPino: Damned if I can remember exactly when this happened (and the Internet is no help), but it must have been in the spring of 1989 because I recall hanging a picture of Grace slugging DiPino in my eighth grade locker. DiPino, then a member of the hated Cardinals, threw a pitch just a bit too inside (there had been some off-the-field problems between the two), and Grace charged the mound, belting DiPino with a wicked undercut. I realized then the Cubs-Cardinals rivalry was not something to be trifled with. Another Grace memory, the 1989 playoffs. Grace batted .647 in the NLCS with an OPS of 1.788. If only his teammates had played half as well.

Mike was never particularly skilled with women, and, though he'd never admit it, I always sensed he took a certain pride in this. Everyone we knew was a newspaper nerd, so it's not as if anybody we knew was out having threesomes and drunkenly taking random women home every night (you know, the stuff you're supposed to do in college), but Mike was unusually sanguine about the whole thing. Not only did Mike not ever try to pick up girls, he never seemed to consider it a legitimate option. This saved him considerable embarrassment—embarrassment the rest of us, particularly me, knew all too well—but it also took him out of the game a little bit. Chasing girls occupies a disproportionate amount of a college student's life, and it never seemed a big deal for Mike. "It'll happen when it happens," he said, "and there's no need to push it." I took this to mean that he was a virgin. I'm pretty sure I was right.

It was unnerving, but a lot about Mike was unnerving to me. He was as affable and loyal a friend as you could ask for, but nothing ever seemed to faze him: He never seemed to go through any of the agonizing soul-searching that's an obligation for college students. He knew who he was and what he wanted to do, and setbacks never brought him down. I secretly hated him for it.

One evening, we sat out on the porch of our dingy hovel across the street from the *Daily Illini,* smoking cigarettes and drinking Mad Dog 40/40. I was wallowing in one of those spates of self-pity that regularly visit during college, reaching heights of self-absorption that only pampered middle-class white people can achieve. I don't know what I was upset about, probably some girl. I told him that nothing meant anything, that the world was a stupid, mean place, that life was just a series of pointless, cruel interludes and that death was our only solace. (The odds are excellent that I was wearing flannel, listening to a lot of Nirvana, and wiping my hair out of my eyes. The nineties were such a dumb decade.) "It's all nothing!" I wailed. "Everything we are doing is impotent!"

Mike, who had always been my trusty sidekick, the low-key reporter counterpart to my histrionic, self-indulgent "columnist," paused and threw an empty pack of cigarettes at my head. "You're being a moron," he said. "The world's just fine. Stop whining. If you ever have a kid who talks like this, I hope you slap him." This was not the talk of an only child. This was the talk of a man with a plan. I laughed, and then we put on the new Smashing Pumpkins CD and played Nintendo RBI Baseball for about six hours.

The summer before our senior year of college, Joan, the cute blonde who worked on the city desk at the paper, finally decided she'd had enough of smarmy, egocentric boys like me and made a move on Mike. She was smart about it: She waited until everyone else from the paper was busy with something else and pounced. She and Mike were an immediate staple. They were both Chicago kids, and she was willing to turn away from the White Sox.

Mike ended up getting that newspaper job. He's now the managing editor for the *Aurora Beacon-News*. It worked out differently than
it was supposed to. The Billy Goat Tavern is now a tourist trap. The
Sun-Times is bankrupt and in a building clear across town. Mike's the
oldest person on staff; they laid off all his contemporaries, and now
he supervises a staff of cheap, disposable recent grads. And he's in
charge of the paper's Twitter page. There's a blogger in town that
keeps ripping on Mike all the time. Says he's not a real journalist.
Says he's old media. Says he don't know nothing. No Pepsi. Coke.

Mike's still pretty cool with it all, though. His casual contented-
ness remains unnerving, and awesome.

KOSUKE FUKUDOME is hitting .136 in the month of September and is
barely playing. Manager Lou Piniella has told him he needs to "Amer-
icanize" his game, though he must not have said it in Japanese, because it hasn't worked. Joel Pineiro doesn't seem to mind any of this:
He walks Fukudome on four straight pitches, and the sky around our
row grows darker.

Fortunately, Ted Lilly is up next, and even though his career stats
imply that he can hit, his batting stance, in which he does a rather
convincing impersonation of someone suffering from spina bifida, is
the first sign of hope I've seen all inning. (Lilly, awaiting the pitch, looks
like he has an itch in the middle of his back he's trying to scratch with
the bat.) Which brings up Soriano. Lackadaisical, heavens-blessed
Alfonso Soriano. With the bases loaded. We'll know real fast how this
is going to work.

MIKE'S TOP FOUR CUBS MEMORIES, NO. 2, BY MIKE

May 28–May 30, 1999: Will Leitch and I attend all three games
of the Cubs-Cardinals series at Wrigley Field. The Cubs sweep
the series. Four years later, Will and I watch the Cubs beat the

Cardinals again, in fifteen innings, on a two-run homer by Sammy Sosa, who's still a dick, regardless.

Unlike today's game, in 2003, in a five-game series over Labor Day weekend at Wrigley Field, the Cardinals and Cubs were both still in the National League Central race. Coming into the series, the Cardinals were tied for first with the Astros, and the upstart Cubs, led by pitching phenoms Mark Prior and Kerry Wood, were just a half game back. This was the series for the Cardinals, winners of the last three division titles, to assert their authority. We had lost Game 1, thanks to that blasted Prior, but I felt positive about Game 2, because this was the Cubs. We all knew the rules.

I sat in the upper deck with Mike and Joan, whom I was visiting from New York. They were living together by then, all normal and grown-up, and I was their madman friend starving while trying to figure out how he could find someone to pay him for typing. We were awfully happy up there, boozing and talking about O'Malley's, but there was a certain muted pity in their mannerisms: Mr. Wild Searching Columnist Guy was a lot less cute in 2003 than he'd been in 1997. Right before the seventh-inning stretch, Joan left to use the restroom, which struck me as strange: Isn't locking arms and singing—singing! everyone all as one!—at the seventh-inning stretch half the point of going to Wrigley Field?

Once Joan was safely away, Mike turned to me. "So listen . . . Joan and I are getting married. And we'd love for you to be the best man. It couldn't be anyone else." I said I'd be honored. I would. Of course. Mike smiled. "Good. You can even bring a date."

"I'll do it as long as the Cardinals win this game," I said, and it wasn't discussed again until the wedding. I gave a lousy speech: I felt like I had too much to say. I think I just talked about the Cardinals. They lost that game in 2003. Jeff Fassero threw a batting practice fastball to Sosa in the bottom of the fifteenth, and he smashed it onto Waveland Avenue, sending everybody home. The Cardinals went 1–4 in the series, and for all intents and purposes, the National League Central race was over. The Cubs ended up winning the division and advancing to the National League Championship Series against the Florida Marlins. Odd: I just *can't remember* what happened next.

Three years later, Mike and Joan had a son, Jackson, the kid in the Edmonds jersey screaming and playing with the Zombies. He's three years old now, and Mike says he hasn't quite figured out the Cubs stuff yet. Jackson doesn't know any of the players—though Mike likes to make him say, "Fukudome," because it's funny—and he has trouble sitting through a whole game, like any respectable three-year-old. But Mike keeps buying him anything he can with a Cubs logo on it.

'Cause hey: If Mike wants to put the indignity of being a Cubs fan on a whole other generation, far be it from me to stop him.

ON A 1–0 PITCH, Soriano flicks his wrists ever so slightly—he will never, ever look like he's trying—and rips a line drive just out of the reach of shortstop Cesar Izturis. Pineiro wasn't going to be able to dance between the raindrops forever. Unfortunately, his defense betrays him again: In his hurry to charge the ball and make a play on the second runner trying to score, Definitive Genius Brian Barton overplays his hand and muffs the play. The ball gleefully skitters past him and goes all the way to the wall. It happens so quickly, so *whipdashwhipdashrewww* that it takes a few seconds to register. Baseball happens like this. It's nothing . . . and then it's everything. One bad pitch, and one bad fielding play, and we go from a nice calm 0–0 game to a 3–0 Cubs lead and forty thousand Cubs fans screaming in my father's and my ears. If I had decided to look at my watch, I would have missed the whole thing. I wish I had.

Mike yells "Yeah!" That's all he does. No other words, not even a change of facial expression. After Ryan Theriot flies out to end the inning on the next pitch, he looks at his phone, opens it, and shows it to me. It's a picture of Jackson in that Cubs jersey. "Ain't he cute?" he says.

"He looks like a fucking serial killer," I tell him. Mike puts the phone back in his pocket and finally allows himself a smile and that little fist pump thing white people do when they're happy but are too repressed to actually show it.

He's earned it. It's 3–0 Cubs. I pat my dad on the back. "Maybe if Barton weren't so busy studying, he'd have gotten that ball," he says. He's lashing out. I understand.

"Make sure you get that in your score book," Mike says. "Three runs. *Three.* T-H-R-E-E."

MIKE'S TOP FOUR CUBS MEMORIES, NO. 1, BY MIKE

Game 6 NLCS, October 14, 2003: I still feel that sickness deep within my gut. Rooting for the Cubs has not been the same. I have not—cannot—be as invested. It hurts too much. Something (the charm of low expectations?) was lost that day.

Watching Mike at the end of this inning, with the Cubs up 3–0 and his fellow fans exuberant and tan, I absolutely do not believe him on this. And you know: I am glad I don't.

KNOWLEDGE YOU NOW HAVE

1. You are only allowed to curse when the Cardinals are behind.
2. Mad Dog 40/40, in 1996, was $4.99 for a full liter.
3. Your father's hero growing up was a fat man known for the unique placing of his thumb.

TOP OF THE THIRD INNING

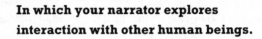

**In which your narrator explores
interaction with other human beings.**

*My father was a youth baseball manager and board member in a
baseball league in a small town in northern West Virginia. This
was during the 1960s, and the league was discussing the issue
of integration. I remember being in the car with my dad as he
described the board meeting where the decision was being discussed and voted on. Pop wanted to let everyone play baseball,
and if the league had not integrated, he would have left the board,
and my brother and I would not have played baseball that summer. The league did vote to integrate. I would drive with my dad
and brother to pick one of our players, an African-American boy.
He did not have a glove, so my dad made me give him mine. Dad
took a moral stand at a challenging time in our country's history
even though he would have had two very disappointed boys if
he had made them quit the team.*

— MIKE McCULLOUGH, Lake Zurich, Illinois

DAD HAS MADE A NEW FRIEND. THIS IS TYPICAL. IF YOU LEAVE
my father alone for as long as thirty seconds, he will start talking to
some stranger. When you're stuck with him at some endless Midwestern wedding where you don't know anyone, by the end of the

night, Dad's usually conducting the band and wearing the bride's garter around his bicep. At the launch party for the release of my last book, my father walked into a crowded Manhattan bar with about a hundred snotty, damaged, bitter media types. By the end of the night, he had signed more books than I had. This is just what Dad does. Dad can talk to anybody.

This is not something that I ever noticed as a child. Dad was not an outgoing man, or at least he didn't seem like one. He was the big scary guy who had an endless number of chores for me, who seemed frustrated by my early desire to read books rather than play sports, who never could disguise his disgust that I couldn't tell which one was a Phillips head screwdriver. He was not the hugging, your-best-pal type dad. He was the quiet, stoic, demanding sort. He never spanked me or called me terrible names, but he wasn't quite sure how to handle the awkward kid who wasn't much help out in the garage. I feared him and desperately didn't want to disappoint him.

That is to say, he was a dad. The role he was playing, I suspect, was his impersonation of his own father. Because he always appeared to be a lot more fun and warm to everyone else than he did to me.

When I was eight years old, playing in the Mattoon Jaycee League, Dad signed up to be my coach and immediately confused everyone on our first day of practice by bringing along my cousin Denny.

Denny was a year older than me, so he was already a one-year Jaycee veteran. He'd played for Pepsi-Cola the year before, under the eye of Coach Simpson, a loud, abrasive, and entirely awful woman whose son, Dustin, was renowned for running out of the batter's box in fear every time the pitcher started his windup.

Denny didn't really like baseball very much in the first place, but under Coach Simpson, he quickly grew to loathe it. Denny was very small—the bat was almost as tall as he was—and Coach Simpson made it far worse. She would typically refuse to play him, but when his father complained, she would stick him in late in the game with explicit instructions, whispering in his tiny, underdeveloped ears, not to swing. "Just stand up there. If you swing, you won't play next game." Denny was so little, it was near impossible to throw him a strike, and he would inevitably walk every time he came up. He would then be replaced with a pinch runner, followed by a nasty glance from Coach Simpson in his father's direction, as if to say, *There's your goddamned at bat*! Once, Denny, if just out of boredom, swung three times, struck out, and was promptly screamed at by Coach Simpson. He quietly cried on the bench.

Dad, because he was family, rescued Denny from Coach Simpson and made it clear there was a new sheriff in town. "Denny is going to be our catcher. Put the gear on, Denny," he said. Now, Denny did own a glove, but under Coach Simpson, he was rarely called upon to use it, and then only as a harmless right fielder. Denny? As a catcher? Any pitch would surely knock him over. Ricky McKittrick, a classy, smart ten-year-old with a firebrand younger brother who ended up in the Coles County Jail, was our best pitcher, and Dad directed him to warm up with Denny. Ricky fired his best heater in there, and Denny, to his surprise, snatched it out of the air with his virgin catcher's mitt. You could see a huge smile through the mask. We had our catcher, and baseball found itself a fan.

The fever swept through the whole Little League team. (We were sponsored by the local VFW, which just meant opponents called us "Very Fat Women." Eight-year-olds are fantastic.) There was this chubby eight-year-old named John Hawkins. He was so obese he could barely swing the bat, and when he did, it was with no extension, a top spinning itself into the ground. He also couldn't catch with his undersized glove jammed uncomfortably over his plump fingers. Once, during batting practice, he was smacked in the face with a pop-up because he'd been chewing on his glove and watching a nearby train pass.

Dad was undaunted. The first game of the season, John was the leadoff batter. He was hit with the first pitch and immediately given the steal sign by Dad. He waddled and belly flopped into second base. That the catcher's throw had sailed into center field was irrelevant. He was safe. His grin could be seen three states over.

Then there was John Branson. A gangly, shy kid from a dirt-poor Mattoon family, raised by a single mother, he would cry every time she dropped him off at practice. He would often refuse to leave his mom's side in the car. Dad would go out and sit with them. After two practices, once he had cajoled John out of the car, Dad began calling him "Bulldog." Funny thing: John started to look a little less scared when he came to the plate, and about two weeks later, he showed up for a game with the name "BULLDOG" emblazoned across his uniform. By his final year, he made the city all-star game, and years later, in the thirteen-year-old league he hit a home run off me that cost us the game. His family remains close with ours.

I hated all of this. I had finally come around on baseball, memorizing Stan Musial's statistics and rattling them off to my parents' friends' amazement, so at the age of eight, if you loved the game, you were already better than three-quarters of the kids out there, who were plopped in the league just so their parents could have a few hours' peace each week. I was good. I was the best player.

Problem was, Dad kept batting me near the bottom of the order, behind John Hawkins and Denny and Bulldog. I deserved to be batting fourth, and pitching, and catching, and playing every damn position on the field if I had to. Why were those shrimps and crybabies batting above me?

Everyone on the team loved Dad instantly, but I didn't see it. Why? All he did was let crappy players on the field when it hurt us the most. We could have totally beaten the Elks Club if I'd have been batting fifth.

Dad plunged onward. He would often drive out of town to pick up players whose parents couldn't make the trip. If a kid wanted his name on the back of his jersey but couldn't afford it, Dad would pick up the tab. He even would encourage me to make friends with the ones the other kids rarely talked to.

Dad also developed this weird habit, inspired by one of John Hawkins's at bats. Despite Dad's attempts to change the laws of physics and motion, Hawkins's girth made it tremendously difficult for him to get the bat around on even the weakest of fastballs. Most of his at bats were strikeouts, walks or a hit-by-pitch. Once, though, Hawkins (who was inevitably known as "Hawk" by the end of the season) happened to time his lunge at just the right moment, and *pow*. The ball had all of Hawk's weight behind it and went soaring over the left fielder's head. Hawk stood there in wonder. *I did that?* Dad stifled a laugh and screamed, "GO!" Hawk snapped out of it and took off, and the sonuvagun ended up on third base. Dad hugged him as he stood, panting, on the base. From then on, any time any player would hit the ball, Dad would yell, "GO!" I'm sure it annoyed the other coaches, but the kids ate it up. The best was when Bulldog drilled one down the first-base line and ended up on third, where he scolded Dad for forgetting. "Hey, you didn't yell 'GO!' "

Eventually, I ate it up too. It was impossible not to get caught up in it.

Dad led our team's charge for three years, all three years I played for the team. We never won a league title, only made the playoffs once, ending up a respectable .500 during his tenure. At the end of the third season, the entire team went out to our house for an end-of-the-year picnic. The team shocked him with a trophy with the names of every player, with the inscription, "Presented to Coach for a wonderful year. Thank you, and GO!!!!!" It remains on the wall of our home, having survived years of moving and chaos and upheaval and all the curveballs growing up and growing old throws you.

To this day, anytime I'm back in Mattoon and run into one of the old VFW kids, he always mentions that team. Many of them played only one more year of organized baseball, and learned that most grown-ups weren't like Dad, that most cared too much about winning and losing, rather than kids feeling like they're a part of something, part of a team. Many of them have kids of their own now. Many of them have faced so much of the tragedy and the heartache and the disappointment and the sorrow that adulthood brings that it's a wonder they can remember childhood at all.

They all remember those teams, though, and they all remember Dad. Dad can talk to anybody.

DAD'S NEW FRIEND is the guy wearing a Cubs T-shirt and the blue Cardinals hat. Quite reasonably, Dad asks him what the deal is with the getup. His explanation is not convincing.

"Well, see I grew up a Cardinals fan, and I *love* the Cardinals!" he says, cheerfully, dumbly. "Willie McGee . . . Ozzie Smith . . . Bruce Sutter . . . remember those guys?"

Dad says yes, he does remember those guys.

"Yeah, yeah, well, you know, I LOVE the Cardinals!" The man is probably around thirty-five, just a couple of years older than I am, but he has the doofus goatee and casual obliviousness of someone who was middle-aged when he was in high school. "I always root for them . . . except when the Cubs are in town, of course."

That Dad keeps a straight face after hearing this makes me think he could survive waterboarding without so much as a facial twitch. "I see, I see . . . Now, why's that? I don't get that."

The man grins. "Well, her, of course!" He points to his wife sitting next to him, who is clad entirely in Cubbie Blue and even has a tiny caricature of Harry Caray painted on her face. She's cute and friendly, but not nearly cute and friendly enough.

"When we got married, we moved here, for her family, and you know, her pops was a Cubs fan, and you know how that goes, right, man?" He's looking at me for some sort of recognition, but he's not going to get it. He frowns for a second and turns back to my dad, who's smiling, somehow.

"So we made a deal," he says. "I could root for the Cardinals as long as they weren't playing the Cubs. And when they're in town, I'd come and cheer for the Cubbies. I mean, what's the hurt? The Cardinals are out of the race anyway. The Cubs . . . this is their year! This is where I live! Everyone's so excited about it! How can you not get on board?"

Mike slaps me on the shoulder. "See, Will? You gotta get on board! No use fighting it!"

I look at the man. "Sir, I mean no offense by this . . . but you're the worst sports fan I've ever met." The numbnuts thinks I'm kidding.

Dad closes this Socratic debate. "Hey, to each his own!" he says. "Everybody's gotta eat!" I have no idea what he's talking about, and I turn away, ashamed, while he and that guy prattle on for a while about something or other.

CARDINALS CATCHER Jason LaRue leads off the top of the third. He's hitting .236 on the season with four home runs, and all you need to know about Jason LaRue is that this is his best offensive season in about six years. Actually, that's not all you need to know about Jason LaRue. You also need to know what's on his face.

Jason LaRue wears a Fu Manchu mustache, which makes him look like an odd mix of Peter Lorre and Charles Manson. It's a look that no one other than a baseball player has tried in about forty years, and it's worth noting that on a baseball player, it almost looks normal. Some enterprising sociological student should write a master's thesis about the dynamics of a professional baseball team's locker room. These are twenty-five men who, for six months out of the year, hang out with only one another, all of them socially stunted but athletically gifted piano prodigies. Imagine a military platoon, except there's no discipline, no noble purpose, and everyone's a millionaire. The group-think of a professional baseball team can be staggering. After the Pittsburgh Pirates traded "star" center fielder Nate McLouth to the Atlanta Braves in June 2009, the *Pittsburgh Post-Gazette* reported the locker room scene thusly:

> On Thursday, at the clubhouse table where McLouth used to play cards with relievers Sean Burnett and Jesse Chavez, a candle bearing McLouth's uniform No. 13 was lit, along with a photo of him in uniform. "We'll miss him," Burnett said.

This is what we're dealing with here: Overgrown adolescents who have no idea how to live in the greater world, boys lacking even the most basic notion of how humans live. This does not make them bad people, and this does not make me cheer for them any less. But it is worth understanding. And it is worth realizing that the most blatant physical manifestation of this twenty-five-men, six-month, basic-training-in-luxury-hotels regimen is the unique facial hair that only baseball players dare sport. LaRue's is an extreme example, but you also have Ryan Franklin's extended chin hair (which could be tucked in his spikes), Scott Spiezio's ridiculous dyed-red "landing strip," and Rick Ankiel's spectacular Tom Selleck mustache. In the constrained, childlike world of a baseball clubhouse, facial hair becomes the lone opportunity for self-expression. There are no women around to tell them the Red Foatee or the Scraggling Goat is a bad idea. This is theirs, and only theirs.

Lilly hangs a curveball to LaRue, who pounces on it, rearing back all his might and muscle, squaring the ball perfectly, grunting and screaming out all the strength within him, and pops the ball about fifteen feet in the air to the first baseman, who catches it for the first out. Derrek Lee has a little half-beard thing going. He kind of looks like Kermit the Frog when he slipped on a disguise.

THERE'S A COLLEGIAL atmosphere to baseball games that I've never found in other sports. Football games, particularly professional ones, are scary visits into a dangerous, gutter end of the gene pool, with painted faces, skull tattoos, and people eating aluminum and injecting the liquid inside. Every time I go to a professional football game, I feel like I'm a Rhodes scholar, and I am anything but a Rhodes scholar. Simply going to the restroom can feel like visiting a war zone.

Baseball is calmer than that, warmer, just fifty thousand people sitting in a park watching people roll around on the grass. There is a sense that we are all in this together, that we're leisurely witnessing something unfurl in front of us, that we can look away for a moment and not worry about the world exploding behind us. We all have plenty of time. The clock is not ticking down.

When I'm at Busch Stadium, surrounded by my Cardinals brethren, the odds are great that I have little to nothing in common with anyone around me. I am a political liberal, a Woody Allen obsessive, a closet death metal fan who spends way too much time playing Tetris on my phone. If he's lucky, the random stranger to my left in the bleachers is none of these things. But if he is a Cardinals fan, then he is my best friend. Whatever our socioeconomic backgrounds, secret fetishes, quiet prejudices, if he's wearing that interlocking STL hat, we have a mutual interest, a common bond, a lifelong passion that eliminates everything else from the equation.

In 2006, I ended up with four tickets for Game 5 of the World Series between the St. Louis Cardinals and the Detroit Tigers. (This game will come up again.) Tickets for my father, my mother, and me, and we sold the fourth one, to a loyal Cardinals fan. He had driven all the way from Florida to meet his brother, who lived in Kansas, outside Busch Stadium to see if either of them could find tickets. Neither was going to miss a deciding game of a Cardinals World Series, and neither was going to pass up the opportunity to experience it with the other. We ran into them pregame as they asked anyone within eyesight for tickets. We said we only had one, and after a few seconds of silent brother communication, the older one took us up on our offer of face value. It would have been wrong to price gouge a fellow Cardinals fan, even if it was the World Series.

We sat next to the older brother the entire game, high-fiving him, hugging him, fretting with him. His brother made it in, to a seat on the other side of the stadium (and at far above face value of the ticket), and they spent most of the freezing evening texting each other back and forth. When Adam Wainwright struck out Brandon Inge to win the game, and the Series, we exploded, an orgy of red-clad corny Cardinal fan dorkiness. It's a seminal Leitch family memory, one of those nights that we'll all remember when we die. The older brother was there with us, for every step. He was a member of the Leitch family that night. I remember nothing about him, except that he was from Florida; I couldn't even guess at his name. In that moment, though, at that game, he was blood.

He took that picture, that iconic capture, mere seconds after the final out. It was his idea. "Hey, I gotta get a picture of you guys . . . WOOOOO!" That picture is in our homes now, in scrapbooks, on computer backgrounds, on freaking stamps. It is a signature Leitch family image.

We didn't think to take a picture of him. Within a minute of taking the shot, he left to go find his brother and have his own family memory.

NOTE: If you are reading this book, and you are that guy: Please do not contact me. No offense; you were awesome. I just think we'll all enjoy each other more in the past rather than the present. It was too cold that night for you to smell Dad, for one thing.

PERHAPS WHAT'S MOST annoying about Dad's new friend is that he was cheering when the Cubs scored those three bullshit runs last inning, and that, after Cesar Izturis's one-out infield single (the only kind of single Cesar Izturis has the power to hit), he looked at his wife before deciding whether or not it was OK to clap. It wasn't.

Fox's Josh Lewin, talking about the importance of postseason experience, points out that if/when the Cubs win today, it will be "the fifteenth clinching in one way, shape or form for Jim Edmonds. He knows how to show the young players how to do it." Yes. The tragedy of rookies being maimed by stray champagne corks is one that has plagued championship sports teams for a century. Thankfully, Jim Edmonds is here to make the Cubs clubhouse safe for unbridled revelry. I can't believe Edmonds doesn't have a mustache.

This inning has promise. Suddenly All-World Ludwick is up with a runner on and Pujols looming ominously on deck. The fear today is that this game will be over before it starts rolling, that the Cubs will pile up a big lead and spend the last five innings doing a celebratory samba. If the Cardinals are going to go down, I want them to be respectable about it. I want them to give us a show. I want them to make this trip worthwhile. I can't stare blankly ahead, pausing only for gallows humor, for three hours. We have to make them sweat. We have to make them earn this. It's already 3–0 Bad Guys. It grows late early. This is the first real chance to make a dent, to cut this off before it gnarls out of control. Our best two hitters are up. It's Ludwick. It's Thudwick! It's a chance to make a dent, it's one sliver of opportunity, it's a truly . . . Aw, Christ, Ludwick hits a dictionary-definition double-play ball, for the aliens, and that is fucking that.

Out of the corner of my eye, I see that the man in the Cubs T-shirt and blue Cardinals hat is jumping up like a big damn idiot and Dad is looking down at his shoes. Only for a second, though. Then he's back talking to the man, back to their previous conversation, whatever that could possibly be about.

BASEBALL BRINGS OUT our better natures. Baseball makes us more neighborly. Baseball encourages us to be more kind. Baseball releases us from our solitary, misanthropic selves, the self-indulgence, the tunnel vision, the xenophobia. It allows us to share in a collective escape, beam ourselves to a leisure place away from time, space, fears, and anything that has gnarly teeth and growls at us before we sleep. We are all visitors to the same planet, together, and we are all friends. Even if that's it. Even if that's the whole damn thing.

KNOWLEDGE YOU NOW HAVE

---

1. Reading Norma Klein books during baseball practice is unacceptable.
2. It is very important that you know your father was an excellent baseball player when he was eight.
3. That's why your middle name is Bulldog. Now, get out of your mother's car.

BOTTOM OF THE THIRD INNING

**In which your narrator tries to
turn this into a reference book.**

*I was at a game with my then-girlfriend, now-wife, with my dad
and her grandfather. Cardinals at Giants at Pac Bell Park in 2002,
and Albert Pujols was just starting to emerge as a superstar, so
he wasn't totally well known yet. Pujols is up, and the guys behind us take notice of Albert's name and start saying things like
"Poo holes? Poo holes? He's a smelly poo hole! Stick it in his poo
hole!" At first they were just sort of saying these things to each
other and laughing. I thought, Well, Grandpa flew jets for forty
years and doesn't hear very well, maybe he's not picking up on
this. But now they're getting louder and louder. Just as I start
thinking of ways to excuse myself or maybe ask Grandpa if he
wants to go get a beer with me, he leans over to me and says,
very quietly, "I think I'd change my name." Just killed me. I told
this story at his funeral, and the mourners roared.*

— ERIC SOARES, Oakland, California

THE CUBS MAKE THREE OUTS ON SIX PITCHES. DERREK LEE FLIES
out to right, Aramis Ramirez grounds out to short, and Jim Edmonds
strikes out. I don't see any of this. I am in the restroom, standing
over one of those troughs, with my score book tucked under my
left arm and my penis held with my right hand. These troughs are

disgusting. I think I see someone's finger is in there, along with a couple of teeth.

WHEN DAD COACHED, my mother kept score for all our Jaycee games, sitting in a lawn chair, drinking a wine cooler, which everyone was drinking at the time. ("Seagrams . . . Golden Wine Cooler . . . *it's wet and it's dry!* . . . Golden Wine Cooler . . . *my my my.*") She used a leather-bound C. S. Peterson's Scoremaster, the "Official Baseball & Softball Scorebook: A Complete Record Of Game And Player." I loved the way my mom kept score. Because we were all eight or nine years old, there was no such thing as an error. If you hit the ball to the pitcher, who threw it past the first baseman, who threw it past the second, who threw it past the third, you had a home run. In eight-year-old baseball, this happens often.

Mom didn't bother with the traditional scoring system: "5" for third basemen, "2" for catcher, so on. She would just write "GO" for groundouts, "FL" for fly outs, "FO" for foul outs and move on with her life. Scoring purists refer to this as "ghetto" scorekeeping, which I find offensive and repulsive and wrong. Mom kept all the old books, and we still have them in our attic. Sometimes I'll visit Mattoon and go look at them. If I'm bummed out, I can hark back to my 5-for-5 performance in 1984 against Mitchell-Jerdan Funeral Home, and pretend it wasn't because of five errors.

When I graduated from college, and entered the scary real world, I found myself drawn back to reminders of a time when matters weren't simpler but felt that way. (Another example of this: this book.) So I decided to buy a score book. To my relief, C. S. Peterson still made the same score books, so I bought thirty, in case they ever went out of business. Each score book holds space for twenty-five games. So far, since I began in the summer of 1998, I've filled six.

Every game in the book is a memory, a straight-faced, stoic, impartial rundown of an event immortalized only by its chronicle. Every moment in a baseball game is imminently forgettable, until it isn't. Every Major League Baseball game I attend, I bring my score book. I've sat in the crowded, freezing bleachers of Yankee Stadium, full of drunken people spitting, and I've sat in the fifth row of Montreal's Olympic Stadium, wondering if they called a hot dog a "royale with relish." I have forgotten my score book only once, and I turned around, drove forty-five minutes back home, and returned. I actually have nightmares about being at a baseball game without my score book, which is truly a lame nightmare. If there were a fire in my apartment, the first objects I would save—the *first*—would be my score books.

I feel sometimes like they're the only way I'll be remembered. Every email, blog post, or online column I've ever written will probably be obliterated when Skylab seizes control of Earth and enslaves the human race, and this book, like the others, will end up being sold for a penny on someone's stoop somewhere. The score books—safely ensconced in the underground panic room, as specifically requested in my will—will be the only proof of where I was, of what I saw, of who I was with, of what happened.

They're the only constant I've had. Since I started doing the score books, I've lived in three different cities, held fourteen different jobs, dated several unfortunate women. Through moves, through packing and unpacking, through the inevitable detritus that flows through our lives every day, the score books are the only tangible evidence that I existed, of who I am, of what I hope will live on long after I am gone. (They might be *all* that shows up in my will.) I wish my father had kept score books, and my grandfather had. Imagine a piece of paper that shows that William Franklin Leitch II of Mattoon was once in the same building as Stan Musial. It feels important. It feels like a document. The score books are the old sepia photos, graying, fraying, but lasting.

That is, at least, the plan. Each entry in the score book contains the following information, the most important information. Let's take a look at the first entry in the book, as an example.

FINAL SCORE: San Francisco Giants 5 (1–0),

St. Louis Cardinals 3 (0–1)

DATE: 26 May 1999

LOCATION: Busch Stadium, St. Louis

WINNING PITCHER: Kirk Rueter

LOSING PITCHER: Kent Bottenfield

HOME RUNS: *Giants:* J. T. Snow, Rich Aurilia;

Cardinals: Fernando Tatis, Shawon Dunston,

Joe McEwing

ATTENDEES: Brian Barker a coworker at the time, someone

I've long lost touch with. I think he called me

a "fag" for bringing a score book.

The attendees are the most important. I always make sure to include it, whether it's my dad, a girlfriend, an old coworker I'll never see again, or just some random fella I bought an extra ticket from. Even with the wonders of Facebook, I can't recollect the names of half the people I went to high school with. Accompanying someone to a baseball game is a sacred thing: It deserves to be remembered.

A look back through the last ten years of score books is a look back at my life, at your life, at everyone's. In case the fire eats the score books before I can get to them, I better write it all down while I have the chance.

(Note: Originally, this chapter included EVERY baseball game in my scorebook. Unfortunately, my editor informed me that it took up about 32,193 pages. What follows, thus, are just the most memorable games. Trust me, my editor did you an enormous favor.)

FINAL SCORE: St. Louis Cardinals 3 (1–1),

San Francisco Giants 2 (1–1)

DATE: 27 May 1999

LOCATION: Busch Stadium, St. Louis

WINNING PITCHER: Heathcliff Slocumb

LOSING PITCHER: Jerry Spradlin
HOME RUNS: *Cardinals:* Mark McGwire
ATTENDEES: Self

When I worked for the old *Sporting News* in St. Louis, I had the night shift, 4 P.M. to 2 A.M., so I had to sneak in afternoon games like this one and still be a half hour or so late to work. It was the first of many McGwire homers I saw, this one in the season after 62, the game, the homer, that changed the world of baseball, the one that healed so many wounds, the one that helped Roger Maris's family absolve the baseball world of all its sins against their late father, the one where McGwire hugged his son, and families everywhere bonded and wept, the one where a classy kid named Tim Forneris gave up a million dollars to do the right thing, the one that no one ever talks about anymore, the one we all pretend never happened.

FINAL SCORE: Chicago Cubs 4 (1–0),
St. Louis Cardinals 3 (1–2)
DATE: 29 May 1999
LOCATION: Wrigley Field, Chicago
WINNING PITCHER: Felix Heredia
LOSING PITCHER: Rick Bottalico
HOME RUNS: *Cubs:* Glenallen Hill
ATTENDEES: Mike Cetera

These were some mediocre Cardinals teams—it was right before Pujols arrived—and the only real reason to watch was Mc-Gwire. Unfortunately, he had the day off, and Joe McEwing—a classic scrappy fan favorite; when McDonald's sponsored "Big Mac Land" in the upper deck of Busch Stadium for McGwire homers, they added a "Little Mac Land" in the lower bleachers for McEwing, which gave everyone in the stadium a free order of small fries if he hit one out there—was thrown out stealing in the ninth inning with the Cards down a run. Mike spent most of the game agonizing over whether or not to get back together with Joan during a brief hiatus. He did.

FINAL SCORE:	New York Mets 7 (1–0),
	Arizona Diamondbacks 6 (0–1)
DATE:	21 May 2000
LOCATION:	Shea Stadium, New York
WINNING PITCHER:	Rick Reed
LOSING PITCHER:	Randy Johnson
HOME RUNS:	*Mets:* Joe McEwing (2), Mike Piazza,
	Edgardo Alfonzo, Robin Ventura.
	Diamondbacks: Steve Finley, Travis Lee
ATTENDEES:	Heather Benz

My first visit to a New York stadium, where I realized quickly that even though Rudy Guiliani had transformed most of the city into a Disney-fied tourist playground, he hadn't quite gotten around to Shea, which vaguely resembled the Thunderdome with surface-to-air missiles. McEwing, my beloved middling middle infielder, had a reputation for being able to hit off Johnson—at the time the most dominating pitcher in baseball—though his lifetime .250 average against the Unit belies that. On this day, though, my Midwestern Cardinals buddy welcomed me to Gotham with a homer and two doubles, and this city seemed vulnerable, conquerable.

FINAL SCORE:	Chicago White Sox 10 (1–1),
	New York Yankees 9 (0–1)
DATE:	17 June 2000
LOCATION:	Yankee Stadium, New York
WINNING PITCHER:	Cal Eldred
LOSING PITCHER:	Jake Westbrook

HOME RUNS:	*White Sox:* Chris Singleton (2),
	Magglio Ordonez. *Yankees:* Bernie Williams
ATTENDEES:	Chris Jenkins

Now that the old Yankee Stadium has been torn down, we remember it as a cathedral to baseball's epic history, but we forget that after the hideous seventies renovation, it mostly looked like a dated ode to urban blight. My first trip broke my heart, though. Before I moved there, I had always thought of New York as a haven for artists, writers, thinkers. I imagined the baseball games would feature recitations of Bart Giamatti poems between innings. Turns out, they sang "Cotton-Eyed Joe" like the idiots back home.

FINAL SCORE:	Atlanta Braves 6 (1–0),
	New York Mets 4 (1–1)
DATE:	29 June 2000
LOCATION:	Shea Stadium, New York
WINNING PITCHER:	John Burkett
LOSING PITCHER:	Rick Reed (1–1)
HOME RUNS:	*Braves:* Andres Galarraga
ATTENDEES:	Fellow employees of Novix Media,
	a hot dot-com company that was going
	to make us all rich (and employed us
	all for precisely forty-four more days)

This was the triumphant return to Shea Stadium by Braves closer John Rocker, who, just six months earlier, had said he hated going to Mets games because of all the "queers with AIDS" and "Asians and Koreans and Vietnamese and Indians and Russians and Spanish people and everything up there. How the hell did they get in this country?" Mets fans worked up all their bile . . . and Rocker still shut down the Mets to earn the save. It was probably the last highlight of Rocker's troubled career. Years later I interviewed him and his black girlfriend in a bar on the Lower East Side of Manhattan, and he drank lots of Red Bull and talked about running for national office someday.

FINAL SCORE: New York Mets 4 (2–1),

St. Louis Cardinals 3 (4–4)

DATE: 29 July 2000

LOCATION: Shea Stadium, New York

WINNING PITCHER: Rick White

LOSING PITCHER: Mike James

HOME RUNS: *Mets:* Mike Piazza (2), Mike Bordick;

Cardinals: Ray Lankford (3), Jim Edmonds

ATTENDEES: Bryan Leitch, Sally Leitch, Jill Leitch

My family's first visit to New York, timed of course to a Cardinals visit. The Leitches did not immediately take to New York. The oppressive heat, the intrusive crowds, the sudden awareness of millions of minorities . . . it was all stacked against the Mattoonians. A highlight of the visit: the family, overheated and exhausted, screaming at one another in Times Square. Right when my sister was about to shiv my eyeball, Cardinals outfielder J. D. Drew walked right past us on the street. We all stopped, looked at one another, said, "Hey, look, J. D. Drew," and then reconvened the screaming. Later, we all had dinner at a T.G.I. Friday's and agreed not to talk about it.

FINAL SCORE: New York Yankees 9 (2–1),

Seattle Mariners 7 (0–1)

DATE: 17 October 2000

LOCATION: Yankee Stadium, New York

WINNING PITCHER: Orlando Hernandez

LOSING PITCHER: Arthur Rhodes

HOME RUNS: *Mariners:* Alex Rodriguez, Carlos Guillen;

Yankees: David Justice

ATTENDEES: Erin Franzman

My first postseason game, I decided to pretend to be a Yankees fan for three hours. By that, I mean, "just assume, no matter what happens, your team is going to win." (This was 2000, at the end of the Yankees Dynasty, when this was a perfectly logical strategy.) David Justice hit a huge (and largely forgotten) three-run homer in the seventh inning, and the Yankees were off to the Subway Series. I hadn't even lived in New York a year and had no idea what that meant. Mostly, I learned that Yankees fans had no idea how the rest of the world lived. One guy noticed my Cardinals hat and asked if the "STL" stood for "Scranton."

FINAL SCORE:	New York Yankees 7 (3–1),
	Tampa Bay Devil Rays (0–2)
DATE:	29 June 2001
LOCATION:	Yankee Stadium, New York
WINNING PITCHER:	Roger Clemens
LOSING PITCHER:	Bryan Rekar
HOME RUNS:	*Yankees:* Tino Martinez, Alfonso Soriano
ATTENDEES:	Mike Bruno

To be honest, I spent the last four innings of this game drinking tequila and smoking cigarettes in one of the terraces in the upper tier. Now that new Yankee Stadium requires you to take your shoes off before you enter, I can't believe you could once smoke in the old one. Despite the tequila, I still kept my score book updated.

FINAL SCORE:	New York Mets 4 (4–2),
	St. Louis Cardinals 3 (4–6)
DATE:	23 April 2002
LOCATION:	Shea Stadium, New York
WINNING PITCHER:	Jeff D'Amico
LOSING PITCHER:	Matt Morris

HOME RUNS: *Cardinals:* Albert Pujols

ATTENDEES: Tim Grierson

Most notable for being the first time I saw The Great Pujols in person. People forget how he was just a gift for the Cardinals dropped from the clouds. He hadn't even been a heralded prospect, and the only reason he made the team out of Spring Training in 2001 was because Bobby Bonilla was hurt. (Seriously.) He must have known I was there and witnessing him for the first time: He hit a two-run homer in the first inning.

FINAL SCORE: St. Louis Cardinals 5 (5–6),

Houston Astros 4 (0–1)

DATE: 23 May 2002

LOCATION: Busch Stadium, St. Louis

WINNING PITCHER: Jason Isringhausen

LOSING PITCHER: Octavio Dotel

HOME RUNS: *Cardinals:* Jim Edmonds (2)

ATTENDEES: Brian Doolittle bachelor party

As you've probably guessed by my simpering, effete tone, I'm not much of a strip club guy. This was the perfect bachelor party: bleacher seats at Busch, a Cardinals victory, and enough Bud Light to kill a Clydesdale. I plan on doing this for all five of my eventual bachelor parties. Albert Pujols was playing third base in this game.

FINAL SCORE: St. Louis Cardinals 3 (6–7),

San Diego Padres 3 (0–2)

DATE: 1 July 2002

LOCATION: Busch Stadium, St. Louis

WINNING PITCHER: Woody Williams

LOSING PITCHER: Oliver Perez

HOME RUNS: *Padres:* Ray Lankford (5);
                      Cardinals: Jim Edmonds (3), Albert Pujols (2),
                      Miguel Cairo, Woody Williams
ATTENDEES: Bryan Leitch, Sally Leitch, Jill Leitch

I begin a yearly homesick tradition of spending one weekend in St. Louis, preferably one against an inferior foe. The starting third baseman this game was Mike Coolbaugh, the minor-league first base coach who was killed by a line drive in a minor-league game five years later. He went 0-for-4 in this, one of his three starts that season, his last in the major leagues.

FINAL SCORE: Houston Astros 5 (1–1),
                        Montreal Expos 3 (0–1)
DATE: 3 August 2002
LOCATION: Olympic Stadium, Montreal
WINNING PITCHER: Octavio Dotel (1–1)
LOSING PITCHER: T. J. Tucker
HOME RUNS: *Expos:* Brad Wilkerson;
                      Astros: Jeff Bagwell, Craig Biggio
ATTENDEES: Amy Blair

Three observations from my lone trip to baseball abroad to see the sadly lamented Expos:

1. The Expos' version of a "hot dog" was 75 percent polyure-thane and came in an antiseptic, limp, cold Styrofoam box.
2. Vladimir Guerrero hit a ball off the roof of the dome. Nobody had any idea what to do, and by the time the ball bounced, confused, along the term, he was panting away at second base.
3. During a particularly "exciting" moment in the game, a child next to me started banging his metal seat against

the chair back. This was quite annoying, so I eyed his father, waiting for him to inform his son that this was an obnoxious way to show one's support for the team. Then I noticed the father was doing the same thing, as were seven thousand other Expos fans. This was the Canadian version of the Wave. I had no idea.

I miss the Expos. Don't you?

FINAL SCORE:	St. Louis Cardinals 5 (9–7),
	Philadelphia Phillies 1 (1–2)
DATE:	18 August 1999
LOCATION:	Veterans Stadium, Philadelphia
WINNING PITCHER:	Matt Morris (1–1)
LOSING PITCHER:	Vicente Padilla (1–1)
HOME RUNS:	*Phillies:* Bobby Abreu (2);
	Cardinals: Edgar Renteria (2)
ATTENDEES:	Bryan Leitch, Sally Leitch, Jill Leitch

After the game, we took Philadelphia's amusing impersonation of a subway system back to my uncle's home. It was a blistering summer, and my sister was wearing a tank top, which caught the attention of some teenagers on the train. Little did they know: Jill was going through a collegiate rebellion phase at the time, listening to a lot of Ani DiFranco and Tori Amos, and she had stopped shaving her armpit hair. When the train hit a bump, she raised her arms to grab the strap above. You could actually hear the guys go "Awwwwwww!!!!" from twenty feet away. She has since shaved the armpits.

FINAL SCORE:	Baltimore Orioles 2 (1–0),
	Boston Red Sox 1 (0–1)
DATE:	5 April 2003

LOCATION: Camden Yards, Baltimore
WINNING PITCHER: B. J. Ryan
LOSING PITCHER: Chad Fox
ATTENDEES: Matt Pitzer, Kate Pitzer, Tyson Kade

I was trying to come up with a metaphor for the odd experience of Camden Yards feeling dated and derivative of all the other new stadiums even though it was the template and the rest are rip-offs. Best I can come up with? *M*A*S*H* (the TV show) seems incredibly mawkish and awkward now, in the wake of shows that took what it did and refined it, but at the time, it was thought revolutionary. Plus, both *M*A*S*H* and Camden Yards feature George Will shooting Koreans.

FINAL SCORE: Oakland A's 5 (1–0),
                New York Yankees 3 (5–2)
DATE: 3 May 2003
LOCATION: Yankee Stadium, New York
WINNING PITCHER: Keith Foulke
LOSING PITCHER: Juan Acevedo
HOME RUNS: *Yankees:* Jason Giambi; *A's:* Eric Chavez
ATTENDEES: Greg Lindsay

This game was about two weeks before Michael Lewis's revolutionary bestseller *Moneyball* came out, confusing Joe Morgan and changing the game of baseball forever. I wonder if Billy Beane knew what he was in for on this lazy May afternoon. In my memories, Bill James was umpiring this game, and he was smoking a pipe.

FINAL SCORE: New York Yankees 5 (6–3),
                St. Louis Cardinals 2 (9–8)
DATE: 13 June 2003
LOCATION: Yankee Stadium, New York
WINNING PITCHER: Roger Clemens (3–0)

LOSING PITCHER: Jason Simontacchi (1–1)

HOME RUNS: *Cardinals:* Jim Edmonds (5);

                Yankees: Raul Mondesi (2), Ruben Sierra,

                Hideki Matsui

ATTENDEES: Bryan Leitch, Sally Leitch

Only the siren song of the Cardinals playing at Yankee Stadium for the first time since 1964 (when my father was fifteen years old and four years away from meeting my mother) could bring the Leitches back to New York. As luck would have it, their visit would coincide with Roger Clemens going for his three hundredth win *and* his four thousandth strikeout. He notched them both and came on the field afterward to roaring, relentless cheers that never, ever stopped. "I'm sad the Cardinals lost," Dad said, "but I'm glad we got to see this. Clemens seems like a class act."

FINAL SCORE: New York Yankees 13 (7–3),

                St. Louis Cardinals 4 (9–9)

DATE: 13 June 2003

LOCATION: Yankee Stadium, New York

WINNING PITCHER: Andy Pettitte

LOSING PITCHER: Matt Morris (1–1)

HOME RUNS: *Cardinals:* Tino Martinez 2 (2);

                Yankees: Jason Giambi 2 (3),

                Raul Mondesi (3), Ruben Sierra (2)

ATTENDEES: Bryan Leitch, Sally Leitch

In the midst of the rainiest summer in record New York history, the Leitches were faced with the fiercest test yet of their fervid Never Leave A Game Early mantra. That is to say: The Yankees took a 4–0 lead in the first inning before a dreary two-hour rain delay. During the delay, I took my parents on a tour of the stadium. When the Bleacher Creatures noticed the Cardinal-red-clad fans looking at them, they began chanting "DAR-YLE KI-LE! DAR-YLE KI-LE!" at us, in mocking memoriam of the beloved pitcher who had died a year earlier. Welcome to New York, Leitches. The Cardinals fell behind 13–2 after the rain delay, but we stayed until the last pitch anyway.

FINAL SCORE:	New York Mets 13 (6–4),
	St. Louis Cardinals 5 (10–11)
DATE:	3 August 2003
LOCATION:	Shea Stadium, New York
WINNING PITCHER:	Jeremy Griffiths
LOSING PITCHER:	Garrett Stephenson (0–2)
HOME RUNS:	*Mets:* Tony Clark 2 (3); *Cardinals:* Bo Hart (2)
ATTENDEES:	Aileen Gallagher, David Gaffen, Kathie Fries

Since I started the score books, this was the last time the Cardinals were within one game under .500. The 2000s were probably the Cardinals' best decade in their storied history. Their record in games I attended? 26–35.

FINAL SCORE:	New York Yankees 6 (9–3),
	Kansas City Royals 3 (0–1)
DATE:	19 August 2003
LOCATION:	Yankee Stadium, New York
WINNING PITCHER:	Andy Pettitte (1–1)
LOSING PITCHER:	Kevin Appier (1–1)
HOME RUNS:	*Yankees:* Alfonso Soriano (2),
	Bernie Williams (2), Karim Garcia
ATTENDEES:	Mike Bruno, Liz Zach, A. J. Daulerio

The years of losing, nonstop, unrelenting losing, have disguised the fact that Kansas City is one of the best baseball cities in the country. Kansas City has the Negro Leagues Baseball Museum, and great baseball writers like Joe Posnanski, Bill James, Rob Neyer, Jeff Passan, and

Rany Jazayerli developed their love of the game watching the Royals. George Brett's a civic hero. It's a wonderful place to watch baseball. They've had one winning season in fifteen years. If the Royals ever become relevant again, no fans will have earned it more.

FINAL SCORE:	Chicago Cubs 4 (3–1),
	St. Louis Cardinals 2 (10–13)
DATE:	2 September 2003
LOCATION:	Wrigley Field, Chicago
WINNING PITCHER:	Mark Guthrie
LOSING PITCHER:	Jeff Fassero
HOME RUNS:	*Cardinals:* Jim Edmonds (6);
	Cubs: Sammy Sosa
ATTENDEES:	Mike Cetera, Joan Mocek

The aforementioned Best Man game. Jeff Fassero should never be allowed to pitch to Sammy Sosa, under any circumstances.

FINAL SCORE:	Boston Red Sox 9 (1–2),
	New York Yankees 6 (9–4)
DATE:	15 October 2003
LOCATION:	Yankee Stadium, New York
WINNING PITCHER:	Alan Embree
LOSING PITCHER:	Jose Contreras
HOME RUNS:	*Red Sox:* Trot Nixon, Jason Varitek;
	Yankees: Jason Giambi (4),
	Jorge Posada (3)
ATTENDEES:	Amy Blair, Erika Croxton

This was Game 6 of the 2003 ALCS, the game *before* Grady Little's Pedro Martinez brain cramp and Aaron Boone's crushing homer. I sat in the bleachers with thousands of drunk, freezing fans giving me wedgies for keeping my score book. But I still didn't miss a pitch. Afterward, my friend Amy, devastated that she didn't see her Yankees clinch a World Series, punched a Red Sox fan in the face. The Red Sox–Yankees rivalry terrifies me.

FINAL SCORE:	Toronto Blue Jays 5 (1–0),
	Baltimore Orioles 4 (1–1)
DATE:	24 April 2004
LOCATION:	Camden Yards, Baltimore
WINNING PITCHER:	Kerry Ligtenberg
LOSING PITCHER:	Mike DeJean (1–1)
HOME RUNS:	*Orioles:* Miguel Cabrera;
	Blue Jays: Carlos Delgado
ATTENDEES:	Matt Pitzer

The Orioles lineup this night: Brian Roberts (mentioned in Mitchell Report's steroid blacklist), Melvin Mora (openly rumored to have taken steroids), Miguel Tejada (Mitchell Report), Rafael Palmeiro (tested positive for steroids), Javy Lopez (openly rumored to have taken steroids), Jay Gibbons (Mitchell Report), David Segui (admitted to having used human growth hormone), Luis Matos (apparently clean), Larry Bigbie (Mitchell Report).

FINAL SCORE:	New York Mets 4 (8–4),
	Colorado Rockies 0 (0–1)
DATE:	23 May 2004
LOCATION:	Shea Stadium, New York
WINNING PITCHER:	Tom Glavine
LOSING PITCHER:	Shawn Estes (0–2)
ATTENDEES:	Greg Lindsay

For any true seamhead, the holy grail of any trip to the ballpark is a no-hitter. This was the closest I ever came. Tom Glavine shut down the Rockies for seven-and-two-thirds innings before a hooking line drive from someone named Kit Pellow just eluded Shane Spencer's grasp for a double, the Rockies' lone hit. I'll never make it farther than that, I fear. I wonder what would have happened if Glavine had finished this off, completing the Mets' first-ever no-hitter. (It's crazy the Mets have never had a no-hitter, by the way.) Glavine was ultimately run out of town by the Mets, and the mere mention of his name causes Mets fans to stab themselves in the head. But four outs more, and he would have been a Mets legend. Every game, every pitch counts, forever.

FINAL SCORE: Boston Red Sox 10 (3–3),

New York Yankees 3 (12–6)

DATE: 20 October 2004

LOCATION: Yankee Stadium, New York

WINNING PITCHER: Derek Lowe (1–1)

LOSING PITCHER: Kevin Brown (2–1)

HOME RUNS: *Red Sox:* Johnny Damon 2 (2),

David Ortiz (2), Mark Bellhorn

ATTENDEES: Heather Benz

Yes, I was at Game 7 of the 2004 ALCS, when the Sox finished that ridiculous comeback against the Yankees. This is less exciting than it sounds: Again, if you're a fan of neither team, the game is merely about spectacle, and this game had little. It was essentially over after the second inning when Damon hit a grand slam to give the Sox a 5–0 lead. I spent the entire game warming in the glow of Jim Edmonds's NLCS Game 6 homer, which I'd watched at a bar across the street from Yankee Stadium right before this game started, and looking up at George Steinbrenner's skybox to see if he'd jumped out. I don't know why I don't just move back to St. Louis already.

FINAL SCORE: San Diego Padres 5 (2–3),

St. Louis Cardinals 4 (12–16)

> DATE: 7 May 2005
> LOCATION: Busch Stadium, St. Louis
> WINNING PITCHER: Adam Eaton (2–0)
> LOSING PITCHER: Chris Carpenter (1–1)
> HOME RUNS: *Cardinals:* Albert Pujols (7), Larry Walker
> ATTENDEES: Bryan Leitch, Sally Leitch, Jill Leitch

Thanks to her recent chemotherapy treatments, my mother had lost her hair and looked a little too much like my uncle for everyone's tastes, particularly my father's. She wore a hat for two innings before throwing it at me. "It's too fucking hot," she said. "I'll just make the beer man piss his pants, I don't care." They gave us free beer the whole game.

> FINAL SCORE: New York Yankees 6 (13–6),
>   Pittsburgh Pirates 1 (0–2)
> DATE: 16 June 2005
> LOCATION: Yankee Stadium, New York
> WINNING PITCHER: Randy Johnson (1–1)
> LOSING PITCHER: Oliver Perez (0–2)
> HOME RUNS: *Yankees:* Hideki Matsui (2);
>   *Pirates:* Michael Restovich
> ATTENDEES: Self

If you want to know what my life was like in June 2005, witness me going by myself to a Yankees-Pirates game simply because it was interleague and both pitchers were tall.

> FINAL SCORE: St. Louis Cardinals 4 (14–17),
>   San Francisco Giants 2 (3–4)
> DATE: 20 August 2005
> LOCATION: Busch Stadium, St. Louis
> WINNING PITCHER: Matt Morris (2–2)

LOSING PITCHER: Kevin Correia
ATTENDEES: Bryan Leitch

My last series at the old Busch Stadium. After the game, my father and I ran into Cardinals reliever Al Reyes, who was in the midst of his best season. He spotted us at a bar, wearing our dopey red Cardinals gear, and said, "Hey, Cardinals fans, lemme buy you a shot!" And he did. Two-and-a-half years later, Reyes punched a police officer at a Tampa bar and was tasered twice. He earned the win for the Rays the next night. Al Reyes is awesome.

FINAL SCORE: San Francisco Giants 4 (4–4),
St. Louis Cardinals 2 (14–18)
DATE: 21 August 2005
LOCATION: Busch Stadium, St. Louis
WINNING PITCHER: Jason Schmidt (1–1)
LOSING PITCHER: Jeff Suppan
ATTENDEES: Bryan Leitch

Fittingly, the last game I ever saw at the old stadium, they lost. Pujols had the day off, someone named Scott Seabol batted fifth, and I spent the last inning on a train to the airport to catch my plane. Just a dreary day all around. I grew up at Busch Stadium, and I left it for the final time like it was a boring opera I couldn't wait to see end. I'll never forgive myself for this.

FINAL SCORE: Los Angeles Dodgers 3 (1–0),
San Francisco Giants 1 (4–5)
DATE: 15 April 2006
LOCATION: Dodger Stadium, Los Angeles
WINNING PITCHER: Odalis Perez
LOSING PITCHER: Jason Schmidt (1–1)
ATTENDEES: Mark Pesavento

I'm not sure enough people appreciate just how gorgeous Dodger Stadium is. Somehow, in the middle of downtown Los Angeles (which might be the least appealing urban center in the country), there's a lovely, leisurely, isolated baseball stadium where it feels like it's 1960 and everyone's wearing fedoras and pretending they're Don Draper in a Hawaiian shirt. It's pure baseball pleasure, and that's even *without* hearing Vin Scully's voice piped through the bathrooms.

FINAL SCORE:	St. Louis Cardinals 8 (15–21),
	Atlanta Braves 3 (3–1)
DATE:	19 July 2006
LOCATION:	New Busch Stadium, St. Louis
WINNING PITCHER:	Chris Carpenter (2–1)
LOSING PITCHER:	Jason Shiell
HOME RUNS:	*Cardinals:* Jim Edmonds (9);
	Braves: Brian McCann (3)
ATTENDEES:	Bryan Leitch

Five minutes before game time, in my first visit to the Cardinals' new park, St. Louis was hit with a tornado. Remember when the spaceships attack the cities in *Independence Day*? When everything's fine, and then all of a sudden the black green clouds converge, and everything is dark and still? That's what it was like. A friend sent me a text message, tongue-in-cheek: "Beware the clouds of death!" The grounds crew brought the tarp onto the field, though it wasn't raining yet. I grabbed a beer and started chatting with the lady who sold it to us. I looked on, curiously, as the American flag waved one direction, then whipped back dramatically in the other.

And then: WHAM. Within a matter of seconds, chaos reigned. The beer tent we were standing under imploded, sending—no!—beer flying everywhere and people scattering in all directions. A television camera fell from just above me. Everyone ducked for cover; one guy ran around with his daughter, screaming that she had a bad heart, though he seemed a lot more scared than she was. I think I heard Joe Buck cry. It was absolutely surreal.

FINAL SCORE:	New York Mets 4 (18–10),
	St. Louis Cardinals 2 (15–25)
DATE:	18 October 2006
LOCATION:	Shea Stadium, New York
WINNING PITCHER:	John Maine
LOSING PITCHER:	Chris Carpenter (2–2)
HOME RUNS:	*Mets:* Jose Reyes (2)
ATTENDEES:	Kristen Pettit

Given the opportunity to possibly see the Cardinals clinch the World Series—they came into this NLCS Game 6 up 3–2—I couldn't turn it down, despite the enemy territory. But after the Cardinals lost, and after hearing everyone around me do backflips while I was in misery, I knew, for Game 7, I needed to find some Cardinals fans. Dewey's Flatiron in Manhattan, and twenty-four hours later, I had about a hundred new best friends, all of whom I had licked champagne off.

FINAL SCORE:	St. Louis Cardinals 4 (16–24),
	Detroit Tigers 2 (0–1)
DATE:	27 October 2006
LOCATION:	Busch Stadium, St. Louis
WINNING PITCHER:	Jeff Weaver (1–1)
LOSING PITCHER:	Justin Verlander
HOME RUNS:	*Tigers:* Sean Casey
ATTENDEES:	Bryan Leitch, Sally Leitch

I might have mentioned this game. If you're host to a World Series–clinching game, you drop the "new" from your name, that's for goddamned sure.

FINAL SCORE:	St. Louis Cardinals 5 (17–24),
	New York Mets 3 (19–11)
DATE:	26 June 2007
LOCATION:	Shea Stadium, New York
WINNING PITCHER:	Brad Thompson
LOSING PITCHER:	Scott Schoeneweis
HOME RUNS:	*Cardinals:* Brendan Ryan; *Mets:* Paul Lo Duca
ATTENDEES:	Bryan Leitch, Sally Leitch

It was around this point of the season that we realized the Cardinals weren't going to repeat as World Series champions—the cleanup hitter was Juan Encarnacion—and just began hoping everyone on the Cubs, who looked light-years better, would start randomly snapping hamstrings. By the way: No worse time for my mother to be wearing a Yadier Molina jersey at Shea Stadium than the Cards' first visit to Shea since the 2006 NLCS. By the end of the game, her hair, now grown back, was 64 percent chewing gum.

FINAL SCORE:	St. Louis Cardinals 5 (18–26),
	San Diego Padres 0 (2–4)
DATE:	9 August 2007
LOCATION:	Busch Stadium, St. Louis
WINNING PITCHER:	Joel Pineiro
LOSING PITCHER:	Chris Young
HOME RUNS:	*Cardinals:* Rick Ankiel
ATTENDEES:	Brian Doolittle, Amanda Doolittle,
	Brian Desmet

The story of Rick Ankiel is an amazing one, sure, but to Cardinals fans, it's not a miracle or a life-affirming tale: It's just the story of a wayward nephew who, finally, seems to have backed away from the abyss and is able to stay clean . . . for now, anyway. This was Ankiel's first game as an outfielder—he was called up from Memphis before the game—and his seventh-inning homer was one of the great sporting events I've ever witnessed. In the dugout, Tony La Russa, who barely budged a muscle when the Cardinals won the World Series, leapt, hooted, and hollered like he'd won the lottery, or the FDA had permanently banned canned meat. He understood. He knew this was about more than just baseball. Anywhere else, Ankiel is roadkill, long forgotten. In St. Louis, he's a permanent part of the skyline. No matter what else happens.

FINAL SCORE:	Los Angeles Dodgers 2 (3–1),
	St. Louis Cardinals 1 (18–27)
DATE:	10 August 2007
LOCATION:	Busch Stadium, St. Louis
WINNING PITCHER:	Joe Beimel
LOSING PITCHER:	Adam Wainwright (1–1)
HOME RUNS:	*Dodgers*: James Loney
ATTENDEES:	Bryan Leitch

Watching my father work his way up the Busch Stadium ticket food chain over the years has been a unique pleasure. When I was a kid, he was in the upper deck. Then to the bleachers. Then the middle tier. Now he's one spot away from box seats: "In a coupla years, I wanna get those seats where you can just push a button and they just bring you beer."

FINAL SCORE:	St. Louis Cardinals 3 (21–27),
	New York Mets 0 (21–12)
DATE:	27 September 2007
LOCATION:	Shea Stadium, New York
WINNING PITCHER:	Joel Pineiro (2–0)
LOSING PITCHER:	Pedro Martinez (0–2)
ATTENDEES:	Aileen Gallagher

I apologize to Mets fans in advance here, but this was smack in the middle of the Mets' collapse, the worst collapse, according to Baseball Prospectus, in the history of the major leagues. When a baseball team falls apart down the stretch, it's worse than anything else in sports, because it happens in slow motion. First it's one, then two, then a spot win, all's fine, then another two losses, then another, then *oh my god this cannot be happening.* Would you rather die by shotgun or by Chinese water torture? The Mets die by Chinese water torture. Shoot them in the head, please. Be kind. Be merciful.

FINAL SCORE:	St. Louis Cardinals 5 (22–28),
	Milwaukee Brewers 3 (2–1)
DATE:	10 May 2008
LOCATION:	Miller Park, Milwaukee
WINNING PITCHER:	Russ Springer
LOSING PITCHER:	Eric Gagne
HOME RUNS:	*Cardinals:* Chris Duncan;
	Brewers: Prince Fielder
ATTENDEES:	Bryan Leitch, Sally Leitch

Eric Gagne career path, with salaries:

2003: Cy Young winner, Los Angeles Dodgers, $550,000

2004: All-Star reliever, Los Angeles Dodgers, $5 million

2005: Mostly injured pitcher, Los Angeles Dodgers, $8 million

2006: Pitches total of two innings, Los Angeles Dodgers, $10 million

2007: Ineffective, hated reliever, Boston Red Sox, accused of taking HGH in Mitchell Report, $6 million

2008: Awful reliever, Milwaukee Brewers, $10 million

2009: Starting pitcher, Quebec Capitales, Can-Am League, $25 per diem

FINAL SCORE:	St. Louis Cardinals 9 (23–28),
	Boston Red Sox 3 (3–5)
DATE:	21 June 2008
LOCATION:	Fenway Park, Boston
WINNING PITCHER:	Mitchell Boggs
LOSING PITCHER:	Daisuke Matsuzaka
HOME RUNS:	*Cardinals:* Rick Ankiel (4), Troy Glaus,
	Aaron Miles; *Red Sox:* J. D. Drew
ATTENDEES:	Bryan Leitch, Sally Leitch, Alexa Stevenson

How badly did my parents want to see Fenway Park? Bad enough that I coughed up $250 apiece for four halfway-decent seats. Bad enough that, for the first time in our lives, my family took a *flight* together to make sure they saw the game in time. (When I was growing up, nineteen-hour drives were the norm.) Bad enough that my endlessly patient girlfriend bought Cardinals socks that lighted up. Was it worth it? My dad: "Fenway smells like Ted Williams thawed out and everyone's too afraid to say anything."

FINAL SCORE:	New York Mets 7 (23–12),
	St. Louis Cardinals 2 (23–29)
DATE:	25 July 2008
LOCATION:	Shea Stadium, New York
WINNING PITCHER:	Mike Pelfrey (2–0)
LOSING PITCHER:	Mitchell Boggs (1–1)
HOME RUNS:	*Mets:* Carlos Delgado (4), Argenis Reyes
ATTENDEES:	Julia Furay, Mike Ryan

My final visit to Shea Stadium ended like so many had before: With the Mets stomping on the Cardinals' larynx. I always thought Shea got a bad rap: Sure, it was ugly and dated and a ratty urban coliseum, but it always had the feel that something *important* was happening there. The place raised its game when it mattered. At Citi Field, the new place . . . it feels like a nice place to go have dinner.

FINAL SCORE:	St. Louis Cardinals 18 (24–29),
	Atlanta Braves 3 (3–3)
DATE:	22 August 2008
LOCATION:	Busch Stadium, St. Louis
WINNING PITCHER:	Adam Wainwright (1–1)
LOSING PITCHER:	Charlie Morton
HOME RUNS:	*Braves*: Greg Norton
ATTENDEES:	Bryan Leitch, Sally Leitch

My favorite tidbit from the biggest Cardinals blowout I've ever attended? Not that the Cardinals didn't hit a single homer en route to scoring eighteen runs. Not that Jason LaRue played left field. Not that the game was still over in under three hours. No, my favorite tidbit was that Joel Pineiro, a starter, managed to earn a save in an 18–3 game.

WHICH BRINGS US TO TODAY.

WHEN I RETURN TO MY SEAT, with more beers, Mike taps me on the shoulder and shows me his left arm, which is partially covered in ink.

"Lee flied to right, Ramirez grounded to short, and Edmonds struck out on a check swing. I figured you'd need that for your scorebook."

I did. Thank you. One more half-inning for the historians.

KNOWLEDGE YOU NOW HAVE

1. Your father was willing to visit a foreign country as long as they played baseball there.

2. The mid-aughts Baltimore Orioles apparently gargled with human growth hormone.

3. Your dad won't be mad if you skip a chapter or two every once in a while.

TOP OF THE FOURTH INNING

**In which your narrator comes to
terms with the Great Pujols, and
the Great Unspeakable.**

*Many people say they have been a fan of their favorite team
since birth, but usually people become fans of their team over
time. Their first game, their first playoff run, whatever it may be.
I have been a Mets fan since birth. I mean it. When I was born in
February of 1985, I was given to my dad to be held in his arms.
He had just become a father for the first time and was overcome
with emotion. He didn't know what to say. What do you talk to a
baby about? Spring Training had just begun for the 1985 baseball season, so he said the only thing that came to mind. He told
me he was excited about Dwight Gooden. What else do you say
to a baby?*

— ZACH LINDER, Brooklyn, New York

ALBERT PUJOLS IS THE TYPE OF HITTER WHO, WHEN HE DOESN'T
hit a line drive off or over something immobile, you're actively surprised. The art of hitting a baseball has vexed great men for generations. Even the preternaturally skilled can be turned into the fool in
their quest for even semi-consistent dominance. One of my favorite
baseball quotes is from Mickey Mantle: "During my 18 years I came
to bat almost 10,000 times. I struck out about 1,700 times and walked
maybe 1,800 times. You figure a ballplayer will average about 500 at

bats a season. That means I played seven years without ever hitting the ball."

I'm not sure Mantle's math is solid there, but his premise surely is: Baseball is *hard.* Even when you're one of the lucky bastards who can do it—on a whim, out of nowhere, it can just go away. In Michael Lewis's *Moneyball,* a fading David Justice comes back to the dugout after flying out to the warning track. Lewis describes Justice's slow plight brilliantly: " 'That used to be out,' [Justice said.] There was something morbid about it, like watching a death, play-by-play." Even when it was easy for Justice, it was never easy.

Albert Pujols flies in the face of this more than any other baseball player I've ever seen. Watching him on a daily basis, like I pretty much have since he showed up in 2001, is like seeing Ted Williams in his prime, crossed with Tony Gwynn in his prime, crossed with Keith Hernandez in his prime, crossed with Mark McGwire in his prime. He is Voltron, a construction of the best sections of exemplary but still lesser beings. When Barry Bonds was launching homers during his grand later Giants seasons, he was a power machine: He either homered, walked, or struck out. There was something lumbering and awkward about him, an assembly line of moonshots that, if you adjusted the settings just one notch, would sputter and break down. There was no poetry to Bonds: Only Bonds could make the parabolic grandeur of a home run turn linear and flat.

Pujols is not like this. But Pujols is not pure and fluid like Ken Griffey Jr. either. Pujols has a strange air about him, like a low-level professor who's voracious for knowledge and ends up trapped in the lab with some scary radiation: He's a genius, serious Hulk. Pujols had to scrap his way to this point. Pujols was not always Albert Pujols. It's what makes him great, and what makes him impossible not to watch.

Nobody remembers this now, but the only reason Pujols made the Cardinals Opening Day roster in 2001 was because Bobby Bonilla, the Proven Veteran that Tony La Russa had slotted to play third base, was injured. Pujols was not a can't-miss prospect like Barry Bonds, or Alex Rodriguez, or even teammate Rick Ankiel. He was a pudgy junior college kid whose family had moved to Kansas City; married with kids; a secret baseball obsessive in a fat kid body. (If you have the opportunity, take a look at how tubby Pujols was when he was a teenager. There is hope for your batter-addled eight-year-old yet, parents!) He was a solid player for Maple Woods Community College, but not heavily scouted, and the teams that watched him play came away unimpressed. (The Devil Rays scout who passed on him later quit his job, quite reasonably.) There was still genius, though, if you could see past the fat to notice it: In Pujols's *first game,* he pulled off an unassisted triple play *and* hit a grand slam. Something was there.

The Cardinals do not deserve as much credit for drafting Pujols as they love to take: After all, Pujols was picked in the thirteenth round—there were 401 men drafted before him—so they obviously weren't *too* concerned about missing out. (They still almost did, lowballing him on a bonus before he called their bluff and they raised it.) As someone who has read every word written about the Cardinals for the last thirty years, let me tell you, Albert Pujols fell from the sky. No one had any idea he was coming. We couldn't possibly have known. He was our special gift.

Pujols lost the weight, quickly, and started tearing apart minor-league pitching, first in Peoria, then Potomac, then in a brief stop in Memphis in 2000. He blasted his way to the Major League All-Star Game that rookie season in 2001, and boy howdy, were we ever *off.* The pleasure of watching Pujols was in watching him adjust. He was not Barry Bonds, a man told he was the next great American baseball superstar while he was still in the womb. That friend of yours who was fat in high school and then thinned down and was adored by every woman you knew in college? That guy learned the right moves by watching the skinny people, learning how they interacted when he wasn't around, and then pouncing when the opportunity struck. Pujols played every game—still plays every game—as if he is that fat kid trying to make up for missed time. He plays like it could all go away tomorrow. He plays like he knows if he rests for just a second, someone thinner, someone for whom this was *supposed* to happen, could take it away.

You see, baseball requires great athletic gifts, but that's a tiny, almost insignificant part of it. Pujols has worked his way into his physical strength, but the reason he is the player that he is is because he started with nothing and must keep ascending, a public school kid trying to outhustle the prep kids with the family accounts at the country club. There are hitters who are stronger than Pujols, with more powerful arms, with more natural speed. Albert Pujols was no one until very recently. He still plays, and improves, and studies, like he's a nobody. It's what makes him great. It's what makes him special. And it's what makes him better, every single year. Albert Pujols is a great American success story: Self-made, upwardly mobile, fiercely competitive. This is what we want our citizens to be. (If just to rub it in, Pujols became an American citizen in 2007 by notching a perfect score on his citizenship test. Show-off.) If he were a white guy playing in New York, he'd be considering a Senate run. His success is a real success. He makes us all want to be better. He shows it can be done.

I doubt Ted Lilly knows all this, though, and I doubt he cares: At six-foot-one, 190-pounds, he's not exactly a hulking he-man himself—of course, compared to me, you, and the vast majority of humanity, he's still huge—and thusly, he's probably had to do his fair share of scrapping. Confidence and vigor aside, he looks far from enthused to be facing Pujols, even though he's leading off, the bases are empty, and all told, if you have to pitch to Pujols at all, it's best to do so with no one on and a three-run lead.

Pujols is eyeing him the way he eyes every pitcher, like the hurler is a burglar who has invaded his home and hasn't yet noticed that Pujols is standing right behind him with something blunt, heavy, and murderous. Lilly is the type of pitcher, theoretically anyway, that Pujols struggles with: a left-handed soft-tosser, a deceptive changeup curveball artist with less heat than most but more heat than you think. Pujols's lone flaw as a hitter is his impatience. Sure, he walks a lot—he is Albert Pujols, and when you are Albert Pujols, walks are inevitable—but there's never any doubt that he'd rather not. When Pujols has no protection in the lineup behind him, which is often, because there is no real "protection" for Albert Pujols short a well-trained gorilla who can handle the curveball, he will strain to make *something* happen, swinging at pitches outside the strike zone and overextending himself in a way that, say, Barry Bonds would never do. (Bonds clearly didn't give a shit: *Walk me, fuck off, who cares, when do we eat?*) When you're constantly batting with no one on base, and you're bored with walking, you start swinging at pitches you shouldn't. Pujols did not create this Albert Pujols to trot leisurely to first base. He does not like it. And a smart pitcher like Ted Lilly knows he does not like it. The Cardinals are down three runs. If there were a way on earth for Albert Pujols to get those three runs back with one swing, he would do it. But even he can't.

So Ted Lilly picks. He lofts a breaking ball here, he floats a changeup there, he butterflies annoying little whimpers over there, hoping Pujols will chase, will poke after one he shouldn't. Unfortunately for Lilly in this at bat, he is locked in. Those pitches just off the corner of the plate, those "pitcher's pitches"? Pujols leisurely flicks them into foul territory. Those pseudo-eephuses (eephi?) that tempt just north of the strike zone? Pujols takes them. He knows Lilly doesn't want to walk him to lead off the inning with a three-run lead. He knows Lilly's going to give him a pitch that's hittable. Maybe not launchable. But hittable.

I've seen Pujols do this often. My favorite was a game against the Kansas City Royals, when he came up with the bases loaded. It was tied 4–4 in the fourth inning, with two outs, and Pujols had terrorized his hometown Royals all weekend, like he always does. (Do not snub Albert.) The Royals, quite sensibly, decided that they wanted to walk Pujols. They weren't going to do it intentionally, because you can't intentionally walk someone with the bases loaded without a court order. But they were walking him. You just knew it. It was worth one run to avoid this careening out of control. The count turned 3–0, and Pujols, almost out of boredom, started nicking pitches far out of the strike zone foul. Two feet outside? *Dink* foul. Almost in the dirt? *Floop* foul. This happened for about five pitches, and the Kauffman Stadium crowd began to sense something amazing happening. Pujols was waiting. He was willing to sit there and foul pitches off until poor Kyle Davies, journeyman, just wanting to get out of there alive, made a mistake. *I got all day.*

Davies, as was bound to happen, caught too much of the plate with a breaking ball, and Pujols's eyes grew wide wide wide. Almost haphazardly, he smashed the ball over the left field fence for a grand slam, the result a foregone conclusion, an afterthought. Even Royals fans applauded him. He was an alien using superior technology to mock us feeble humans.

Pujols is locked in like that now. Lilly knows it. But he's not going to just walk him, and he's a far better pitcher than Kyle Davies. If Pujols is that locked in, Lilly's going to make sure, no matter what happens, no matter how hard he hits it, that the ball isn't going over the wall. At best, a dent in the brick and ivy. Keep the ball *down.*

On the seventh pitch, pitcher strategy and batter strategy converge. Lilly throws a low, slightly inside fastball that Pujols decides is to his liking—fastball, hittable, per Pujols's plan—and he smashes it—on the ground, per Lilly's plan—between short and third. Aramis Ramirez, who was a lot more useful for Cardinals fans when he was an underachieving Pirate as opposed to a Cub realizing his true place in the world, is honed in and dives to his left, snatching the ball with the most flimsy, fragile part of his glove. This part of his glove is enough. He falls flat on his face and then, with the precision of a military pushup, bounces right back up and flings the ball to Derrek Lee at first. But Ramirez, with all the diving and jumping and pushing and thrusting, is off balance and throws far short of Lee, who has to dive and leap himself, off the base, just to catch it. Then, as he's falling over, he yanks his left arm in the air as Pujols passes by him, hoping to brush the great one, pure luck, stab-in-the-dark stuff. *And he gets him.* Pujols, despite controlling every aspect of every interaction, despite ending up with the exact result he was looking for—Ball! Hit! Hard!—is out, out just as much as you or I would be had we gone up there with a Styrofoam Nerf bat. All that trouble. All that focus. All that strength. All that work. And he's out.

All it took was three professional baseball players performing at the peak of their abilities, showcasing athleticism they didn't know they had, benefiting from the random physics of the gods. It took three men doing everything perfectly to get out Pujols. Barely.

You really are actively surprised he ever makes an out.

NOT EVERYONE is so self-made. Some need shortcuts. Which brings us to Troy Glaus.

This is a book about baseball, so I suppose there has to be a mention of performance-enhancing drugs. I don't like it, you don't like it, ain't nobody like it, but there it is, regardless: I can't ignore the pretend elephant in the pretend room. I trudge onward, battered, defeated, but hopeful that, someday, maybe my children, maybe my grandchildren, will be able to write books about baseball without having to mention steroids. We can only hope to leave the earth in better condition than we found it in.

About a year before this game, Glaus, a slugging third baseman who was a key part of the 2002 World Champion Anaheim Angels, was outed as a recipient of human growth hormone. In case you are one of the fortunate human beings who has been watching baseball games for the last decade on mute and then reading not a word about the game before or afterward—which is not the worst idea in the world—here is how HumanGrowthHormoneSales.com, a Web site that's obviously impartial and lacks any sort of agenda, describes human growth hormone:

> Injectable HGH human growth hormone, also called somatropin, is produced in the anterior of the pituitary gland inside the brain. It is one of the most abundant hormones secreted. It influences the growth of cells, bones, muscles and organs throughout the body. Clinical studies suggest that symptoms associated with aging may be due to the decline of growth hormone levels in our bodies. HGH is vital in helping prevent the aging process. Injectable HGH human growth hormone is one of many endocrine hormones, like estrogen, progesterone, testosterone, melatonin and DHEA, that all decline in production with age. While many of these hormones can be replaced to deter some of the effects of aging, human growth hormone reaches far beyond the scope of any of these hormones. Growth hormone not only prevents biological aging, it promotes weight loss, builds muscle mass, improves memory, significantly enhances sex drive, increases energy and many other symptoms associated with aging.

Well, jeez, that stuff sounds fantastic! When he received the shipments of HGH through "an allegedly illegal Internet distribution network," Glaus was on the disabled list, dealing with shoulder injuries that had plagued him ever since the World Series. Because HGH was not banned by baseball—and because he hadn't actually tested positive for it anyway; *Sports Illustrated* found receipts with Glaus's name on them—Glaus received no punishment. As it was, his shame was overshadowed by a similar revelation concerning Cardinals pitcher-turned-outfielder Rick Ankiel, and all told, most people don't even remember Glaus ever took HGH at all. (At least until I brought it up. Sorry.) After his injury rehab—the time he was taking the HGH—he signed a four-year, $45 million contract with the Arizona Diamondbacks and went back to doing what he did best: hitting home runs. He launched thirty-seven for Arizona, then thirty-eight the next season after being traded to the Toronto Blue Jays. (He made the all-star team that year too, and doubled and scored the winning run in the ninth inning.) More injuries came in 2007, and four months after the HGH allegations, the Jays traded him to the Cardinals for Scott Rolen. Glaus, to this day, has never commented on the HGH allegations, and, after being interviewed for the Mitchell Report, "the Commissioner's Office announced that there was insufficient evidence of a violation of the joint program in effect at the time of the conduct in question to warrant discipline of Glaus." And that was it, and that was that.

As he stands at the plate here with two outs in the fourth, he's proving to be worth every penny the Cardinals are paying and definitely worth trading the injured and La Russa–phobic Rolen. He's batting .266 with twenty-four home runs and ninety-four RBIs and has been splendid at third base. He also, more to the point, has remained healthy. I've watched about every Cardinals game this year, and I have not once—not *once*—heard a single fan even bring up Glaus's supposed HGH use. Nobody cares as long as he hits.

Of course, Troy Glaus is not Albert Pujols. It doesn't come easy to Pujols, but it *really* doesn't come easy to Glaus, particularly overcoming injuries. Glaus was looking at free agency back in 2004 and needed to make sure he could convince potential suitors he was healthy enough to take a chance on. So he took a drug that wasn't banned by baseball, a choice we only know about because of some enterprising *Sports Illustrated* reporters. Sure, most people don't care. But the main reason most people don't care if Troy Glaus takes performance-enhancing drugs is because most people don't care about Troy Glaus. Barry Bonds was a different kettle of fish. Roger

Clemens was a different kettle of fish. And Albert Pujols would *definitely* be a different kettle of fish.

ON A SEPTEMBER NIGHT in 1998, Mark McGwire hit his sixty-second home run of the season, breaking Roger Maris's record in front of a frenzied crowd in St. Louis. The moment was perfect.

People forget now, but much of the joy of that night revolved around not McGwire, but Maris's family. When Maris had broken Babe Ruth's record in 1961, he had been showered with scorn and derision, and the media was so hard on him that his hair famously fell out. (You might have heard something about this from Billy Crystal.) Maris ultimately hightailed it out of New York and found solace in St. Louis, of all places, where he was embraced as a fellow crew-cutted, square-jawed Midwesterner. (If you can count Maris's North Dakota as "Midwestern.") Maris died in 1985, still bitter about his time in New York and the home run record he had grown to consider a curse.

The fanfare McGwire received thirty-seven years later was, indirectly, an affirmation of Maris: his children, who were in Busch Stadium that night, were able to finally receive the accolades that had been denied their father. When McGwire hugged his rival (and blasted Cub) Sammy Sosa and hoisted that tubby son to the heavens, it wasn't just a celebration; it felt as if something had been healed, a mistake corrected.

In just a decade-plus, the night has turned from symbolizing everything that was right about sports into representing everything that is wrong. Now whenever the highlights of that night are shown, they're usually accompanied by foreboding music and interspersed with the infamous images of McGwire and Sosa testifying before Congress about steroids. Bernie Miklasz, the fine *St. Louis Post-Dispatch* columnist, published a book of his best columns, and prefaced the one about that night's game—the column of his that has probably been read by more people than any other—with the notion that there was a temptation to "bury this event and pretend it didn't happen."

These days, McGwire finds himself about three hundred stubborn, scolding minds away from the Hall of Fame, and Sosa is probably even farther. If you were touched by that evening, you are now supposed to feel duped—that it was all a facade that has eroded away.

But it hasn't. One name that hasn't been mentioned much in the last few years is Tim Forneris. Remember him? He was the young groundskeeper who ended up with McGwire's home run ball. Though collectors would have paid millions for the ball—McGwire's seventieth ultimately went for more than $3 million—Forneris, caught up in the spirit of the moment, gave it back to McGwire, saying it belonged in the Hall of Fame.

Forneris's decision was derided by the cynics, but most fans applauded him: The moment was too inspiring and uniting to be sullied by something as ugly as rampant consumerism and greed. It was sports in its purest form, a feel-good moment that was unscripted and unrehearsed. It was perfect. And now, if you believe the sports consensus, we're supposed to be ashamed of that night, to see it as some dark blotch on the history of sport.

Whatever your thoughts on steroids and McGwire's and Sosa's murky history with them, that night really did happen, and all the optimism and warmth that came out of it was real. Tim Forneris really did give back that ball. McGwire really did embrace his son and provide a real-life *Field of Dreams* moment for fathers and sons everywhere. (Dad called me seconds after the homer, called McGwire "a class act," and still has the game on videotape.) The Maris children really did cry and honor their tortured, maligned father. We were all touched by these moments, and why wouldn't we be? They were real.

Sportswriters can cast their votes of "protest" all they want—and we can reserve our right to suspect they're full of bunk. Mike Lupica of the *Daily News* has made a second career as a fierce voice against McGwire and Sosa and their "hypocrisy" . . . but his first career involved banking a tidy sum off *Summer of '98*, his memoir about following that home run chase with his sons.

That night in 1998 isn't going away and we shouldn't pretend it didn't happen. It did. And you know what? It was good. It was a great night.

THERE HAS NEVER BEEN any evidence that Albert Pujols has ever taken steroids. Pujols appeared on the cover of *Sports Illustrated* before the 2009 season with the cover line: "Albert Pujols Has a Message: Don't Be Afraid to Believe in Me." He has established himself as the best player in baseball, but just as important, he is now the face of post-steroid baseball, the guy who will set the baseball record book straight, the guy who Did It The Right Way.

I'm not sure most fans see it this way, generally; fans are much better at making their peace with "cheating" baseball players than media folk are. Witness Glaus, or Ankiel, or Andy Pettitte, or Ryan Franklin: If we happen to like the player "caught" using performance enhancers, we tend to let it go in a way we never do with Bonds, Clemens, or Alex Rodriguez, polarizing figures in the first place. Our innocence was lost a long time ago, and unlike sportswriters from the time who let the steroid scandal pass gleefully under their noses, we're not particularly angry about it. It's sports. It's baseball. It's entertainment. It's distraction. We'll move on with our life, regardless. Sports isn't a morality play for us: It's a place to escape morality plays.

But Pujols . . . it feels like Pujols would be different. It feels like his brand of excellence—the up-from-bootstraps, hardworking, obsessive kind, the kind no one noticed until he grabbed a bat and whacked them in the face with it—is steeped more deeply in the real, in the work, in the This Could Be You. I think it would be difficult for people. I think that's why Pujols is on the cover of *SI*, telling us it's OK to come out and cheer without fear, telling us that it's all good, nothing to fear here.

That's the thing, though: We can't trust anyone anymore. Why would we? Whether we believe steroids to be the secret, festering evil rotting the soul of our greatest game, or we believe it's just the latest "impurity" that supposedly eats away at the game but in actuality couldn't so much as make a scratch . . . it is naïve and silly to just acquit someone, across the board, when we know nothing about him and never could. Steroids were everywhere. They might still be. It is not a witch hunt, or hysterical, or even apathetic, to understand that.

To be 100 percent clear: I do not think Albert Pujols is using steroids. I'm just saying . . . what if it happens? What if it turns out that we *can't* believe in him? Does that invalidate everything he's done? The pure beauty of watching him bat? The fans like me who wear his jersey? (I have four.) Does it matter?

It doesn't. Those times we watched Albert, or McGwire, or Bonds, or whoever, they were real. Those moments were ours. They belonged to us before they happened, during, and afterward. The only one who can ruin them is us. If Albert Pujols had secretly shot the pitch Brad Lidge threw him in the 2005 NLCS out of a cannon without anybody noticing, and we just found out about it now, it wouldn't change that my father and I called each other to explode, together, fifteen hundred miles apart, rapturous, incredulous, fantabulous. That was our moment. Not Pujols's. Not The Sacred Game Of Baseball's.

Because it's not just Albert. It's all of us. It's the game we love and worship at the altar of. It's a game that can be destroyed by nothing. Our memories, our screams of joy, our shrieks of Bartman pain . . . they are ours. They belong to us. Nothing can change that. Nothing should.

GLAUS POPS UP to the shortstop, and the Cardinals go down in order. Six more batters until Pujols. Fifteen more outs to go.

KNOWLEDGE YOU NOW HAVE

1. Human growth hormone was once not standard issue at birth.
2. The reason your mother keeps making you clean your plate is because we want you to get fat and turn into Albert Pujols.
3. Your father hates talking about steroids.

BOTTOM OF THE FOURTH INNING

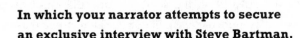

**In which your narrator attempts to secure
an exclusive interview with Steve Bartman.**

*I am a Red Sox fan and so is my father, and I was born in 1984.
One of my earliest memories is of playing a game of catch with
my dad, probably around 1988. He was throwing the ball to me,
and I was probably heaving, lobbing, rolling, or doing whatever a
four-year-old can do that resembles throwing. One of my throws
was a classic fifty-eight-footer, landing in the grass in front of my
dad. He bent over to field it, but it dribbled between his legs. I
pointed at him, laughed, and yelled, "Bill Buckner! Bill Buckner!"
I was four. This was two years after the '86 Series. My dad turned
around and yelled back, "What did you say?!" Buckner's error
was apparently common knowledge among pre-kindergartners
in Maine in 1988. No, from his tone, he was obviously angry that
his son had compared his fielding prowess to Buckner's. "Don't
say that! That's not nice!" he scolded. Some baseball wounds
take a long time to heal.*

— JOEL BARKAN, San Diego, California

GEOVANY SOTO HITS A LINE SHOT ON ONE HOP TO GLAUS, AND IT'S
too fast, it's too much, and Glaus muffs it, and here we go again,
there's a leadoff base runner. Tony La Russa informs us in his always
awkward dugout interviews with FOX broadcasters that Pineiro's

wife just had twins, so he's probably a little tired, but he's "gutting it out just fine." Part of me wonders how Pineiro's wife feels about that. She hasn't exactly had the most comfortable and relaxing thirty-hour stretch either.

Mark DeRosa, who a year from now will be playing for the Cardinals but right now is a soulless monster who once ripped a man's heart out to show him how black it was before he died, hits a long, massive fly to deep left field. Barton, still obsessing on parabolas, can't field it, and by the time he finally tracks it down, Soto has scored, DeRosa's standing on second base, and the Cubs are up 4–0.

Baseball does not have a clock, and it's so meticulously fair that it makes sure everyone has an equal chance, equal opportunity, equal hope. But clock or no, there is a point in every baseball game where one gathers the palpable sense that matters are streaking out of control. Dad calls it the "five-run homer" rule. When a game cannot be tied with a grand slam, you are too far behind to hold onto much semblance of hope. You hold onto some. But not much. It is now 4–0. It is only the fourth inning.

Two minutes later, Ted Lilly squeezes home DeRosa from third base and is safe at first himself. It is now 5–0. It is still only the fourth inning.

The Brewers are tied 1–1 with the Reds. Signs are trending downward. This game needs a spoiler alert. It is so grim. I look over at my father, and he is looking downward again, mouthing "Jesus Christ" as tens of thousands of Cubs fans rhapsodize around him. Mike is no longer being modest. He's screaming. He's clapping. He's stomping. How could he not?

It remains strange and disorienting to see Cubs fans so happy. They can smell it.

I look to left field. Every time I go to Wrigley, I look for it. People still sit there.

———

2003. MOISES ALOU was already feisty at the end of the seventh inning. With runners on first and third base, Alou had a chance to truly put Game Six of the National League Championship Series away once and for all. Florida Marlins reliever Chad Fox had just given up a single to Sammy Sosa, and the Wrigley Field crowd felt history stripping off her garter. The Cubs were just six outs away. Alou had a chance to make those six outs pass by right quick.

On a 1–1 pitch, Fox, clearly reeling, threw a mistake pitch, a meat ninety-three-miles-per-hour fastball on the bottom half of the plate, right where Alou is famous for liking it. (It was such a relief when Alou finally retired in 2008: It seems like he was perpetually hitting low line drives down the line, just past whatever hapless soul the Cardinals had on third base, for whatever team Alou happened to be playing for.) As usual, Alou wasn't wearing batting gloves, because Moises Alou says he urinates on his hands to "alleviate calluses," which is a strategy, one supposes. (That's why I do it.)

Alou's eyes lit up and he reared back for the swing of his life. You could see his eyebrows rise slightly when he sees the pitch coming. And . . . he flicked it harmlessly into left field, landing in the glove of 2003-skinny Miguel Cabrera in right field. Alou, realizing he's missed the perfect opportunity to secure his Cubs legend, hops and spins in the air after he makes contact, angry with himself, clearly feeling the pressure of this massive moment. It's a familiar sight to Cubs fans. That would not be the last time Moises Alou would jump into the air and spin angrily that evening. He'd do it again about fifteen minutes later. People remember that one.

Here is what Thom Brennaman said on FOX as the top of the eighth inning of Game 6 of the National League Series began, as the center field camera panned over Wrigley Field, capturing all for posterity. This was a big moment for Brennaman. This would be the highlight of his broadcasting career.

"39,577 at Wrigley Field in Chicago, for Game 6 of this National League Championship Series. On this October 14, 2003. It was on this date in 1908, ninety-five years ago today, that the Cubs defeated the Detroit Tigers 2–0, to wrap up their second straight World Series championship. With a victory tonight—as he said, he did not go around on the pitch there [Mike Mordacei had a check swing off Mark Prior, and the first base umpire gave the safe sign]—with a chance to win their first title since this day, 1908."

The camera cut to the important figures: Marlins third baseman Mike Lowell looking forlorn in the visitors dugout. An elderly woman wearing an oversized Cubs sweatshirt and blue beads around her neck. The obligatory photo of the 1908 Chicago Cubs, all sepia and dead and about to be resurrected. An easy fly ball to Alou in left field.

You can't see Steve Bartman in the shot. He's there, but the camera doesn't catch him.

How excited he must be. He's sitting out there, in Aisle 4, Row 8, Seat 113, nice seats, quality seats. For a regular season game in 2009, that seat runs you about $125 on StubHub. What a gift, really, for a guy like Bartman, a lifelong Cubs fan who cared about his team as much as I care about the Cardinals, as much as any of us care about anything. Bartman was twenty-six years old, single and working a dull desk job, coaching a youth league team in his spare time. The Cubs were the center of his life. He talked to his father about them all the time. He traveled to their Spring Training in Mesa. He listened to the game on his headphones, an old school move, a true fan move. It is almost surprising he didn't have a score book. God, he is just like me.

How many years had he listened to Ron Santo ache and moan on the broadcasts, sneaking his Walkman into class at Notre Dame, refreshing MLB Gameday on his office computer? He lived three miles away from Wrigley, away from Wrigleyville, where all the pretty frat people drank away their days and nights, checking out the game in between attempts to talk that girl from Naperville into their one-bedroom just a few blocks away. Those Cubs fans weren't real Cubs fans, not really. The Cubs were just a conversation topic, a phase in life, way back when, when they lived by Wrigley and partied, man, partied until grown-up life caught up with them and it was off to Lake Forest, for an easy commute into the city and quality school for the inevitable children. Baseball was fun, it was an excuse to go out, but that's what it was to them. Not Steve. Not Bartman. Not him.

He was serious about this.

He was exactly the type of person who deserved seats in the second row just off the left field foul line, and exactly the type of person who rarely gets them anymore. No one knows how he procured the ticket. He wouldn't have been able to afford them, not at his salary. He must have waited a long time. He must have felt that this was the year, and stowed away a little money *this* week, a little more *that* week, hoping this moment would come, preparing. My, how lucky he is! He has front row seats—well, second row—to the most important moment in Cubs baseball in sixty years. He has earned this. He's at the game by himself, for cripes sake. Only diehards go to baseball games by themselves. Only the ones who truly, deeply care. Only people who think the other twenty-one hours of the day are just the time in between the last pitch and the first pitch. People like me. People like Bartman.

How excited he must be.

At this point, Mark Prior had just thrown his one hundredth pitch. Manager Dusty Baker wasn't worried, though: Young Prior has been throwing tons of pitches all season. In his last start of the regular season, he threw 133 in a 4–2 win over the Pittsburgh Pirates. It was his eighteenth victory of the season. Mark Prior was terrifying. He was the Perfect Pitcher. His delivery was smooth, structured, and infinitely repeatable. There was no reason to worry about him. There were only four outs to go.

On a 2–1 count, Juan Pierre, just trying to avoid a strikeout, slapped a curveball foul into the left field stands. It was about eight rows up, but it was around the general vicinity of where Bartman was sitting. I wonder if he stood. I wonder if he thought he had a chance at it. *Oh, just a little high. Damn. It would be pretty cool to grab a ball tonight, of all nights. That would be something to tell my kids about. "That ball up there over the fireplace? That's a ball I caught the night the Cubs clinched a trip to the World Series."* It had to have been in his mind. It would have been in mine.

Good Lord was it ever loud at Wrigley Field. When people think about Game 6 of the National League Championship Series, they imagine everything being perfect and wonderful and glorious and then all of a sudden One Thing Happened and everything collapsed. Going back to watch the game again, that's what I remembered too. Nope. After reaching for his put-em-away pitch on Pierre, Prior tries to waste a fastball away but touches too much of the plate, and Pierre slaps it down the left field line—left again!—for a double. Analyst Al Leiter says, "Prior is strong enough to make sure the exterior distractions don't get in his task and focus," which probably makes sense, somewhere. The tying run is on deck.

I was not at the stadium that night—as mentioned, I was watching the game in an Inwood bar downstairs from my apartment, depressed about what was clearly about to happen—so I can't say what the mood was after Pierre's hit, but you have to think there was *some* apprehension, right? Sure, the Marlins needed to put another runner on base to have a chance, but come on, it's the Cubs. Surely the Cubs must have sensed something.

I bet Bartman did. I bet he bit his hand, or kicked the back of the guy's chair in front of him, the guy who did some business with the Cubs and had the nice seats but deep down didn't know much about baseball and kind of liked the White Sox more anyway. True baseball fans do not cheer for their teams to win: They cheer for them not to lose. Victory does not come with joy; it comes with relief. Losing causes only pain. When I sat in Busch for Game 5 of the 2006

World Series, I was not counting down outs. I was not preparing to celebrate a title. I was terrified that this was all going to veer wrong, that, once again, all the time and effort and emotion I had put into this team, this lovely precious elusive team, would be for naught. I would watch them blow out. And, like all fans, I feared deep down that it would be my fault. That if I hadn't have gone to the game, they would have won. It doesn't make any sense. It's irrational. But nothing about being a baseball fan is rational. The goal is not to watch your team dominate. The goal is to escape without being embarrassed. Baseball is not a sport for dominators. Baseball is a sport for survivors.

I bet the Dread was in Bartman's gut right then. He'd come too far, and been through too much, for it not to have been.

Watching it years later, maybe I don't sense much Dread in the hearts of Wrigley fans. The center field camera pans again, this time over Waveland Avenue outside the left field fence. It's packed with people who just want to be close. They're here to see history. They will.

On a 1–1 count to Luis Castillo, Prior is handed an awfully friendly strike call on a pitch that looked a few inches off the plate. It's 1–2. It's all locking into place. Dusty Baker is confident; there's no one up in the bullpen. Prior is throwing his 110th pitch. Nothing to be concerned about. It's ball three. The count is full. Another foul ball. Another foul ball. Baker has a twinge, a pang, Spidey Sense kicking in a tad late, and Kyle Farnsworth stands up in the bullpen. Bartman must see him. He's walking to the bullpen mound right in front of him. It's the first tangible sign that he's not the only one worried anymore.

Bartman stands, listening to Santo. Everyone's standing now. I bet Bartman doesn't want to stand. I bet this is all becoming a bit much for him. It's not feeling like history right now, a culmination, the Cubs' coronation after years of misery. Not to Bartman. It feels like the Cubs need five more outs. And that feels like a lot of outs. It always does.

On a 3–2 pitch, in the eighth pitch of that at bat, Castillo hits a fly ball down the left field line. The ball stays in the air for precisely four seconds.

> *"There are few words to describe how awful I feel and what I have experienced within these last twenty-four hours. I am so truly sorry from the bottom of this Cubs fan's broken heart.*
>
> *"I ask that Cubs fans everywhere redirect the negative energy that has been vented towards my family, my friends, and myself into the usual positive support for our beloved team on their way to being National League champs."*

—STEVE BARTMAN,
hours after the foul ball that would make him famous,
and the last public statement he ever made

THREE PEOPLE went for that ball. Nobody remembers that, but there were three. One was wearing a gray long-sleeved T-shirt with blue stripes on the arms. One was wearing a blue pullover sweatshirt. And one was Steve Bartman. The ball was closest to him. But it could have been any of the three.

What if Bartman had caught it? What if it had fallen *smack* right into his hand, and it had stayed? It would have been difficult to be mad at *that* guy, wouldn't it? If he had come away with it clean? Hell, people would have loved that. The Cubs might have gone on to win, and Steve Bartman would have been the awesome dude who made that funny play in the eighth inning. Perhaps more important, it would have stopped Moises Alou.

Alou, in an instinctive reaction that made matters about 80 million times worse, began waving his arms and leaping around as if someone had inserted a scorpion in his jockstrap. He had not calmed down since his frustrated leap after the fly out in the seventh inning—one suspects Moises Alou had been feeling the Dread for a while, even if his manager hadn't—and he exploded when he didn't catch this ball. If Alou had just calmly walked back to his position, no one would ever know the name Steve Bartman. The whole at bat would have passed without incident. The Cubs might have made it to the World Series. Or maybe they wouldn't have. But this incident wouldn't have mattered. No one would have noticed.

That's not what happened, though. Alou stalked off, cursing and stomping his feet, looking back and glaring at the fan, screaming "motherfucker" and "what the fuck?" The boos began immediately. Steve Lyons on FOX wasn't much help. When Brennaman pointed out that "that was a Cubs fan who tried to make that catch," Lyons screamed, "Why? I'm surprised someone hasn't thrown that fan onto the field." In Wrigley, the Dread had taken over. After Prior threw a wild fastball for ball four, the crowd began chanting "Asshole! Asshole!"

Meanwhile, there sat Bartman.

God, look at him. Within seconds of the walk to Pierre, the FOX cameras found him.

Look at him. He's the only guy sitting down. He still has his head-phones on. He is almost certainly listening to WGN Radio broadcast-ers talking specifically about him. Dread has entered the hearts of everyone in the stadium, people are booing and screaming, Wrig-ley's freaked out, everything is going wrong. And there he is, sitting back down in his seat, ready to cheer his team back on to victory. His Cubbies are still five outs away from the World Series. That hasn't changed. But the rest of the galaxy has.

He has about four minutes left. In four minutes, the Cubs will have collapsed, and he will be ushered out through the back halls of Wrigley by armed policemen while fans throw beer at him. One fan tries to attack him before being stopped by another Cubs fan: They proceed to fight with each other. Bartman, bless his heart, covers his face with his jacket when he notices a camera on him. He wants to put the toothpaste back in the tube. This has all happened so fast. This has happened in four seconds.

For this second, for that moment captured in the screengrab above, Steve Bartman thinks the Cubs can still win the World Se-ries. He doesn't quite realize that his life has forever changed. And if I had to wager a guess, I bet, at that second above, he doesn't actu-ally care. There are runners on first and third, but there's already one out. Ivan Rodriguez hits into double plays all the time. That was quite the little hullabaloo there, *hoo boy,* but come on, boys, let's get back to business. Just five outs to go. Just five little outs to go.

It breaks your heart. It breaks my heart. That was me. That was you. That was all of us. Forget about reaching for the ball: Anyone would have done that. No, Steve Bartman is a man who, within sec-onds of one of the most famous plays in baseball history, a play that *directly involved him,* straightened up his headphones, dusted him-self off, and sat back down in his seat to watch the game.

If the Cubs had acted like Steve Bartman, had they put it behind them and concentrated on the task at hand, they might have won that

World Series. They should have followed Bartman's lead. Everyone should have.

But they didn't. The Cubs, clearly panicked, had a big meeting at the mound, allowing the crowd enough time to focus solely on Bartman and not on what they were there for in the first place. And Prior stayed in the game.

About forty-five seconds after the above screengrab, FOX shows a Wrigley security guard walking up to Bartman and positively identifying him. He then takes out his CB radio and tells the other guards to come meet him. From three seats over, the man in the gray long-sleeved T-shirt with blue stripes on the arms rushes over to talk to the guard. We can't see what he's saying, but he doesn't seem angry. He is not strangling Bartman. He looks sad, he looks guilty, he looks like he, more than anyone else in the stadium, in the entire viewing world, understands what's happening. He stands over Bartman, his girth protecting him from the camera, his last line of defense, a last-ditch effort to shield him from what he cannot be shielded from, from what is coming.

Bartman sits there, still. All he can do is try to look around this wide Good Samaritan. He is trying to see the game. This is the most important moment in Chicago Cubs history. He saved up a ton to get these seats. He's been a Cubs fan his whole life. He just wants to see the Cubs make it to the World Series.

On a 1–2 pitch, Ivan Rodriguez smashes a hanging curveball into left field for a base hit. On the next pitch, skinny Miguel Cabrera hits an easy ground ball to shortstop Alex Gonzalez, who, distracted by Dread, bobbles it. Everyone's safe. The bases are loaded. The die is cast. History is sweeping over. Everyone sees what's happening now. What is on the field is too gruesome to witness. So they look away. They look to Aisle 4, Row 8, Seat 113. They look for Bartman.

But he isn't there. He doesn't see any of this. He has been whisked away, gone.

Bless his heart. Bless his Cubs fan's broken heart.

BARTMAN DIDN'T end up with the ball. Neither did the other two people who grasped for it. The unnamed fellow who did, someone in a red hat and gray jumper who snatched it from the ground while Bartman looked down and Alou did his hopping fit, sold it a year later to a Chicago restaurateur named Grant Deporter for $113,824.16. They blew up the ball a few months later at Harry Caray's restaurant. Harry would have liked that, I bet.

I've watched that play in slow motion upward of one hundred times while working on this chapter, and I can say with 95 percent certainty that Alou would not have caught that ball. He was leaping over a tall railing without a clear look at the ball even *without* six hands in his way. Had no one touched the ball, at *best,* it would have bounced on the bottom of his glove. Alou couldn't have seen well enough to know when to close his mitt or where the ball was landing.

Alou, years later, is still being an asshole about this. In 2008, Alou told an Associated Press reporter, "You know what the funny thing is? I wouldn't have caught it, anyway." Yeah, boy, that *is* hilarious. Two months later, he changed his mind again. "I don't remember saying that. If I said that, I was probably joking to make [Bartman] feel better. But I don't remember saying that." To Alou, it must be so funny. It must be such a joke to him. One crazy game for a team he hasn't played for in years. He's already won a World Series. He suited up for seven different teams in his career. Out of eighteen years in the majors, he was only with the Cubs for three. They were just another employer to him. He didn't make the catch, threw a shit fit in front of everyone, and then moved on with his life. Real fuckin' easy for him to say.

None of that matters now.

Obviously, none of this was Bartman's fault. Gonzalez made the error, Baker inexplicably kept Prior in, Prior gave up a game-tying double to future Cub Derrek Lee, Farnsworth and Mike Remlinger gave up five more runs, the Cubs lost Game 7, and the Marlins beat the Yankees in the World Series even though they don't have any fans.

No one remembers Alex Gonzalez, or Dusty Baker, or Mark Prior, or any of them. They only remember Bartman. He even got his own *Law & Order* episode.

But Bartman disappeared. After that public statement, he never said another word. He never did a wacky commercial, he never showed up on a reality show, he never started a blog. He just went *poof.* Earlier in the 2008 season, a site called SportsBuy.com offered Bartman $25,000 simply to show up at a signing, no questions asked, no obligations. He didn't. In today's media culture, this is a heroic act. It's the last Walden act of purity. And it makes absolute sense. I know Bartman. I understand who he is. All that matters is his team. Everything else is noise.

The only proof we have that Bartman is still alive are his friends who continue to guard his privacy and a 2005 ESPN.com story called "Searching for Bartman" by writer Wayne Drehs. Drehs, a Cubs fan sympathetic to Bartman, actually waited for Bartman outside his workplace to ask him questions and (mostly) apologize for what has happened to him over the years. Bartman, in a "Mr. Rogers voice," politely refused and went back in his car.

Except for one moment. After Drehs revealed he was a Cubs fan, Bartman perked up.

"Hell of a game today, huh?" he told Drehs, referring to a Cubs' spanking of the Red Sox. "They were hitting the ball all over the place."

Of course he was still obsessed with the Cubs. Through it all, through everything, Bartman was still that guy with his headphones, sitting down in his seat, staring straight ahead, just wanting everything to be normal so he could go back to watching the game, to living solely in the world of baseball. All else is background—the fake fans, the steroids, the gossip rags, the angry screeds, the *Around the*

Horn, the longtime-listener-first-time-caller, the circle of madness that surrounds something so pure and hopeful and open. It's all nothing. It means something to love a team that much. It's *important*.

Bartman, on just an average day at the office, which will never, ever be "average" when you're Steve Bartman, sat at his desk all day, refreshing Gameday like he always did, getting updates on the Cubs' meaningless Spring Training, eager for the new season, hopeful that this time, maybe this time, it would be the year. Not for himself. Not for any kind of absolution. Just for his Cubbies.

I bet Bartman feels worse about the Cubs losing that game than he ever has about what happened to him in the wake. That's what I bet. I know I would. I'm damn sure I would. Because it could have been me.

If this all goes wrong, if the Cardinals lose this game, and the Cubs do what everyone in this park thinks they're going to do and win the World Series, I will be miserable, my father will be miserable, every Cardinals fan on earth will be miserable. But I'll be happy for Bartman. For about ten minutes anyway. Maybe five.

Or maybe just four seconds. Those four seconds will have to be enough.

KNOWLEDGE YOU NOW HAVE

1. Your grandfather has a T-shirt that has a picture of a red bird excreting on a baby bear on the front and "Bartman 2003" on the back.
2. He finds this hilarious.
3. Your father doesn't.

TOP OF THE FIFTH INNING

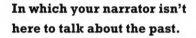

In which your narrator isn't here to talk about the past.

As I was pitching to my four-year-old son at a park, a ten-year-old boy and his father—who was still dressed in his business casual work clothes—started kicking a soccer ball to each other nearby. After five minutes of tripping over the ball and themselves, the father retreated to his chair by the soccer field and the boy wandered over to where we were playing baseball. His name was Kyle, and he asked if he could play with us. I told him he could. When it was Kyle's turn to bat, it was pretty obvious that he didn't have any experience playing baseball. After a few hopeless flails and some minor adjustments I made to his swing, he starting fouling pitches off. When he finally hit one in the right direction he looked over at his dad, beaming with pride, and said, "I wish my dad could have seen that." I cringed and thought, "I'm glad your dad didn't hear that." Moments later as I walked by him to retrieve a few of the balls he had missed, he looked over at me and said, "You're cool. I wish you were my dad." I looked over at his dad, who was too far away to have heard the comment, and I felt awful. Before Kyle ran over to his dad to tell him how well he had been hitting, I tried to redeem the moment as best as I could. I had to say something. "I might be cool to have as a friend," I told the

kid, "but your dad is the best person in the world to be your
dad." I'm not sure if he bought it or not, but it was all I could
think to say.

— BRYAN ALLAIN, Intercourse, Pennsylvania

2009. I ATTENDED THE 2009 ALL-STAR GAME, HELD ABOUT NINE
months after the game at Wrigley, in St. Louis, with my parents and
my father's friend Jeff, a farmer who came across some late-in-life
money and now pretty much spends every weekend hectoring my
father into zipping down to Busch Stadium and drinking all day. Dad
does not require much hectoring.

Those who think the United States federal subsidy system is too
friendly to the American farmer will find considerable evidence to
support their viewpoint in Jeff. He owns an unnaturally high amount
of farmland on the outskirts of Mattoon, most of which is rented out
to the government for "future projects." He cashes an inordinate
number of happy Obama checks, and as far as I can tell, about two
months out of the year are his "busy season," and the rest of the time
he's hanging around the Leitch house, drinking beer. Nice guy, sure,
and a fun guy to have a six-pack with. After that, you start to wonder
what's going on, you know, at *his* house.

My dad is Jeff's idol. Dad knows how to fix tractors, plant grass,
build houses, install insulation, unclog pipes, and all kinds of manual activities you'd think a farmer would know how to do. Jeff comes
by, and Dad puts a new engine in his Jeep and changes the oil in
his tractor, and, as payment, Jeff trots along with Dad to Cardinals
games because I'm out in New York and therefore unavailable. Like
most parents, mine were too busy dealing with wild-eyed children
to hang onto their twentysomething friendships, and now that the
kids are out of the house, they need something, and someone, to fill
their time. For them, that guy is Jeff.

Jeff is a baseball fan of a kind that most normal, non-obsessive people are: casual, generally uninformed, and loud. I don't mean this as an insult, not necessarily. Jeff hates Tony La Russa, hates Albert Pujols, hates Busch Stadium, hates beer vendors, hates St. Louis, hates city drivers, hates the upper deck, hates the lower deck, hates the Cubs, hates the Cardinals. Jeff is one of those people who thinks everything in baseball is wrong.

At the 2009 All-Star Game, I sat in section 452, with my parents and Jeff. I had bought tickets for my dad for his sixtieth birthday, and Jeff came along with us. That was fine. Jeff is a nice guy. (I am emphasizing this fact, and not just because he'll read this.) But this is an All-Star Game. This is the game that doesn't count. This is a game to relax and have fun.

Jeff is like most normal people who watch a little bit of baseball, kind of. Jeff is not one to relax and have fun. Baseball is to be complained about.

THE 2008 CHICAGO CUBS, the ones kicking the Cardinals' asses that day at Wrigley, had eight different players named to the 2008 All-Star Game in Yankee Stadium in New York. Half of them played the game at Wrigley: left fielder Alfonso Soriano, catcher Geovony Soto, third baseman Aramis Ramirez, and center fielder Kosuke Fukudome. At the top of the fifth, four of them sat on the bench or in the bullpen, desperately waiting to run onto the field and spray champagne in disparate directions: pitchers Ryan Dempster, Kerry Wood, Carlos Zambrano, and Carlos Marmol. That was more all-stars than any other team in baseball, and the most all-stars the Cubs had had on the team in their history. This was the year of the Cub. You might have heard.

The Cardinals only had two, and neither of them batted in the fifth inning: Pujols, of course, and Ludwick, whose hot first half earned him a surprising trip to Yankee Stadium. During all-star week in

Gotham, I headed out to Fifth Avenue for the annual all-star parade, mostly to see Ludwick, who must have been bewildered to be there. (Before 2008, he'd never hit more than fourteen homers in a season.) When Ludwick's "float"—actually a 2009 Chevy Silverado—made it to my section, I was the only person paying any attention to him. Because I am a thirteen-year-old boy, I yelled, "Hey, Ryan! Go Cards! Congratulations! Welcome to New York!"

Ludwick turned and smiled widely. "Thanks! Gotta love New York. I wouldn't want to live here, but for a couple days, it's great!"

I hear this sentiment a lot from friends back home. "I don't know how you live there, but I'd like to come visit sometime." Allow this Midwesterner to translate that statement for those in the Northeast Corridor: This means, "you people are fucking morons for living in New York."

Ludwick's appearance on the all-star roster allowed me to continue a nearly decade-long tradition: buying an all-star jersey, each year, of whatever Cardinal happens to make the team. And no repeats:

2009 (Busch Stadium)—Yadier Molina
2008 (Yankee Stadium)—Ryan Ludwick
2007 (AT&T Park)—Albert Pujols
2006 (PNC Park)—David Eckstein
2005 (Comerica Park)—Jim Edmonds
2004 (Minute Maid Park)—Scott Rolen
2003 (U.S. Cellular Field)—Edgar Renteria
2002 (Miller Park)—Matt Morris

You probably think all this all-star stuff is silly. You're wrong.

A NATURAL PART of growing older is realizing how infantile some of your childhood passions turned out to be. As it turns out, the Teenage

Mutant Ninja Turtles, Vanilla Ice, and *Saved By the Bell,* alas, are pretty lame. My sister, living a perfectly happy hippie life at the age of thirty, wouldn't admit that she once had a New Kids on the Block bedspread even if you plucked out her toenails, one by one. We enjoy simple pleasures when we are young, because when we are young, we are stupid and have no taste.

But we can take it too far the other way too. Sometimes we can segue so far into adulthood that we forget the purity of shiny colors, surreal landscapes, dogs and cats living together. We look too far behind the curtain rather than just absorbing the giddiness of what's in front of us.

When I was a child, my favorite event of the year was the Major League Baseball All-Star Game. It was a kaleidoscope of crazy visions for a ten-year-old. Ozzie Smith batting against Roger Clemens? Tony Gwynn and Dale Murphy in the same outfield? Cal Ripken shaking hands with Dwight Gooden before the game? Yes please! The All-Star Game unites the gods in one location, at one time, in a way that's breathtaking for a young baseball fan. It was like *Who Framed Roger Rabbit* when Daffy Duck and Donald Duck played a piano duet together, or a comic book in which Batman and Spider-Man joined forces. It blew my mind. It still kind of does.

Sure, in a theoretical sense, interleague play and extended player movement has diluted the All-Star Game, but that's just a theoretical thing: Something you bring up as some sort of data point for whatever agenda you have rather than an actual reason not to watch the All-Star Game. Sure, it doesn't *really* mean anything, it's just an exhibition game, the home-field advantage for the World Series thing is pointless. So what? It's a game where you just watch the greatest baseball players in the world play baseball for four hours.

Baseball's All-Star Game is the only all-star game that matters precisely because baseball is a sport that cannot be altered dramatically if the players don't care, like in the NBA and NFL. Baseball is just baseball, and it's a sport that focuses on the individual in a way perfect for the All-Star Game. Tim Lincecum against Derek Jeter? Albert Pujols versus Roy Halladay? Yes please! It's the All-Star Game! Look at all the different uniforms! Everybody's all in the same place! What more do you people want? If you can't appreciate that, you are old and cranky and I am not sure we can be friends.

AT THE 2009 All-Star Game, hometown hero Yadier Molina came up with runners on first and third and two outs in the second inning. Molina might have to dodge flaming arrows every time he visits Flushing, but at Busch, he's just a notch below Pujols on the adulation chart. I've found that Yady is particularly popular among the female contingent of Cardinals fans. This is not because he is strikingly attractive; he is not Grady Sizemore, and these are not Grady's Ladies. I think it's because he's kind of pudgy, kind of awkward, kind of cuddly, and always smiling. I also suspect the "Yady" nickname helps; it's difficult to come up with a cute moniker for the scowling, scary Pujols, and it's impossible to morph either "Albert" or "Pujols" into something that ends in a y. Yady is warm and accessible, and you just want to buy him a pie and watch him eat it, then buy him another one, and watch him eat that too. You want to wrap him up in a blanket and tell him jokes. He would be an active giggler.

It's a big moment for Yady, the local product shining on one of baseball's grandest stages. National League manager Charlie Manuel, a baseball lifer who once managed the Cleveland Indians with a colostomy bag next to him after undergoing treatment for cancer, paced around the dugout. The NL was already down 1–0. This was as important an at bat as the game had seen so far, and St. Louis's own was at the plate.

And Jeff was screaming.

"Get 'em out of there!" he yelled. "You gotta have a bigger bat up there! Molina ain't gonna hit one out! Step on their throat."

My parents, typically quiet and studious at the game, looked down at their feet, and I stared straight ahead hoping no one in our section connected *me* to *that guy*. Jeff did not allow this.

"Will, Will, you know this guy managing?"

"Yeah," I mumbled. "Charlie Manuel. The Phillies manager. They won the World Series last year."

"Well, he's an IDIOT! Is he like La Russa? I bet he's like La Russa! He has to be! Boooo!"

Never mind that Yadier Molina, in front of the Cardinals red fans, had yet to actually bat in an all-star game. Never mind that, had Manuel actually pinch hit for Molina in that situation, Tony LaRussa and Albert Pujols would have had a race to see who could insert a Louisville Slugger in Manuel's anus faster. (I like Albert's odds.) Never mind that Jeff had probably never heard the name Charlie Manuel in his life.

No, Charlie Manuel was *the manager,* like Tony La Russa was *the manager,* and the manager exists, to Jeff, and fans like Jeff (normal people), to be the evil minion standing in between them and everything they believe and know to be "true" in the world of baseball. Tony La Russa, and Charlie Manuel, and every other manager in baseball history, have devoted their lives to baseball, to dissecting every possible scenario, to planning for all situations. They have seen more baseball than any of us can imagine: They breathe and excrete baseball. It is a sport that keeps them on the road for six months out of the year, that ruins any semblance of a normal family life, that breaks their heart, that flashes over their eyelids when they attempt to sleep at night. They care more about baseball than any of us care about anything. They have traded everything. This is all they know. They are the pulse of the game. We are just visitors. This does not mean they are always right. That is their curse: Their decisions, wrung out of sweat and blood and bile and years of emptiness, are simply decisions. It can all go wrong, and when it does—and even when it doesn't—they have farmers screaming at them for being a fucking moron, from the stands, from the radio, in the restaurant when they just want to have a few beers and be left alone for a while. They love it so Jeff can hate it. They are there so that we might destroy them. Neither can exist without the other.

Charlie Manuel got this grief from Jeff, and surely thousands others, for making an *obvious* decision. And so few decisions are obvious.

Managers understand, the good ones, anyway. They understand that part of baseball's value lies in its capacity to inspire such rage. The game makes us all helpless. We refer to it as "second-guessing," to be nice, but it's really lashing out at what we cannot control. We expect baseball to be perfect, all the time. And it is perfect. But it is run by human beings, who are far from perfect, who are not even close. We hold it against the game. We hold baseball to a higher standard. It must be as idyllic in reality as it is in our dreams.

"He must be like Tony La Russa," Jeff repeated, through his beer. "Boooo!" Yadier Molina hit an RBI single, and everyone cheered, including Jeff, who smiled and said, "Still should've pinch-hit. This guy, what's his name, Manny, he doesn't know what he's doing." Jeff and I clinked cups. Yady hit that ball hard.

EVEN THOUGH it's now the most profitable professional sport in the country and is being watched by more people on earth than at any other time in human history, baseball is rarely at its best when it's trying to put on its fancy Sunday clothes. The MLB Network, pretty much the only channel playing at Will Leitch Brooklyn Headquarters, is renowned for this, dressing up baseball history in sepia-hazed Things Were So Much Better Then Bubble Wrap. Ken Burns laid down the foundation for this, and everyone at Major League Baseball Productions has followed his lead, romanticizing baseball's past into some sort of pretend Elysian Fields, where the sports was uncorrupted by capitalism, nobody looked for unfair advantages, and all players floated a foot about the infield. Major League Base-ball cashes in on this, but a little less each year: This sort of happy nothing-to-see-here revisionism inevitably produces diminishing returns.

The flip side to this, and the ultimate result, is the unstated no-tion behind every truthless whitewashing of the past: *The good days are behind us. Baseball has lost its way.* When people say the strength of baseball is in its history, or in its numbers, what they're really saying is *Back in my day . . . we understood what baseball re-ally was.* They've packaged the past and fed it to us wholesale, and it makes baseball look like a game primarily enjoyed by men in fe-doras, responding to spunky, gritty utility infielders with shouts of "Zounds!" and "Egads!"

The NFL and the NBA mostly ignore their history, constantly sell-ing you on the idea that what you are seeing right now is the pinna-cle of their sport's potential. It has never been better than this, and it never will be. Until the next time you want to buy a jersey. Baseball plays up the opposite too much. It turns the past into something that cannot be replicated. And it makes everybody pissed about every-thing that's happening now.

Because this is a book about baseball, I feel obliged to leap to baseball's defense. Everyone is wrong. Trashing baseball is indicative of intellectual laziness. Allow me a little debunking.

MYTH: *Steroids have ruined baseball's record book, which is the true source of baseball's supposed mystic power.*

Baseball is gorgeous whether it's played by steroid monsters or Little Leaguers. But to hear it the last few years, baseball is nothing but big historic numbers to be discussed as relevant or not.

So: Who cares that Pete Rose is the all-time hits leader? Who cares if Barry Bonds has more homers than anyone else? Who cares if Roger Clemens won the most Cy Young Awards? When did baseball become about that? Baseball is three hours of Shakespeare sixteen times a day, and, somehow, we've turned it into a math problem about longevity.

If Alex Rodriguez had never been busted for steroids, and he had eradicated all of Bonds's records, Barry Bonds would have still existed. A record broken doesn't mean the achievements (or their dubious sources) went away. You can't erase the past. You can't relive it, either. You have to let it go.

More to the point: Saying that baseball is ruled by its record book is another, roundabout, faux-analytical way of saying it is ruled by its past. No other sport claims to be ruled by numbers, because no other sport would be so perverse as to imply that the action on the field is somehow secondary to some imaginary, elusive theoretical construct. The game is the source of the numbers, the players, the teams, the uniforms, the fans—everything. The bases are still ninety feet apart from one another, at least until China takes us over and turns the measurements into their metric system equivalents. It is always the same. We're the ones who screw it up.

MYTH: *Baseball is in constant need of saving, whether it's by Babe Ruth, Cal Ripken, Mark McGwire, or whomever. Eventually you'll run out of saviors.*

Take your pick: cause and effect, before and after.

Time Baseball Died: the 1919 Black Sox scandal
What Brought Baseball Back to Life: Babe Ruth and the
    American erection caused by the booming home run

Time Baseball Died: the cocaine scandals of the late seventies
    and early eighties.
What Brought Baseball Back to Life: the speed (velocity, not
    amphetamines)-dominated game of the mid-eighties,

led by Whitey Herzog and his Cardinals, along with the
spinning pile of special lunacy that was Rickey Henderson

Time Baseball Died: Pete Rose gambling on baseball
What Brought Baseball Back to Life: The world deciding that it
   didn't like Jim Gray

Time Baseball Died: the 1994 players' strike
What Brought Baseball Back to Life: Cal Ripken deciding to
   never skip a game, ever, no matter how much his skills might
   be declining

Time Baseball Died: the 1994 players' strike
What Brought Baseball Back to Life: The Great 1998 Home Run
   Chase between St. Louis Cardinals first baseman Mark
   McGwire and Chicago Cubs outfielder Sammy Sosa, two
   people who were not actually friends at the time, no matter
   how much they pretended to be

Time Baseball Died: Steroids!
What Brought Baseball Back to Life: Sorry! Still dead!

All of these "scandals" have one thing in common: They all took
place during periods of baseball growth. Because baseball inspires
such starry-eyed demands for perfection, there is a tendency to
frame it in some sort of narrative. There is no overarching baseball
narrative, as much as Ken Burns might like there to be. Baseball
scandals are the same as political scandals: helpful in selling newspapers (or Google ads on blogs, whatever), effective in inspiring
drive-by media traffic, and far more noteworthy in the short term
than the long term. Scandals allow people who aren't paying attention and are therefore easily disenchanted with Just How Different
Baseball Is From When We Were Young to come gawk for a while

and label it The Reason I Don't Watch Baseball As Much Anymore. Baseball has "survived" everything thrown its way, because it is baseball, not a novel. Had Cal Ripken not broken Lou Gehrig's record, had Babe Ruth not hit five hundred-foot moon shots in between drunken threesomes, had the Yankees and Diamondbacks not played a brilliant World Series right after September 11, baseball would still be chugging along just fine.

MYTH: *Baseball is for nerds. Football is the new great American pastime. More people care about football than baseball. Baseball is boring and lasts too long.*

Well, baseball is for nerds. I can't combat that, I suppose, particularly because you're about to pull my underwear over my head and tie it in a nice bow around my neck. It looks pretty, now that I'm in front of a mirror.

Football is an easy sport to watch casually on television. The quarterback goes back, throws the ball, the camera pans over, the wide receiver catches it, touchdown. What went into that play? Did someone miss his coverage? Did the offensive coordinator notice a flaw in the defense's game planning? Did the quarterback just make a perfect throw? Does the wide receiver possess the ability to levitate at great speeds? The television tells us none of this: We just saw a guy throw the ball and another guy catch it. It's a misleading juxtaposition that confuses us into thinking we saw an explicit cause and effect. We didn't. We just saw what we wanted to see and nothing more.

Football is once a week. You can pay little to no attention to football, and it's still always there for you on Sundays and Monday nights. It requires no effort, no investment, no obsession. Anyone can sound like they know football, and anyone can appreciate its violence. But it asks little of you. You can like football, a *lot,* and no one will really notice. It does not require you to love it. It does not require much at all. There are people who love football, who obsess over it, who follow it the way millions of others follow baseball. They are the minority. Football does not breed diehards.

People who think football is a better sport than baseball do so because they watch sports the way people watch reality television: They want it quick, they want it simple, and they want it obvious. There's nothing wrong with that: We're talking about sports here, not literature. But baseball offers more. It always has. And it always will.

What's great about all this? I still have no doubt that Jeff enjoyed the All-Star Game just as much as I did. Baseball is an addiction for me and millions of other fans . . . but that doesn't make it any more fun for me than it does for non-addicts, normal people. It takes all kinds.

How great is baseball? I've just spent this endless chapter singing its praises, defending it to its detractors, and interviewing myself about its glories . . . even when my team is down 5–0 to their hated rivals as 100,000 Wrigleyville denizens prepare to swoop into a drunken orgy everywhere around me. No use waiting for rain anymore either, not that there's a cloud in the sky: With the easy 1-2-3 in the top of the fifth, this game is now official. Even when you're watching a dispiriting, wrenching baseball game, it's better than doing anything else. Fedora or no.

KNOWLEDGE YOU NOW HAVE

1. Your father greatly enjoys Jeff's company and merely used him as a stand-in for a point he was trying to make. He is being as clear as possible about this.

2. Ken Burns hasn't watched a baseball game in fifteen years.

3. Football players used to always beat up your father.

BOTTOM OF THE FIFTH INNING

In which your narrator won't go there.

My sports-loving and generally all-American dad had the misfortune of having three daughters and no sons. He dutifully took us to Mets games every baseball season and always arranged these outings on giveaway days. When we went to the beach, we had Mets Snoopy towels and various Mets hats with designs from the 1980s and 1990s. The house was full of plastic Mets cups for a time. A few years ago I was explaining at a family gathering that my dad was a big Mets fan. He interrupted: "No. I'm a Yankees fan." I was confused. Why had we been dragged to all of those Mets games as kids? "They gave away better free stuff."

— MEGHAN KEANE, Brooklyn, New York

1994. ONCE, IN COLLEGE, I CAME HOME FOR A WEEKEND WHEN I was somewhat depressed, for those vague, completely stupid reasons people get depressed in college. It was springtime, and the Cardinals were playing an afternoon game at Wrigley; I was supposed to meet my father for lunch to watch it. I drove to his office, the CIPS Electric Company substation, where a bunch of electricians had *Playboy* calendars and posters of Camaros peppering all available wall space.

My dad works, essentially, as a troubleshooter for the electric company. You know those big unwieldy metallic configurations with the power company's logo slapped on a chain-link and barbed-wire fence? They're usually siphoned off away from everything else, because they're highly dangerous. When your power goes out, because of a storm or something—sometimes a kamikaze bird will do a death dive right into a transformer, shorting out half the town—it's because one of those has broken down.

Well, my dad's the guy who fixes those and makes sure nothing goes wrong with them. He's been doing it my whole life, and he's very good at it. He has developed a reputation among his coworkers and bosses as a guy who never does a job half-ass, never complains, and never leaves work for others to do. Troubleshooting can be hazardous; while on the job, Dad has watched a man be electrocuted to death, only a few feet away. When I was in junior high, an accident once chopped off his middle finger at the knuckle. They put it in iced milk and sewed it back on. You can poke his middle finger with a needle, and he can't feel it. It's kind of fun.

About fifteen years ago, my father's union was threatening a strike. Management had been considering the possibility of locking the workers out as a preemptive maneuver, but they weren't quite sure if the union was bluffing. A large part of my father's job is overtime; he's on call twenty-four hours a day, because you never know when your power's going to go out. In twenty years, my father had never once, for any reason, turned down overtime; when they called, no matter what time of day, no matter what he might have had going on (he once left halfway through opening Christmas presents), he always dropped what he was doing and did the job. The union, as a matter of protest, distributed word throughout its ranks that, as a show of solidarity, when the dispatcher called, they would feign sickness to let management know they meant business.

At 8 P.M. one night about two weeks before my high school graduation, our phone rang, and I answered. The dispatcher said, "Will, is your dad there?" I handed him the phone and watched as my dad, saddened, going against his very nature, said, "Sorry, Bob, I'm, um . . .

I'm real sick. I can't make it." If Bryan Leitch was turning down over-time, management knew the union wasn't kidding around. They locked out the workers the next day. Eventually management caved. There were a lot of guys like my dad in that union.

Anyway: The day I went to go meet Dad for the Cards-Cubs game, Buck, a guy my father has worked with forever, saw me pull in and told me Dad was stuck on a job just outside of town and wouldn't be back for half an hour. We shared a cigarette and he asked me about college. "You still writing about the Illini for your student paper? I've had just about enough of Lou Henson; he should retire." I told him I was, in a dismissive, this-is-a-waste-of-my-precious-time type of way. I was sure he didn't care about my newspaper columns any more than my dad did; my father had famously lectured me on the foolish-ness of majoring in journalism, where no one did anything but write pointless, usually inaccurate stories, and besides, there weren't any jobs anyway. I had a big chip on my shoulder about my family in col-lege. I think most college students do.

Buck told me I should just wait in Dad's office—which didn't re-ally have a desk; it was mostly a card table where he ate lunch—until he returned. I scowled and pouted my way through the endless pa-rade of work trucks, with ladders and hooks and big metal things I'd never know how to use stacked loosely on their sides, past the weld-ers and the sparks and all the real work, and made my way to Dad's office. He shared the large room with about ten other guys, and it was empty.

I threw my backpack next to his desk with disgust and slouched in his chair. I then looked up. The first thing I noticed was a picture of my sister in her cheerleading uniform. This was before my sister had discovered the counterculture, back when she was a gymnast and a popular kid. She was carrying pom-poms and flashing a bright braces smile. Next to that was, to my shock, my most recent sports column for the *Daily Illini*, surrounded by a whole collage of others. My father's desk was covered in his son's newspaper clippings. He even had one

I'd written about the annoyance of incompetent teaching assistants; that story must have had as much cultural significance to my father as an exposé of the oppression of Muslim women in Iran. I'd had no idea he'd ever even read the *Daily Illini*. I'd had no idea he even cared.

I sat quiet for a moment, then grabbed my backpack and headed out to my car. I'd wait for Dad there. I didn't want him to see me seeing all that at his desk. It would have been embarrassing for both of us.

ON A 2–0 PITCH, Derrek Lee flies out to right field. Somehow Adam Kennedy, who looks bewildered to be playing right field in the first place, gets a good read on the ball and it lands safely in his glove.

Dad is on another beer run. The short top of the fifth, the looming sense that this game is already over, the fear that Dad's big trip up north was pointless and unnecessarily painful, has me in a self-pitying mood. This was dumb. We are idiots. My team sucks. When your baseball team looks helpless, the world's a forlorn place. You feel impotent. You feel like real life.

For distraction, I decide to dip briefly into that real life.

"So, Mike, how're your parents, anyway?"

Mike's parents are lovely, lovely people. When he and Joan were married, they invited my parents, and everyone became instant friends. His mom and dad are wide-necked Chicago folk: thick Dah Bears accents, deep dish pizzas, bighearted Catholic traditionalists. I have an urge to hug both of them every time I see them. I try to be subtle about it.

"Oh, you know, fine," Mike says. "Ma's been having some health issues, but she's hanging in. They're excited to be grandparents. That kind of freaks me out, actually. My mom is a grandma."

"Nevermind" is on classic rock stations now. I actually remember what it was like to be in college and not have an email account. Baseball players I cheered for growing up are fat bald men now.

Flecks of gray are sneaking into my own hair. Four drinks give me a hangover. I'm thirty-four.

My grandfather died at the age of sixty-six, the age my father will be in six years. I like Dad's odds of making it past that. By the time my grandfather died, he'd had lung cancer, three heart attacks, and painful, debilitating arthritis. He wore false teeth, which he would take out and rub up against my ear to freak me out. (It worked.) None of this stopped him from smoking on his deathbed. He was old. He was elderly at sixty-six.

Dad is not that old yet. He was born in 1949, and modern medicine has served him well. He's been on blood pressure medication since he was my age, he has a hawkish nurse for a wife, and he stopped smoking twenty-five years ago. He's never had a heart attack, and even though he's developed a substantial beer gut in the last decade, it's a thick, sturdy one. He's thick all over. He has the muscular arms and legs of a man who has been doing manual labor his entire life. I could spend three hours in the gym every day, and I'd never look like that. I'm not sure anyone should be more muscular and strong than his dad. Dads are different. They're just bigger.

It's getting near now, though. I have accepted that I am growing older, that I am a grown man, that I am an adult. I kind of like it: Age has a way of giving humans a gravitas that they haven't earned. Like most people, I have essentially the same personality I had at twenty-two. But because a decade has passed since then, I'm given more authority now. I'm thought of as wiser. I'm not. The same shit will happen in another decade. I'll still be the same guy. But "wiser." And as much of an idiot as ever. I like it. I could get used to this adult business.

Parents grow older too, though, and I could do without that. My father needs to be forty-two forever, speckled gray beard, but vibrant, powerful, able to play on the CIPS company softball team, drink beers and laugh in the outfield, toss pop flies to me that soar infinitely heavenward, my eyes growing massive, in awe of just how high that went. He is indestructible at forty-two. He is going to live forever.

My father is still strong. He conceded to needing glasses a few years ago—he has those cool older guy glasses like Tampa Bay manager Joe Maddon wears—but there is no cane, there is no limp, there is no walker, there is no hearing aid, there is no wheelchair. He is the same guy he has always been.

But he's a little different. He's a little more emotional: He's not as *taciturn* as he used to be. He'll tell my sister he loves her. He'll talk more openly about his life, about what he's feeling. This is a man I have seen cry exactly once: When his father-in-law, my mother's dad, my grandfather, died, Dad, a pallbearer, lowered the coffin into the ground and came back to the car with me. He was quiet for a few seconds and then burst into tears. It lasted about three seconds. He then coughed, and it was over. "My underwear must have been too tight," he said, and it was never discussed again. That was twenty-one years ago. I haven't seen him cry since. My mom and sister say he has. They say he'll get misty-eyed over something as simple as a sad episode of *House.*

He'd never get misty-eyed around me, though. He knows how hard that would be on both of us. I prefer to think Mom and Jill are just lying.

He gets lonely more. I think of my father as an old Western cowboy, content to work on his own, spanning the frontier, content in quiet and open space. But I know this isn't true.

My dad plays a lot of video poker. In our house—one that he built with his brothers, drawing up the plans himself, buying the materials, doing the whole damn thing on his own—he has fashioned the basement as a home for his long-dormant id. There are bar posters and neon lights all over the walls. An enormous Chicago Bears mural hangs next to the bar he's installed. A blonde in a bikini is straddling a Miller Lite bottle. My father drinks only Natural Light, no hard alcohol, but nevertheless the bar is stacked with whiskey and vodka bottles, for decorative purposes. They are filled not with liquor, but with colored water that has been sitting around for months. I found this out the hard way.

Dad has set up an entertainment center down there, with a huge TV, stereo surround sound, and access to the satellite dish. Every time the Cardinals play, he grabs a six-pack, sits at the bar, and screams at the television. Dad is never satisfied. Cardinals games at home are glorious routines of obscene verbal gymnastics for my father, and even if the game is boring, he never is. "Jeee-zus Ka-RYST! God-DAMN it, Wellemeyer! Get him out of there, LaRussa! Son—Of—A—BITCH!" My favorite part is when the Cardinals are trailing late and appear likely to lose. Dad, who has been setting off Richter scales in Iowa every time an ump's call goes the wrong way and has developed a frightening vein that sticks out about six feet from his forehead, begins to rationalize. "You know, this isn't really that big of a game. If they lose, they'll be fine." (I suspect, at the beer stand at Wrigley he's at right now, in 2008, he's looking at that 5–0 score and doing the same thing.) If the Cardinals mount a comeback, he begins jumping up and down. I've never seen my father jump in life. Only during Cardinals (and Illini basketball) games. And maybe if he sees a spider.

The real highlight of the basement, though, is his poker machine. It's set up in the corner, out of the way, but you can't miss it. It flashes, beeps, sets off sirens. It's simple, just like any old poker machine. If you get two kings, or a flush, you have the option of trying to double your points in a game fittingly called "Double Up." You have to guess if the next card is higher than seven or not. Every time you guess correctly, a digital picture of a naked woman pops up. Dad loves that part. "I have to shut those off when the neighbor kids come over."

Dad is addicted to this game. One night over the holidays, when Mom was working all night at the hospital, where she works as an ER nurse, he called my cell. "Hey, I'm over at the VFW. Want to grab a beer?" The VFW is my father's favorite watering hole; he is an Air

Force man. I braved the cold and drove the six blocks, because no-body walks in Mattoon. Dad was sitting at the poker machines. In fact, he was sitting at the exact same poker machine he has at home. Except he was putting money in it this time. Twenty after twenty after twenty. This is not Vegas; this machine does not give money back. But off they went, twenty, twenty, twenty. He even asked me if he could borrow a twenty-spot when he ran out, so he didn't have to run to the ATM. I watched my dad drop a hundred bucks into a machine that doesn't even pay out.

Because he doesn't like sitting in that basement, that basement he built for that very purpose, by himself. It unnerves him. "Too quiet down there. Spooky."

A FRIEND OF MINE, an older friend, disappeared for about two weeks once. We were close enough friends that I noticed he was gone, but not close enough to know why, or to ask. This happens a lot more than it used to. Age turns us into far less attentive friends.

Realizing belatedly that I hadn't talked to him for a while, I dropped my friend an email. He wrote me back within seconds.

> Sad news, man. My Dad passed away in his sleep last week. As wrenching as it is, there's also a sense of relief. No man as vital as my father who ran a company til he was 80 and got "stuck in" til he was 85, should have to live as he did the past few months, shuttling between hospitals and nursing homes. A few days before he died, in a rare moment of lucidity, he said, "we had a great run."

Two days later, he and I were drinking heavily at a midtown bar. We small talked for about an hour, yakking baseball and publishing and large-bottomed women, before I put my best Dr. Phil face on. "So . . . how *are* you, sir?"

I'd rather not have asked this. The notion that someone's father could just be *gone,* just like that, was more than I felt comfortable dealing with. To allow that my friend's father could have died would be to allow that *all* fathers could die.

But I had to ask. I couldn't be *that* selfish.

He pulled a long swig of Stella. He held it in his throat for a while, and it bubbled up and filled his cheeks before he yanked the rest down.

"You know, they say it's the worst thing that can happen to you, that you never can be prepared for it no matter how much you think you are," he said. "They're completely fucking right."

I'd never met his father, and actually I'd only heard him come up in conversation a few times. My friend proceeded to tell me an hour's worth of stories, about growing up, about family troubles, about old flames, his own and his father's, about giving the eulogy, about what kind of man he thought his father was when he was a kid, about how different Dad turned out to be when he was older. He talked about the whole process, working through it all like he was just thinking about it for the first time, though he surely wasn't. Every moment was raw and gaping, a big, throbbing wound kicking with every word. He wasn't calling attention to himself through this. He just looked like he was in the middle of a war and was giving a news report from the front to a concerned citizen back home. It was a war he was losing. He wasn't particularly upset about losing it, or even surprised. He was just beaten down. He was just reporting facts.

I couldn't handle it. I listened and listened, and when he appeared spent, I raised my own glass. "To your dad," I said, because that's what you're supposed to say in that situation. "Cheers."

He wanly cheered, and I steered us back to more about baseball and publishing and large-bottomed women. He left twenty minutes later, out into the world, unprotected, just plodding forward, the night a little longer. I didn't talk to him for another few weeks. Too much. We become such worse friends as we get older. We really do.

———

WITH A 1–2 COUNT on Aramis Ramirez, Tim McCarver uncorks this gem about the baseball playoffs:

> Josh, I once heard someone whimsically say that since the wild card started back in 1994 but didn't get a chance to get off the ground until 1995, that a Major League season was like a scientist studying elephants, and then in the postseason, that same scientist studying parasites. Because what that scientist has to do is put things under the microscope in the postseason.

Hmmm. Go on, Tim.

> If you think about it, a 162-game season, and now all of a sudden, the first round is a maximum of five. So the Cubs and the other teams in postseason play will, without a doubt, be under the microscope.

I see.

I'VE NEVER TOLD my father I love him. Well, that's probably not true: I'm sure when I was, like, four years old, I said it all the time, though probably not nearly as often as I said it to my stuffed ALF. I mean since I was a sentient, walking-around-earth-with-awareness-of-my-surroundings human being, I've never said it.

The Leitches are not one of those families. I have friends who toss in I-love-you's at the end of parental conversations the way most people say "Bye." I think this is great and totally insane. We are solid Midwesterners, taciturn, fearful of the touchy-feely. If something is wrong, you rub some dirt on it and walk it off. "I-love-you's" are not what we *do here.*

My father came from a family of eight children, with a father who worked his can off for ten hours a day and, by the time he came home, just wanted to smoke his Pall Malls in peace. With that many kids screaming, it was no wonder he retired to his study to read the paper and find some quiet. (Fortunately for him, he had a wife who, after dealing with those same eight kids all day, apparently was perfectly fine with this arrangement.) There were no heart-to-hearts in that family. There was no time, and there was no interest. Seven other kids were sitting around to keep you company and remind you that love divided eight ways is divided awfully thin.

It wasn't until my grandfather grew older that my father had many meaningful conversations with him, and even then, they were mostly about Grandpa's health. Dad was the de facto liaison between Grandpa and the rest of the family, because he had named his son, William Franklin Leitch, after him, and because Dad was married to a nurse who could take care of his father. But even then: No I-love-you's. Mom once told me Grandpa wasn't into that "queer shit." You put your head down, you worked to put food on the table, you left everybody alone, and you expected to be left alone, and you retired to a quiet bed at the end of the night, and dammit, that's what life was supposed to be about.

Dad married a more fiery woman, and ended up with two slightly loony kids who felt compelled to pretend they were "interesting" somehow. (When adulthood came, my sister moved to San Francisco. I moved to New York City. Mom jokes that we just went in opposite directions until we hit water.) My dad's more open than my grandfather, a little more world-wise, a little more accepting of people who roam the planet in a different fashion than he might be used to. He's a more social guy, funnier, cruder, less stoic, less closed-off. My dad is a likable guy in a way I suspect my grandfather was not. My dad even text-messages now. I could do without that. I know technology has revolutionized the way human beings

communicate, but all told: I don't think it's *supposed* to be that easy
to communicate with your father.

None of that love crap, though. It's a holdover from his father,
and I'm certain, when I do it with my son (and I will), it'll be a holdover from my dad. It's just something you should *know*. Those
meals he paid for? That roof over your head? That college tuition?
Those phone calls to check in? The big Christmas tree he insists on
chopping down every year? The stocking with the name of the cat
on it? The way, after you say good-bye to him and get on the plane,
you always find a $100 bill he hid somewhere on you? The way
those newspaper clippings and cheerleader photos surround his
desk even though he never told you about them? *That's* "I love
you." Every day is one big "I love you." No need to say it. No fucking
need.

You know when I'm supposed to tell my dad I love him? When
he's on his deathbed. When he knows he's going, and I know he's
going, and I take his hand and I finally, finally tell him. That's when
he wants it to happen, and that's when I want it to happen. If one of us
ends up dying before that moment occurs? Well, one more pain, one
more thing to rub some dirt on and walk off. That's the way it works.
Them's the rules. I'm comfortable with that.

AFTER EVERY Cardinals game, I call my father. I'm in New York, he's
in Mattoon. I'm living a dramatically different life from him, not better, not worse, just different. I'm still years away from a child of
my own. When he was my age, I was eight. We have a picture of
Dad, and the whole family, from when he was thirty-four. Our insur-
ance agent was friends with then Cardinals general manager Dal
Maxvill, and the agent had secured us dugout passes before the game.
We met Whitey Herzog and Ozzie Smith and Darrell Porter. But for
whatever reason, we only secured photographs with two players:
left-handed reliever Ken Dayley and fourth outfielder Tito Landrum.

The photos are still on our wall at home, right next to the bar with the liquor bottles filled with water. I'm carrying a score book and have a pencil behind my ear and my socks pulled up to my knees, and I'm wearing a T-shirt that reads "I Root for Two Teams: The Cardinals and Whoever Plays the Cubs." My sister is wearing oversized sunglasses and a big toothless smile. My mom has a camera around her neck and large bangs. And there's my dad, young, fit—fitter than I am at thirty-four—with a tank top, short black hair, and a mustache. He's staring into the sun, wincing, waiting for whoever to just take the picture already. The kids are surely antsy, Jill probably needs to use the bathroom, and the Astroturf field holds the heat like a catcher's mitt. Pete Rose, playing for the Montreal Expos, is shagging balls at first base, and he's my favorite player who doesn't play for the Cardinals. I want to watch him. Dad's just trying to keep everybody together. The Cardinals do that. Only for a short while, though. Eventually, everyone will scatter.

Ken Dayley is in one picture, and Tito Landrum is in the other. Dayley is only twenty-five years old and has just started his Cardinals career. He'll play in St. Louis for six more seasons, then head to Toronto for two before retiring at the age of 34. Landrum began his career with the Cardinals, was traded in August of the season before to the Baltimore Orioles, where he won a World Series, and then was traded back to the Cardinals that March. He'll play two-and-a-half more seasons with the Cardinals, then rattle around Los Angeles and Baltimore before retiring. He'll also be thirty-four when he hangs 'em up.

It is a tiny snapshot of one tiny moment, the Leitches as close to their family obsession as they will ever be, actually *on the field at Busch Stadium.* And Dad looks like he's about ready to run out the door. He looks happy. We all look happy. But there are more adventures out there, and besides, it's really hot and look there's Pete Rose.

After every Cardinals game, Dad and I bitch and we moan and we cheer and we make plans to get together, every season, one weekend at the new Busch, just the two of us, drinking and watching baseball, our Cardinals, in quiet. It's my favorite weekend of the year, and I suspect it's his. I don't know for sure. I wouldn't dare ask.

It can only be that one weekend out of the year. Phone calls can only do so much, but I have business in New York, and he has his home in Mattoon. The Cardinals are our one constant and our one tether, but the rest of the world is chaos, and it is much bigger. Eventually there will be a family of my own, and we will start our own traditions, our own constants. I'll still be in New York. He'll still be in Mattoon. Time will keep going.

Then he will grow old, and then he will die. I can't talk about it.

DAD RETURNS with the beer—as always, three, breaking all the Wrigley rules—right as Jim Edmonds hits into a double play to end the inning. Dad hands me a beer and then high-fives my empty hand. He is more optimistic about this 5–0 deficit than I am.

"All right!" he brays. "Come on now! Plenty of time! We need some base runners!"

Mike smiles at him, and so do I. For reasons I don't understand, I pat his knee when he sits down. It was there. I don't know why. He looks at me oddly. "What, did I spill some nacho cheese on there? It's a long way down to the seats." I tell him no. It wasn't cheese.

You see, life's like studying an elephant, and age, and time, are like parasites. What you have to do is put things under the microscope.

KNOWLEDGE YOU NOW HAVE

1. There used to be something called "labor unions."
2. Your aunt Jill was a cheerleader. Oh, and yeah, tattoos: She's good at hiding them now.
3. Shhh: Your father loves you. You didn't hear it from me.

TOP OF THE SIXTH INNING

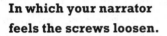

**In which your narrator
feels the screws loosen.**

*My father was not an athlete. Not even close. I'm not exactly sure
how he spent his summers as a youth, but it sure wasn't playing
baseball. When I finally turned eight and was old enough for
Little League, I begged my father to sign me up. I was from Boston and 1986 had just happened. My father took me to the local
sports store to go buy a glove, but when we got there, he was
just stumped looking at the aisle of glove upon glove, clueless as
to which one to pick. He declared that since I was a lefty that
meant I should get a glove that went on my left hand. It took
three long months until Dad realized that the glove should have
gone on the other hand. (It had taken my coach about five seconds.) If my Dad was embarrassed, he didn't show it, and he
still went to all my games. Some fathers pressure their kids into
playing sports, other fathers learn to play at the same time.*

— MIKE RANEN, Salem, Massachusetts

ANYTIME SOMEONE TRIES TO EXPLAIN WHAT TWITTER IS TO
someone who doesn't use it, both people walk away from the conversation fairly certain the other person is an idiot. The Twitter user
sees the Twitter-resistant as close-minded to new technology and
modes of communication; the non–Twitter user can't understand

why anyone would feel obligated to inform the planet when he or she uses the restroom. Both are wrong, and right.

I use Twitter, but only sparingly, and never (so far, anyway) in a fashion that's excretory-inclusive. As a writer, I work for several different publications, so for me, Twitter is a marketing tool: Here's my new magazine feature for *New York,* here's my *Sporting News* column. That's how I "use" Twitter, in the form of "use" that people are generally referring to. But how I *really* use Twitter is as a follower.

I love newspapers, in a way that only people who grew up with newspapers will ever love newspapers, and a way no one ever will again. But I love receiving specifically focused information, news that only I care about, a lot more than I love newspapers. Twitter is a news feed designed exclusively for me. It has facts and opinions about topics that I care about, and it excludes everything else. This is not going to make me a well-rounded intellectual, kept abreast of all the world's goings-on, even those (especially those) that I wouldn't search out otherwise. It is, however, making me an expert in topics I want to be an expert in.

I know everything there is to know about, as soon as there is anything to know about, the following topics:

- Woody Allen films
- Early reviews from film festivals
- Recently discovered Nirvana bootleg concerts
- Baseball Prospectus injury and transaction reports
- Illinois basketball updates from *Champaign News-Gazette* reporters
- Instant reviews of *Mad Men* and *Lost* by trusted television critics
- Who Sarah Palin believes will kill one of her children this week
- Which bars my friends are currently at, mocking me with their active social lives

- Which family members of mine are currently fighting
- What talk show William Shatner is about to appear on
- The next live appearance by the brilliant Louis C.K.
- What Shaquille O'Neal happens to be doing at that exact moment
- When Larry King was able to find the space bar on his computer
- The St. Louis Cardinals

Back in the days of yore—about five years ago, to be exact—the paradigm of sports reporting was simple. A newspaper would send two or three gentlemen to a baseball game, where they would sit in a big air-conditioned, comfortable, and fully catered room, taking notes and making snide, belittling comments to one another. (As a former blogger, now occasional press-box denizen, let me tell you: There is no place more snarky on earth than a baseball press box.) Before the game, they would head down to the locker room and briefly talk to a few players, mostly chitchat, *how ya feelin' out there today looks like it's gonna be a hot one* and so on. Then they would head upstairs, eat dinner, sit down, and "report." The game would begin, and they would "cheer" for a short one, so they could be home at a decent hour, and when the game was over, they would go downstairs and listen to the team's manager explain what they'd just seen for the last three hours, and then they'd head to the locker room to chat with the Important Players. Then they would schlep back upstairs, open up their computers (or, depending on how long ago we're talking here, unpack their typewriters), and write up a game story, which would weave quotes from the players and the manager into an overarching narrative of the game that most of us fans had just watched or listened to. If the game was over in time, that story would appear in the paper the next morning, perhaps accompanied by a man-bites-dog sidebar, a "Lugo Bewildered By Leopard Attack In Fourth." If the game went into extra innings, or was played on the West Coast (for those in the East), there would be no game story the next morning, and we fans would have to wait another twenty-four hours, usually after another whole game had been played, to read the report of what happened. If, say, the rookie starting left fielder had been run over by a tarp, rendering him unable to play in the World Series (*hypothetically speaking*), we would not have access to that information from our trusted reporters until twelve to thirteen hours after it happened, and perhaps even longer. This was the way it was. This was the way reporters liked it. You chilled out, talked to some people, wrote your story, went home, did it again the next day. We all made do.

Obviously, in an Internet age, this is no longer sustainable. Some reporters have bristled at the industry's change, making themselves into martyrs of a new age, blasting sports reporting's transformation as the death knell to all that they hold dear. I understand. I worked at an old small town movie theater in high school and loved when the film canisters for new releases would come in Wednesday evening. I would splice them together that night, and then, after all the showings were over, screen them for my coworkers to make sure I hadn't made a mistake combining the reels. It was great: I was able to stay out until two in the morning when I was only seventeen, and I watched every new movie for free while making out with my girlfriend in the back of an empty theater. It was the life. Now there are multiplexes, with digital prints downloaded and programmed right in. The job I loved no longer exists. That makes me sad. But it does not make me blame the digital prints. Movies look better now too.

Of all the teams in Major League Baseball, no team is covered by more people who have embraced the new sportswriting paradigm than my beloved Cardinals. The Cardinals beat reporters use Twitter. (Or "tweet," if you will.) At the *St. Louis Post-Dispatch*, it's Derrick Goold, Joe Strauss, and Bernie Miklasz. At the local radio station, it's John Marecek. At the Cardinals' official site, it's Matthew Leach.

Heck, even Tony La Russa is on Twitter. Twitter, and more broadly the Web, have changed the way beat reporters work. No longer can they just sit around and eat and gab while waiting for the game to start. Now they're tweeting lineups and injury reports from the locker room before the game, they're providing regular updates while the game is going on, they're still discussing everything that has happened long after the game is done. Baseball is not something that can be described in an 850-word game story once a day. There is too much happening, too often, too subtly to be captured without constant attention. And not just that: Each of these guys is interacting with fans *while the game is going on*. In the past, you had to break some knuckles just to make a beat reporter put his email address at the end of his stories. Now we're all a part of the process. Want to know what the Cardinals beat reporter, the guy who is paid to watch this team *every single game of the year,* thinks of a certain development within seconds of it happening? Now you can. It has dramatically enhanced my enjoyment of the Cardinals. It's what beat reporting should have been in the first place. It has made the fans a part of the process.

More specifically: It has made *me* a part of the process. Because of my constant prattling about my Cardinals love, the Cardinals beat reporters got to know me, and my work, long before Twitter. (I feel as if they tolerated me the way a professional musician would oblige his twelve-year-old nephew's beginner screechings on the guitar. *Aw, that's nice, you want to write too. Good for you!*) By the time we were all on Twitter, we were chatting with one another throughout every game, debating, arguing, commiserating, comparing notes. I respected their work and their devotion to providing fans with all the information they wanted, as soon as they wanted. Most sportswriters aren't willing to take that extra step. They were.

So, thus, there we were in late June 2009, after a tough Cardinals afternoon loss to the Mets at Citi Field (Johan Santana outdealt Chris Carpenter), at Foley's New York, an old sportswriter staple, I, Derrick

Goold from the *Post-Dispatch,* and Matthew Leach from MLB.com. If it weren't for Twitter, they'd have never given me the time of day. But we felt like we knew one another now. We felt like colleagues.

It was late, and they all had planes to catch back to St. Louis the next morning, so they only sipped beers while I pounded vodka tonics. We did what all of us loved to do most: We talked baseball.

Goold and Leach are the main two reporters on the Cardinals beat, which means they're pretty much following the team around all the time, from Spring Training to all the road trips and everything in between. They are around each other every day for six, seven months out of the year, competitors in name, but mostly the two guys who know the team better than anyone other than La Russa. They know the players' personalities, their secrets, their eccentricities, their politics (Todd Wellemeyer is the furthest right wing on a team full of economic conservatives, like most athletes), their forthrightness, their phoniness. And perhaps most of all, they know each other. We all have a work wife/husband, the person we spend the most time with, the only other human who understands the job as well as we do. These guys are that person for each other. They are beat reporter spouses. (When they were in Cleveland, they visited the Rock and Roll Hall of Fame, taking pictures of each other in front of the museum.) I watched as they bickered over which players were enjoyable to deal with and which ones were dicks, the way that only they, the two people that are close to them all the time, could. They were funny and smart and excellent guys. I wished their plane would never leave.

And I couldn't help but feel sorry for them.

I watch the Cardinals every day of the year, living and dying on every pitch and every swing, but I have never actually met a single Cardinal. I haven't wanted to. I cheer for them as abstract representations of a familial and cultural bond that will outlast them as players. They are not people: They are Cardinals. I do not need to know them as people. I do not want to.

Goold and Leach didn't think I felt this way, and therefore they were disappointed, I suspect, that Mr. Famous Cardinals Fan wasn't asking them what Rick Ankiel was really like, whether Brendan Ryan was a friendly guy, what the musical preferences of Adam Wainwright were. (I'd have to think he's a Travis Tritt guy.) They had access to those men, all of them, every Cardinal, for hours every day. It was their job. They were fantastic at it. But there was a disconnect.

They confessed to cheering mostly for quick games. They often groused when a certain pitcher would come in, knowing how irascible he was, knowing they'd have to pry quotes out of him afterward. There was an inevitable layer of professional cynicism about the game to them. If Ryan Ludwick turns out to be an asshole . . . well, that thin strain of fiber that separates real life from baseball life would be snapped. And then what?

Late in the evening, I asked Leach what he thought about the Cardinals' upcoming series with the Twins back in St. Louis. His response was succinct: "I'm just happy to be coming home. I've been on the road for three weeks. I'd like to see my wife, you know?" I understood. And I didn't.

All that said: I asked what they did during their last day off of the last road trip. They looked at each other and shrugged. "Went to a bar and watched baseball," Leach said. "What else would I do?" It grabs us all and shakes us.

CATCHER JASON LARUE leads off the top of the sixth. I know I've mentioned LaRue's facial hair already . . . but you really can't overstate it. It is epic.

You know what it looks like? Remember those magnetic Wooly Willy things, the ones that allowed you to try out different facial hair styles on a hairless imp? You know them. LaRue looks like you took one of those, filled it entirely with gunpowder and rubber cement and put it in the microwave.

Wooly Willy also hits about as well as Jason LaRue does, probably better: LaRue flies out to Jim Edmonds in center field, and suddenly, God this game just flew by, the Cubs are just eleven outs away from their second consecutive National League Central title.

"Boy, this thing's about over," Mike says, not gloating, just stating facts. It occurs to me that through nearly two hours and five-and-one-sixteenth full innings, my father and I haven't had a single incident worth cheering about. The Cardinals have accrued three hits and zero walks. Only one man has reached scoring position, way back in the second inning. Lilly has shut down nine batters in a row, expending just more than thirty pitches to do it. If you were orchestrating a game solely to please a beat reporter with reservations at Gino's East at 8 P.M., this is how you would do it. It is one thing to watch your team lose. It is another to have *nothing* positive occur. This is like a video game with the two teams set on opposite levels: The Cardinals are on Rookie, and the Cubs are on Legend. This is eight-year-olds against varsity. This is an unarmed David against forty Goliaths on angel dust. This is good versus evil.

I've spent most of my decade in New York City arguing the superiority of the Cardinals–Cubs rivalry to the Yankees–Red Sox. This is not an easy argument to make to those who grew up on the Eastern Seaboard, mostly because the Midwest is an imaginary place to them, not unlike Atlantis, or a deep dish pizza restaurant, or Afghanistan. But it's true. We've been around longer, we're less rigidly geographic—the Yankees-Sox battle is about two cities at war; the Cardinals-Cubs is like an ongoing civil land dispute over whether my land begins at the creek, or yours does—we're warmer to each other (sometimes), and all told, a weekend series is not an excuse to set random strangers ablaze. When Cubs fans come to Busch Stadium, they are not pelted with beer and batteries, and when we head to Wrigley, we are allowed to survive. The Yankees and Red Sox fans treat baseball like South American soccer; we treat it like baseball. We are also aware, as fierce and combative as the rivalry is, that there are other baseball teams on the planet other than the Cardinals and the Cubs. The other twenty-eight franchises are not supporting characters in our story.

That is to say: We're not East Coast media elites, with the death panels and the cheeseless meat.

But they do have one thing on us, and it's a big one: postseason series and pennant chases. The Yankees and the Red Sox, partially due, yes, to their massive payrolls, are typically among the best teams in the American League, and they're in the same division. So every season becomes an arms race between the two of them, with the rest of the league caught in the cross fire. Other than 2008's wild Tampa Bay Rays run, the Red Sox and Yankees have finished 1–2 in the AL East every season since 1998. That's a hot pennant chase, every single season. They're usually not even done there: They've met three times in the postseason since the wild card was added in 1995, and all three series have been epic. When the Red Sox and Yankees are playing each other, typically, there's more than just the rivalry at stake.

We cannot say that. Cardinals fans and Cubs fans alike have been waiting for a late-September massive series with vital playoff implications since the National League Central was invented in 1994, and it has never happened. The closest we came was 2003, when the Cardinals came into town over Labor Day with a one-game lead, lost four out of five, and were never heard from again. The Cardinals and the Cubs have never been in the playoffs at the same time, let alone *faced* each other in the playoffs, and it's never really been considered a possibility. It's strange too: Either the Cardinals or the Cubs won the division every single season of the aughts (Houston tied with the Cardinals for the 2001 title), but they've never been able to coordinate contending seasons. They tend to alternate. That's in the Midwestern tradition—sharing, passing the baton back and forth, even if that's not actually how batons are passed. But it hurts our rivalry. It makes us look small time to the rest of the world. We've always imagined what a Cardinals-Cubs National League

Championship Series would be like: I'm guessing apocalyptic, but corn-fed and cheerful.

It's not happening this year either. The Cardinals were out of the Central and wild-card races long before this game began. It's the Cubs' turn. It almost seems right. My father's first trip to Wrigley Field couldn't end with the Cardinals' temporarily thwarting the Cubs' division-clinching dreams. That's not what 2008 is. If we wanted that, we should have picked a Cardinals season. I should have brought him then. I chose the wrong year.

And then shortstop Cesar Izturis singles to center field.

IN APRIL 2009, I was working on a feature story for *New York* magazine about Yankees outfielder Nick Swisher.

(The general premise: "This new Yankee is CRAZY! He's a CHARACTER!" Then I interviewed him for a while and realized he was exactly like every other baseball player I'd ever met, but louder. He was on Twitter, he loved Rascal Flatts, he liked to play pranks on his teammates and sometimes, after games, he liked to go out and hit the clubs. Only in the empty hagiography of a post-Steinbrenner landscape would this be considered subversive.)

This required me to sit in the press box.

The press box is the worst possible venue from which to watch a sporting event. It's antiseptically quiet, as if you were looking at the game on the other side of a fish tank; I found myself tapping on the press box window to see if I could make the tiny gilled players notice me. The reporters up there have been trained to drain themselves of every drop of joy, numbing themselves to not react to the games unfolding below them. Even if I have no rooting interest in the game I'm watching up in the press box, I find I still need to muzzle myself: It is instinct, pure human reaction, to respond to something exciting occurring in front of you. If you have willed this out of yourself, even if it is in the name of professionalism, I am not sure I trust you to accurately describe the events to me afterward.

Anyway. I'd talked to Swisher before the game—"I'm just trying to BE ME, BRO!"—and we settled in for an afternoon tilt between the Oakland A's and the New York Yankees. The game was tight throughout, and a single by future Cardinal Matt Holliday in the top of the seventh tied the game at 7. After that, every moment, even for April, was tense. It went into the tenth inning, then the eleventh, then the twelfth. It was free baseball. It was all you adore about the game: What started out as a normal, lazy April afternoon game turned into an epic test of stamina, two teams still feeling themselves out early in the year, every pitch a referendum on a season, able to turn one way or the other in a split second. I was riveted.

I was alone in this. Around the press box, as each inning ended with the score still tied, the grumblings grew louder.

"Well, looks like this is gonna fuck up dinner reservations."
"If you can't score off Dan Giese, why the hell are you even here?"
"When this game began, Cody Ransom weighed three hundred pounds."
"You know, I'm just gonna go take a nap in the back room here. Wake me up when it's time to head downstairs."

The game made it to the thirteenth inning, and the press box was near revolt. On a surface level, I understand: There are deadlines to be met, and appointments to be kept, and lives to be led. But this is not what baseball is supposed to be. Baseball is not supposed to be a chore endured. When Robinson Cano flew out to deep left field to send the game into the fourteenth, the groans were audible. I couldn't help but get caught up in it. I *was* supposed to meet some friends back in Brooklyn that night, and those plans were now kaput.

I still had to talk to Swisher afterward. This game is crimping my style. How long was this gonna go? Didn't they know we had *plans*?

"Fuck it," one scribe said. "I'm just deleting the whole story and starting over now. I'll be here all night anyway." I found myself nodding. *It's just a dumb April afternoon game. No one will remember it in a month anyway.* I texted my girlfriend: "cancel dinner. i'm never getting out of here."

With a 1–0 count in the bottom of the fifteenth, one out, runner on first, Dan Giese hung a breaking ball to Melky Cabrera, who destroyed it, sending it deep into the right field seats. Not a wind tunnel–aided homer, this one. It was a shot.

This inspired a first for me: Everyone in the press box began cheering. "Thank fucking God," a guy from the *New York Post* exclaimed, and everyone began applauding. It wasn't happy applause. It was kiss-the-ground-because-the-Iranians-just-released-you applause. It was muted and tired and defeated.

Then I looked onto the field. The Yankees poured out of the dugout, jumping up and down, screaming like little kids, little millionaire kids who surely had more interesting plans that evening than the people in the press box did, throwing cream pies at each other, tossing their hats in the air, smothering Cabrera in a wall of pin-striped flesh as he crossed home plate. They ran around the field, enraptured, cleaned, *Holy Ghost Power, stomp on the devil,* delivered, sent home. They were batshit happy.

I watched them for a moment as the press box folks grimly passed by me to the elevators down to the locker room. I was surprised. The players weren't ready to go home. They were riveted. They were ecstatic. They were the kids we all used to be. They can stay young forever.

RYAN LUDWICK strikes out while Cesar Izturis stands bored at first base. He feels the vibe in the air as well. Cubs fans are so in tune to the moment, the History, that they almost forget to boo Albert Pujols when he comes to the plate. A couple drunk guys pick up the slack, almost out of obligation. Albert Pujols is no threat, not right now.

Lewin on FOX chimes in: "Everyone here at Wrigley knows what's at stake here. A win here, and they will party deep into the night." Not with Wrigleyville's parking restrictions they won't.

Ted Lilly considers Pujols more of a threat than his fans do, and he walks him on four pitches. I glance at my score book and look at Dad. "You realize this is the first time all day the Cardinals have had two men on base, right?"

He grins. "Well, then, HERE WE GO!" The guy in the Cards hat and Cubs jersey chuckles, and his wife nudges him in the ribs playfully. Oh, aren't they so freaking happy.

"They're making him work a little bit, at least," Dad says, and he's right. Lilly has thrown more than twenty pitches this inning, the first time that's happened all game, and with a 1–1 count on Felipe Lopez, he fakes a move to second base. It's clearly a stall for time, a chance for a rest: The Cardinals are down by five runs with two outs. If Cesar Izturis were to try to run here, Tony La Russa would sprint out onto the field and tackle him.

Lilly looks back in . . . and fuck me, Izturis and Pujols are *running*.

The pitch is way outside, both runners are safe without a throw. (La Russa does not appear to be coming onto the field.) A single here, one measly freaking single, would bring the Cardinals within three runs. That's still a large deficit with only ten outs to go. But it is smaller than five.

Ball three. Mike sits up a little straighter. I'll give him this: He never feels truly comfortable. He cheers not to win, but to not lose. Like Bartman. Like me.

The last thing Lilly wants to do is walk Lopez, giving the Cardinals another free base runner, so he grooves one. Lopez, though, because he's a *second baseman pretending to be a cleanup hitter,* pounds it just to the left of shortstop Ryan Theriot. Frenchy McFrencherson stumbles for a moment and happens to land right where the ball happens to be. Of course.

But! He gets wobbly with the pickup, then stumbles again, before limply shot-putting a throw from his knees to first. Lopez is safe, easily. The stolen base, the one I thought Lilly was idiotic for worrying about, gave the Cardinals their first run. It's 5–1. Not enough to make anybody start fretting, not even Mike, who forgives Theriot with a "tough play, there." But we at least are on the board. Dad high-fives me. "It's somethin'!" he yells. "Gotta start somewhere." I don't like the high five, but I love it when Dad high-fives me.

Then, before I even have a chance to mark Izturis's run in my score book . . . Troy Glaus deposits a hanging slider deep into the left field bleachers.

As I watch it, more than a year later, you see Glaus do a little lick of his lips. This is Glaus's tell: I've watched Glaus bat enough to know when he's desperate to swing at the first pitch. I couldn't notice this from my seats. But I notice it a year later. He's waiting. This inning has gotten away from Lilly a little bit, and he wants to get ahead of Glaus in the count, wrest back control of the situation. Glaus has been playing baseball a long time. He's aware. And he's ready. Then: WHAM.

The ball lands in around the eighth row, but it could have landed in Bourbonnais and I wouldn't have noticed. As soon as Glaus swung, it was obvious: The ball was gone. I leap into the air, my hat flying a row behind me, and Dad screams, "Go!!!" like he was yelling for John Hawkins to run to first base way back in Little League. It is instant pandemonium. What had been lost, what had been helpless, has returned to us. I yell like I never yell at any other time in my life other than when I'm at a baseball game. I am not a thirty-something man with a job and an apartment and a girlfriend and hopes and dreams. I am a fifteen-year-old kid popping wheelies on my DMX bike in the neighbor's driveway. So is my dad. We hug each other and do a little chest bump, something I've never, ever done with my dad, and will hopefully never do again. The ball is gone. It's a 5–4 game. It happened so fast. It happened like *that.*

A few thousand Cardinals fans scattered around the stadium make a quick clatter, but Wrigley Field is mostly silent. But not where we are. Not in our seats.

And it's a one-run game.

KNOWLEDGE YOU NOW HAVE

1. The MultiNational United Corporation that owns all the banks, universities, and half of Congress was once known as "Twitter."

2. Your father, who is barely a mammal, is jealous of people who have facial hair and often makes fun of them for it.

3. It is possible for people to spend a thousand words bitching about sitting in an air-conditioned box and watching a baseball game for free.

BOTTOM OF THE SIXTH INNING

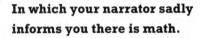

**In which your narrator sadly
informs you there is math.**

*Friday, October 31. Halloween in Philadelphia. The Phillies had
just won the World Series. I took a super-impromptu day off
from the post-college job I had started only a few months earlier,
and my dad did as well. At the time, my dad owned a direct-mail
advertising franchise, so he set his own hours. And he made it
clear that his hours that day would be zero—he wanted to be at
the parade with me, his oldest son. But I didn't want to see him.
I wanted to spend time with my friends, drink Yuengling from
cans and whiskey from giant plastic bottles, to scream and holler and curse and do everything you don't normally do when
your father is around. So I avoided him. Cell reception was bad
enough in the city that day, with so many people congregating in
one spot, that he could barely get through to me as it was. But
just as we were getting camped outside the gates surrounding
Citizens Bank Park, my phone rang. "WHERE ARE YOU?!" he
yelled. Without an excuse, I said, "Right outside the gates!" "I'LL
BE RIGHT THERE!" he yelled. And ten minutes later, there he
was. He had a beer with us. He talked to all my friends about the
last Phillies parade in 1980. But most of all, he huddled with me,
and told me how amazing this all was, and how I needed to
cherish it, and how glad he was to be there with me for it. The
parade rolled by an hour or so later. And my friends and I took*

my father (he's about four inches shorter and thirty pounds
lighter than the smallest of us), propped him on our shoulders,
and carried him around, screaming and cheering and laughing
and crying. There's a picture of it. He has a huge smile on his
face. He was having a ball. And so were we.

— STEVE CIMINO, Medford, New Jersey

WHEN THE TOP OF THE SIXTH INNING BEGAN, MY ST. LOUIS
Cardinals, centerpiece of my flawed universe, had a 4 percent chance
of beating the Chicago Cubs on this clear September afternoon.
Those were the worst odds they'd faced all afternoon.

The game, as all games do, had started out with a 50 percent
win probability on both sides. Ryan Ludwick's one-out double in the
first inning brought the Cardinals up to 52 percent odds, but that was
the best odds we had all day; the Pujols groundout and Felipe Lopez
strikeout that inning dropped us to a 45 percent chance. Alfonso
Soriano's single that went past Brian Barton in left field in the second
inning dropped our odds to 19 percent—we'd been at 43 before that
pitch—and the three Cubs runs in the fourth plummeted us all the
way down to 6 percent. Since then, our odds were never better than
7 percent and never worse than 4. Until Glaus's homer.

The fundamental statistic, the invention that has allowed this
florid, romantic discussion of the beautiful game, is called "Win Probability," and I figured it all out using a device called the Win Expectancy Finder. The Win Expectancy Finder was invented by a very
smart man named Christopher Shea, who runs an excellently named
Web site called Balk Off Balk. The idea of the tool, which tracked
more than a decade of games as data to find the percentage of times
a team in a certain situation went on to win the game, was to track
the wisdom of managerial moves.

In an example another great site, called the Hardball Times,
uses to show the Win Expectancy Finder's utility, imagine your team

has a runner on first base with no one out in the bottom of the ninth. The Win Expectancy Finder, at that point, gives your team a 71 percent chance of winning the game. Many managers, most managers, if they had a hitter not named Albert Pujols at the plate, would bunt the runner over to second base, putting him in scoring position and avoiding the murderous double play. But hold it there: The Win Expectancy Finder shows that your team's odds of winning with a runner on second base and one out—the result of a successful sacrifice bunt—are . . . 70 percent. The out you just gave away cost you more than the benefit of the runner making it to second. Historically speaking.

It's an extremely useful little knickknack. For a manager.

The Hardball Times, in a 2004 essay by Dave Studeman, was blown away by the discovery. "Next time you watch a ballgame," Studeman writes, "use it to track the ups and downs of the game. It will change the way you watch baseball."

I did use it to track the ups and downs of the game. I still do. I can't make it stop.

Now that I am aware of the Win Expectancy Finder, I am acutely aware that: Troy Glaus had not hit a home run that brought the Cardinals within a run and the Leitches to their feet. He had merely increased the Cardinals' win probability from 8 percent to 28 percent. That's what we were really jumping around and screaming about. Apparently.

EVERYONE LIKES TO SAY that baseball's statistical revolution started with a seed planted by Bill James, the bearded Kansan and increasingly cranky but always brilliant grand Socrates of baseball who whittled away the hours working as a security guard at the Stokely-Van Camp plant in Lawrence writing little observations and essays on baseball that would change the course of the game for the next decade. (I've never met Bill James, and I'm not sure he'd like me too much—my unabashed enjoyment of scatological humor would vastly annoy him, I suspect—but it still strikes me as strange that a company would hire the professorial Bill James as a *security guard.* The Lawrence Stokely-Van Camp plant must have had few invaders and lots of free time for its security guards.)

The key to James's genius—and I do think it's genius—was not that he invented new statistics or was some sort of abacus-wielding counterrevolutionary. Most of the statistics he came up with have been either disproved or dramatically modified since he created them. It's that he came to the game from the outside. He didn't play baseball, he didn't broadcast baseball, he didn't report on baseball, he didn't even *watch* much baseball. (Like any good Midwesterner in the mid-seventies, he listened to games on the radio. Fortunately for James—who once quit writing about baseball for a few years because of a few dozen angry letters readers *mailed* to him— there was no Internet back then.) But he cared enough about the game to study it from a perspective that those inside the gates couldn't have.

Jack Shafer, the media critic for *Slate* magazine, once criticized the late, angry Robert Novak for putting the emphasis on day-to-day mundane scoops rather than placing those events in a larger perspective. He wrote it much better than I just did: "One problem with Novak-style scoop journalism is that reporters don't always know what's in the water they're carrying." In baseball, the players, the coaches, the executives, the managers, the broadcasters, the reporters . . . they didn't know what was in the water they were carrying. James was a revelation because he had both the analytical mind and the vast distance from the inner workings of the game: If he hadn't had both, it wouldn't have worked.

James did not start throwing math darts at baseball, nunchuck-ing the game with advanced physics. Of all of James's innovations, my personal favorite is Win Shares. *Win Shares* was a book James wrote in 2002 that was breathtaking in its ambition: It attempted, essentially, to attach to to every player on every team a number that captured and quantified exactly what that player had contributed to his team's success. This is baseball's version of a Theory Of Everything; if you could translate this to humanity itself, you'd be able to solve every mystery of the universe, as well as streamline online dating. James's methodology was flawed, because, Christ, how could it not be? But it brought us a little closer. It was sprawling in what it aspired to. It was ridiculous and fantastic. It tried to change the world.

It did. It made us all look at the game differently, and smartly. But it did not make it more fun.

GEOVANY SOTO reaches on an infield single and Mark DeRosa flies out to center field. This is how the last two innings have looked so far, as charted by Baseball-Reference.com, the premier historically stat-based baseball Web site in the galaxy:

INN OUT ROB R/O PIT(CNT) WWPA WWE SCORE @BAT BATTER PITCHER PLAY DESCRIPTION

BOTTOM OF THE 5TH, CUBS BATTING, AHEAD 5-0, CARDINALS' JOEL PINEIRO FACING 3-4-5

b5 0—O 3,(2-0) -0% 95% 5-0 CHC D. Lee J. Pineiro Flyball: RF
  (RF Line)

b5 1—7,(3-2) 0% 96% 5-0 CHC A. Ramirez J. Pineiro Single to LF
  (Line Drive to Short LF)

b5 1 1—OO 4,(1-2) -1% 95% 5-0 CHC J. Edmonds J. Pineiro
  Ground Ball Double Play: 2B-SS-1B

0 runs, 1 hit, 0 errors, 0 LOB. Cardinals 0, Cubs 5.

TOP OF THE 6TH, CARDINALS BATTING, BEHIND 0-5, CUBS' TED LILLY FACING 9-1-2

t6 0—O 5,(2-2) 1% 96% 0-5 STL J. LaRue T. Lilly Flyball: CF
(Deep CF-RF)

t6 1—2,(0-1) -1% 95% 0-5 STL C. Izturis T. Lilly Single to CF
(Line Drive to Short CF)

t6 1 1—O 4,(1-2) 1% 96% 0-5 STL R. Ludwick T. Lilly Strikeout
Swinging

t6 2 1—5,(3-1) -1% 95% 0-5 STL A. Pujols T. Lilly Walk; Izturis
to 2B

t6 2 12- 3,(1-1) -1% 94% 0-5 STL F. Lopez T. Lilly Izturis Steals 3B;
Pujols Steals 2B

t6 2 -23 R 5,(3-1) -3% 92% 0-5 STL F. Lopez T. Lilly Single to SS
(Ground Ball to Weak SS); Izturis Scores; Pujols to 3B

t6 2 1-3 RRR 1,(0-0) -20% 72% 1-5 STL T. Glaus T. Lilly Home Run
(Fly Ball to Deep LF Line); Pujols Scores; Lopez Scores

t6 2—8,(3-2) -2% 70% 4-5 STL A. Kennedy T. Lilly Walk

t6 2 1—O 3,(0-2) 4% 74% 4-5 STL B. Barton T. Lilly Groundout:
SS-1B (Weak SS)

4 runs, 3 hits, 0 errors, 1 LOB. Cardinals 4, Cubs 5.

BOTTOM OF THE 6TH, CUBS BATTING, AHEAD 5-4, CARDINALS' JOEL PINEIRO FACING 6-7-8

b6 0—4,(2-1) 3% 77% 5-4 CHC G. Soto J. Pineiro Single to 3B
(Ground Ball to Weak 3B)

b6 0 1—O 2,(0-1) -3% 74% 5-4 CHC M. DeRosa J. Pineiro Flyball:
CF (Deep CF)

BASEBALL IS a game understood better in a macro sense, from thirty thousand feet up, than a micro one, with players and coaches and managers too close to the action to understand it. You need the distance, you need the space, you need to be able to stand back and soak it all in. One game is just one game: It's a "small sample size." You can't tell *anything* from one game. It is, in the grand scheme of matters, meaningless, a random occurrence. It doesn't matter what your eyes *see;* it's what the stats *show.* Our best teams, our brightest minds, have embraced this philosophy. This is what's being accepted. This is close to the rule of law. This is what sabermetrics is. It is science rather than art. It is truth.

Except, well . . . uh . . . actually . . . now that I'm looking at it . . .

A whole season, the long tale of following a baseball team through 162 games, can't be simulated or run through in five minutes. Watching a team every day, its struggles, its glories, its problems, its assets, its joys, its pain . . . that's what being a baseball fan is *about,* right? Following these players, learning their weaknesses and strengths, seeing how they react to different situations . . . that's the whole point, right? If my team wins, I am happy. If my team loses, I am sad. This is the fundamental aspect of being a sports fan: Whatever is going on in the world, that nasty mean confusing gray world, cheering for a team provides a three-hour respite of black-and-white. Win = happy. Lose = sad.

The more we understand about baseball statistics, the more we gather the facts and the more we research and learn . . . the more we realize that, at its core, Win = Lose = Meaningless. One plate appearance is nothing. One inning is nothing. One game is nothing. These are facts. And they *suck.*

The problem is that you can only watch one game at a time. I happen to be watching a game right now. It doesn't feel like a small sample size to me. It feels like a baseball game.

ON THE FIRST PITCH to Kosuke Fukudome, Geovany Soto is thrown out trying to steal by about, oh, ninety-six feet. Why was Soto running? An odd maneuver, one would think: It is actually Soto's first stolen base attempt as a major leaguer. (He was 2-for-12 stealing bases as a minor leaguer, which is not so good.)

He was running because Cubs manager Lou Piniella had called for a hit-and-run, and Fukudome—in another example of why he'd been in Piniella's doghouse all season—by the way, if you've ever wondered what it means to be in a manager's "doghouse," it involves him tying you up and throwing lunch meats at you—had missed the sign. I notice that Fukudome doesn't even look at the third base coach, who is surely glaring at him. He just looks down at his feet, with the sad Charlie Brown music playing in his head. I hope he doesn't commit Harry Caray.

The hit-and-run is one of the most exciting plays in baseball. It requires all kinds of moving parts to work in unison: A runner has to secure a good enough jump on the pitcher to force the second baseman into covering the bag, the pitcher has to throw a pitch that's somewhere near the strike zone, and the hitter has to hit it exactly where the second baseman was just standing. When executed perfectly, it's heavenly: It has the ideal mix of talent, luck, and wiles that make you stand up and holler every time it locks into the place. You feel like you're getting away with something: *You thought we were doing* this, *but we're doing* this. It always makes the manager look quite smart. Tony La Russa loves the hit-and-run. It's a cat burglar move, and it's thrilling.

It's also, in a macro world, a terrible strategic maneuver: It's essentially like a sacrifice bunt, but dramatically more risky with a lower reward ceiling. It sure looks pretty when that ball sneaks through the hole and, in an instant, you have runners on first and third, but just as often, if not more, a line drive ends up in the hands of an infielder for a double play, or the batter misses the pitch and the runner is thrown out, or he swings at a terrible pitch just to protect his runner and makes a cheap out, or he just misses the sign all together, like Fukudome. Statistics show that it's almost never worth it.

But man, it's so much fun when it works.

Oh, and the caught stealing increased the Cardinals' odds of winning from 26 percent to 30 percent.

MY FAVORITE PLAYER (and Dad's) growing up was speedy Cardinals center fielder Willie McGee. He was paradoxically lackadaisical and thrilling to watch, a spiraling cacophony of limbs flying in all kinds of directions, flipping all over the place, eventually ending up in the spot he was heading for faster than everybody else. He had occasional power, he played defense like crazy, he flung triples into the gap, he jumped over the wall to steal home runs, he once reversed the Earth's rotation so that he might save Lois Lane from a crack in the San Andreas Fault. He was my hero. He was the hero of many young Cardinals fans. He won an MVP, he won two batting titles, he once inspired George Steinbrenner to say that trading him was one of the biggest mistakes he'd ever made. When he returned to the Cardinals at the end of his career, in 1996, he was greeted with standing ovations every time he so much as coughed. When the Cardinals opened their new stadium in 2006, he stood next to Cardinals legend Bob Gibson to catch the first pitch at the fancy, shiny digs. No one questioned that he deserved to be there. A picture of Willie and an eight-year-old Will Leitch is on the wall at our home in Mattoon. Just hearing his name makes me smile.

So. It turns out: He wasn't very good. Well, that's overstating it. It's more that he was simply an average player. Despite his seven Gold Gloves, stats show that he didn't cover nearly as much ground in center field as it looked like he did—poor routes to the ball seem to have been the culprit—and man, did that guy hate to walk: In 652 plate appearances in 1985, his MVP season, he only walked 38 times. His career OPS, the preferred and generally accepted best practices stat for determining hitting prowess, was .729 ... which is lower than the current major league average of .753. Willie McGee looked like an amazing player to me: I would have sworn it to every court in the land. Watching him play made you feel like baseball was the most electrifying activity imaginable. Willie McGee is the person who made me fall in love with baseball in the first place. Dad dragged me away from my Bugs Bunny cartoon one Saturday morning and drove me to Busch Stadium, where the Cardinals were facing the then-potent Montreal Expos. Keith Hernandez hit a home run, Ozzie Smith made one of his gravity-defying double plays, and Willie McGee stole three bases. It was breathtaking. I was hooked. I never looked back.

And he was *a below average player.* I accept this as a fact. I do not think the statistics are lying. But I hate it. It makes me feel stupid. I want to ignore it. I want to throw it away.

Seattle Times columnist Larry Stone once wrote a story about Kansas City Royals pitcher Brian Bannister, about how Bannister was attempting to study advanced baseball statistics in order to make him a better pitcher. Stone was amazed: A player who not only knew about VORP and BABIP, but found a practical use for them in his performance. Stone wrote that baseball had come a long way.

> Trust me, this is not the prevailing point of view in the clubhouse. More typical is the response of Willie McGee, whom I covered in the early 1990s. I once asked Willie, then with the Giants, about some statistical anomaly in his résumé—an uncommonly high average in day games, if I recall.
>
> "I don't know about that," he said dismissively. "I ain't no Bob James."

I MADE THE MISTAKE one time of informing my father that the advanced baseball statistics book I was reading claimed that Willie McGee wasn't a very good player. Remember how Dad reacted when

I told him at the age of thirteen that I didn't think I would make the major leagues? That's the look he gave me. "You read too goddamned much."

AS PINEIRO strikes out Kosuke Fukudome to end the inning, the Cardinals have a 21 percent chance of winning going into the seventh. They will face Lilly, who has a similarity index of 56 and is most comparable, in a historical sense, to Floyd Bannister, Jerry Koosman, Gary Peters, and Chris Short. Lilly has thrown eighty-nine pitches so far, at the ebb of his traditional limit, with batters posting a 5.00 ERA against him, pushing him to a value level just barely above a theoretically constant replacement player. The likely Cardinals leadoff batter will be Josh Phelps, who notched a .376 EQA with Pittsburgh last year with a WARP3 OF 1.8 and with a PECOTA Breakout rate of 19 percent heading into next season. In his career, Phelps's OPS is .069 higher against left-handed pitchers than right-handers.

Um . . . yay? Go Cards?

KNOWLEDGE YOU NOW HAVE

1. Everything you enjoy right now will eventually be revealed to you as stupid.
2. This is why your mother is always telling you about how, after your parents got married, your dad exclaimed, "We've increased our Procreation Expectancy Rate from 53 percent to 74 percent!"
3. Do not talk to your grandfather about Willie McGee.

TOP OF THE SEVENTH INNING

In which your narrator's physical deficiencies are revealed and rationalized.

At about five years old, my dad took me to my very first Chicago Cubs game. I really don't remember much of it, but my mom sure loves to tell the story. So there was my dad, his good friend, and me sitting in the middle of the bleachers on a hot summer day. Throughout the game I watched them with other bleacher bums, telling old stories, sitting out in the sun, shirtless, drinking beers. Apparently, I was consumed with not only counting the runs in the game but the number of beer cups in everyone's cup stacks. I was also very confused on why the woman in front of us was removed for taking her shirt off. So when I returned home I was excited to tell my mom about my male bonding time, including how many beers my dad drank, the woman flashing us, and the new vocabulary of profanity I had learned. I was not allowed to return to the bleachers with my father until about fourteen years later.

— GEORGE LOBB, Chicago, Illinois

ONCE, SEATTLE MARINERS THIRD BASEMAN ADRIAN BELTRE veered to his left to field a hot ground ball at the hot corner. The ball took a goofy hop and hit him right in the groin. Beltre was not wearing a cup. It did not end well. He ended up with a "severely bruised" testicle and "internal bleeding." I am not certain which is worse.

In the aftermath of the "issue"—Beltre immediately went on the disabled list and played the position with eyes crossed the rest of the season—several major-league players emerged to confess that, now that you mention it, they didn't wear cups either. Oakland second baseman Mark Ellis and Detroit counterpart Placido Polanco said they avoided cups out of "comfort," and most players admitted they'd never heard of an outfielder wearing such protection. (In football, no one wears cups, which is insane.) Most fans were stunned; major leaguers don't wear cups? They hit the ball *hard* in baseball. Mark DeRosa, playing for the Cardinals in 2009 (long story!), had the most rational reaction: "I tell you what, I don't take the team picture without wearing a cup."

But I understand. When I played baseball, I didn't wear a cup either. And I was a *catcher.*

Like any baseball fan, I'm convinced that this life—the one where I write and edit and type, the one where I smoke and drink and generally lay waste to the body I was given—is the wrong one, a mistake. Again: I'm hardly unique in this. One of the irrational pleasures of watching baseball is to delude yourself into thinking that it's an accessible game, that it's one *you* could play. Professional baseball players don't run that much, they can be a little overweight, no one is body-slammed to the ground by four-hundred-pound men. *Heck, if I'da caught a break, that could have been me. It ain't so hard. Why those players complaining about their contracts? I'd play baseball for free.*

But seriously: I was supposed to be a major-league baseball player. If you ask my father here, he'll agree with me, even though he's lying.

It's not my fault no one discovered my talent in time. There is nothing, nothing in this world I miss more than playing baseball.

I've looked around for recreational leagues, but that's all softball, a bunch of fat guys drinking beer in the outfield, complaining

about their jobs and their wives and their kids and their hemor-
rhoids. (I am now one of these people.) There is no real baseball,
the way it's supposed to be played, with fastballs on the inside corner and picking the runner off first, waving a guy home, sprinting
away from the pitcher's mound and heading for the stands because
you just hit a batter with a pitch and now he's running after you and
you are scared.

I haven't played actual organized baseball, actual baseball, in
sixteen years. Since June 17, 1994, to be precise.

Throughout the Mattoon public youth baseball leagues, I had always been known as a bit of a throwback. Typically, our baseball-
mad town would force-feed any kid between the ages of seven and
fifteen into one of the locally sponsored teams. The dads would coach
the kids, usually screaming at their sons to compensate for their own
misspent youth, steering them quickly from the game. Most of those
kids, by the time they were sixteen and had a car to get the FUCK
away from Mom and Dad, did so and were too busy screwing in the
backseat to have time for baseball.

I loved the thinning of the talent ranks though. In the youth summer leagues, thanks to those kids who decided baseball was too
cerebral and bolted for factory jobs, I got my chance. We didn't have
enough players for an actual league, so we just corralled all the
seventeen- and eighteen-year-olds left into a traveling all-star team.
By the time I was eighteen and home for the summer from college,
I was ready. It was my last chance at glory, the last time I'd be able to
play baseball for a long, long time.

All the kids were younger than me, just out of high school at best,
and I was the big college boy back in town. I was the grizzled work-
horse, the Crash Davis, the vet making one last tour of duty. Everyone
knew how much I would have missed playing, so I started every
game at catcher, in Cerro Gordo, in Moweaqua, in Teutopolis.

We came down to the final games of the season, a doubleheader
in rival city Effingham on, of all days, June 29. (We had a very short

season.) Because it was a doubleheader, I only played catcher the first game, considering that two consecutive games would tire a catcher out the way a physical sport, such as basketball, tires people out. In baseball, that is not acceptable.

Early on, when I was learning the fundamentals of catching, I was taught that the best way to make sure no pitch in the dirt ever sneaked past you was to throw your mitt in front of your crotch and dive in front of the ball, allowing it to hit only your mitt or your chest protector, nowhere else. I was known as an excellent defensive catcher, but I was still looking for an edge. So in order to make certain that I instinctively thrust my mitt where it needed to go, which is the elementary nature of catching after all, I secretly—because no youth league coach in his right mind would allow a player to go without—refused to wear a cup. It never came back to bite me. My glove was where it was supposed to be; jeez, what more do you want from a catcher? Question my tactics, but do not question my results.

My coach, a happy guy who later ran for mayor, made a compromise with me: "In good conscience as a coach, I can't let you catch both games, Will. But how about we put you at, say, third base for the second game? It's the same principle, right? Knock down what's in front of you?" Even though it had been so long since I'd played the field that I had to borrow a teammate's glove, I agreed with him, and so it was.

By the way, Dad was supposed to come to this game, and he admits now that had he known it was my last game, he would come. "I couldn't have imagined your last game would be when you were eighteen years old." What a depressing thought.

In the first game, I threw a runner out, forgot to back up first base on a groundball that cost us a run, went 2-for-4 with 2 RBIs, and walked in my last at bat. We won 8–5. I took off my shin guards and chest protector for the last time, sighed, and grabbed some guy named Bill's glove and headed to third base for my final game. I fielded the first couple of ground balls, warm-ups tossed by the first baseman, with ease, and when the first batter stepped to the box, I even started up some "hey batter, hey batter" chatter, because that's what you do when you know you're playing the last baseball game of your life. Our pitcher, an outfielder by position and ultimately a plumber by trade, walked the first guy on four pitches.

A short kid, about fifteen, scampered to the plate. I was ready, crouched in anticipation of the double-play ball, ready to scoop, pivot, and fire, the way Ken Oberkfell and Terry Pendleton used to do it.

Short Kid gets an inside "fastball" and slaps it down the line. Hard. So hard, in fact, that it takes one hop, spinning wildly, whistling, and plants itself in my crotch a split second before the glove can make the trip.

As you know, there is a brief second, before the gnashing and screaming and fuck fuck fuck happens, where you are able to rationally and disinterestedly understand that you have just been hit in the genitals, and it doesn't hurt yet, but it's about to crush you, and it'll happen any minute now . . . *then it happens.*

I collapsed, and the spectators gasped, followed by those giggles we catch every time we see someone hit in the groin. The coach came out with an assistant and carried me off the field. That Bill guy with the glove took over.

And I spent the last seven innings of my baseball career with an ice pack under my shorts, keeping score, wondering when school started again.

JOSH PHELPS strikes out, immediately, as Josh Phelps is wont to do, and Joel Pineiro's day is over. He gave up five runs in six innings, and I'm kind of proud of him.

Josh Phelps, despite the statistical pretzel-twisting I tried in the last chapter, is not a very good player. As it turns out, after this game, he batted seventeen more times, collected two more hits, and never played in the major leagues again. His career was like so many in baseball: completely irrelevant. There are countless guys like this: Crash Davis folks, who play in the majors for a couple of weeks, are never really noticed, and then disappear. They can say they were major leaguers. They can say they reached the Big Time. To fans, they're jokes: The horrible Neifi Perez will be a punch line among my baseball nerd friends and me for the rest of my life. But it is an epic achievement. Making the major leagues requires years of effort, training, talent, and sweat. It is the culmination of years of work, and is only achieved by the very best. To reach that level of success in any other field would make you a captain of industry, a real Tom Wolfe Master of the Universe. In baseball, you get to be Josh Phelps. In baseball, jerks like me get to make jokes about you.

According to Baseball-Reference.com, there are 720 non-pitchers in baseball history who played in a major league game and never got a hit. The most famous of them is Moonlight Graham, immortalized in *Field of Dreams*. But he never had a chance to bat. He only played the field.

Even though my baseball career stalled as the backup catcher on the 1993 IHSA Big 12 Conference Champion Mattoon Green Wave—I still have the T-shirt to prove it—I take a certain amount of pride in my lifetime spotless major-league record. We think of baseball players as otherworldly athletes blessed with physical gifts beyond our imagination. This is true, of course, but sometimes, we improve on those gifts simply by staying out of the game altogether. That is to say: I think, by way of never making an out in the major leagues, I had a better major-league career than someone who did. That's the theory. That's what I'm hanging onto.

Fifty-two of those 720 actually had *ten* at bats without a hit. The leader of the pack is Larry Littleton, an Indians outfielder, who came to the plate twenty-seven times in 1981 and never so much as singled: He walked three times and even knocked in a run with a sacrifice fly. I'm not sure I could hit the ball far enough for a sacrifice fly.

So for the sake of our discussion, the worst player shouldn't have an RBI, or even a walk.

That leaves New York Giants catcher John O'Neill (who actually spread his fifteen pointless at bats over two seasons at the turn of the century) and Gus Creely, a punchless shortstop for the 1890 St. Louis Browns. Bah: Those were more than a hundred years ago. We need to think more recent.

Thus, this decade's ten-and-upper, and my personal favorite, is Josh Labandeira, a 2004 Expos shortstop who, just to be comprehensive, also made one error in his six chances at the position. I like Labandeira for two reasons. One, in 2008, he was signed and released by three different teams (the Giants and the Rays cut him within a month of signing him); afterward, he took the hint and retired. The other reason I like Labandeira is because he's five-foot-seven. Not only was my professional career better than his, but I'm also taller.

Josh Labandeira, who went 0-for-14 in his career, with a double play in there for good measure, might have had the least successful career in baseball history. And somewhere, in Little League, in youth league, in high school ball . . . he was the best player any of his teammates had ever seen.

DAD STILL HAS A TROPHY, down in his basement, that commemorates his 1963 Babe Ruth League Sportsmanship Award. It's not all that prominently displayed, hanging on the wall with kleig lights on it or anything, but he's not exactly hiding it either. It had never occurred to me to ask him about it before now because I am a bad son.

"How'd you get that trophy?"

I was a catcher. Some big sumbitch from Windsor came barreling around third base and lowered his shoulder as he came near me. Just smashed it right into my chin. I went flying, but I hung onto the ball. I remembered that there was a runner on first, so I popped up and fired to third and threw the guy out. When I got to the dugout,

everyone was grab-assing me, telling me how great of a play it was.
They asked me if it hurt, and I told them it didn't, I said it didn't hurt.
But it hurt. It hurt like a goddamned bastard.

"Is that why I was a catcher?"

I didn't want you to be a catcher. You were too small. That was
your idea.

"Whenever I got barreled over by the runner and hung onto the
ball, I always stood over him and dropped the ball lightly on his
chest, so he knew that he hadn't beaten me."

That's probably why you never won the sportsmanship award.

"How about a hitter? What kind of hitter were you?"

Lousy. I probably hit about .250. I didn't strike out much, but I
didn't have any power. I was only in the lineup because I was a good
catcher and I liked playing more than the other kids did. I don't think
I ever hit a home run. I did a lot of bunting.

"Could you hit the curveball?"

No. But you couldn't either. I still think that runs on your mom's
side of the family, though.

WHEN I WAS SIX years old, Dad decided his bookish son—the one
who had been chided by teachers for reading *Mom, the Wolf Man*
and Me during recess—needed to start playing baseball, if just to get
him off the couch. In Mattoon, five- to seven-year-olds were herded
into something called T-ball, where you attempted to hit the station-
ary ball off a piece of black plastic, and since you couldn't strike
out, you just had to sit there, with parents and mean-ass kids staring, until you just hit the friggin' thing, for Christ's sake. For kids
like me, for whom a baseball was that thing the other kids threw at
you while you were reading Judy Blume, this was a laborious process. In the field, a coach once had to run out and remind me to face
the batter and, for the love of God, please quit chewing on my glove.

In retrospect, I realize how difficult it must have been for my dad, who had to watch as his son ran to third base when he finally hit the ball. As a last-ditch effort, my father dragged me to Busch Stadium. It was breathtaking. It was like watching magic: It was watching humans sprout wings and fly. To Dad's amazement, I was hooked. Something about it was otherworldly. What an odd game. Standing around, thinking, watching the planes pass, mulling . . . and then, suddenly, ACTION. I always liked to think before I did anything. This made me more cautious than other kids, less violent. And this made me perfect for baseball. It felt like it was specifically invented for me.

By high school, I was indeed backup catcher. Our cross-county rival was Charleston, and thanks to some sort of fan initiative, our team was slated to play at Busch before a Cardinals-Phillies game. This was back when old Busch had Astroturf and players' legs would go careening off into center field when they rounded second. His hand forced by public sentiment, Coach Jackley was going to let everyone play, even the schleps with the pencils.

Like all bench riders, when I was finally given my chance to shine, I was going to prove everyone wrong. My teammates, constantly startled by my encyclopedic knowledge of former Cardinal Dane Iorg's on-base percentage with two outs against left-handed pitchers in the fourth inning, surprised me by rallying around me in my quest for Busch Stadium glory. One even remarked to the local paper, "He's the biggest Cardinal fan we know. We really want him to get a hit."

We entered the stadium through the players' gate—"Hey, check it out, Pedro Guerrero's car!"—and walked onto the field. It was even bigger than I'd imagined. It felt like we were playing baseball on a faraway planet, a planet with an Arch. Glancing at the lineup card, I noticed I was batting fourteenth and playing right field in the third and sixth innings.

The third inning arrived, and I trotted out to right field, with Mattoon ahead 3–0. The trot to right was slow and ponderous. Every second had to be documented. I was playing at Busch Stadium.

It had rained the night before, and many of us were panicked the game might be canceled. We played, but the field was still wet. With two out, a runner on second, and a sandy-haired corn-fed kid at the plate, our pitcher threw an outside fastball that was lifted into, of all places, right field. I camped comfortably under the lazy fly.

The night before the game, thanks to a defective air conditioner, we'd hurriedly gathered our things and switched hotels. I didn't realize that I'd left my cleats in the room until I was dressing for the game. I kept my sneakers on and hoped no one would notice.

As the ball floated toward me, I stepped six inches to my right . . . and my shoe gave way. Before I could understand what was happening, I was lying on wet turf with my sneaker sitting next to me and the ball far, far, beyond me. My one shoe and I sprinted to the wall, where I grabbed the ball and fired it back toward the infield, but the sandy-haired kid had long since crossed the plate. In the next day's paper, Jim Kimball, the late, beloved sports editor of the *Mattoon Journal-Gazette,* listed his hit as a home run and didn't even mention that I had fallen. Bless his soul. And the sandy-haired kid can tell his grandkids he hit a home run in Busch Stadium and have the proof to back it up.

In the stands, a man sitting next to my father said, "Yikes, who is that out there?"

"Um, I think it's that Alexander kid," my dad responded.

No one gave me the grab-ass in the dugout.

I COVER THE world of sports professionally. Sometimes I interview athletes, sometimes I interview reporters, sometimes I just blithely muse in prose form. I cannot do what they do. I am an observer, commenting on the actions of others but not acting myself.

There was this kid I went to high school with named Kevin Trimble.

Kevin was the best athlete to come out of Mattoon in twenty years. He was the star in football, baseball, and basketball—taller, faster, and with inherent agility and grace. Kevin's big coming out party as an athlete was his freshman year, when, at a school assembly, the principal, desperately trying to be hip, dressed inexplicably like a Blues Brother, tossed him a pass from half court that Kevin threw down with a ferocious dunk. We had never seen anyone like Kevin at our school.

Kevin and I didn't interact much. I usually tried to stay out of the way of guys like Kevin. He wasn't a jerk, really, but he was just the most blessed, impressive student in school and tended to live his life that way. Whenever Kevin was in the room, he *was* the room; his presence elevated everyone else into something bigger than they were. *We're sitting here next to Kevin Trimble,* we'd think. *This will be something to tell our kids someday.*

Kevin was the star center fielder for the Mattoon Green Wave, and I was the backup catcher/scorekeeper. It was my senior year, his junior, and two years, the Seattle Mariners would draft Kevin in the twenty-third round of the amateur draft. Before he went into the on-deck circle, he walked over to the quiet kid with the score book.

"Hey, Will, how many hits has this pitcher given up today?"

"Um, six. You've got two of 'em."

He looked at me as if he were a paleontologist who had just come across the fossils of a specimen he'd long thought fictional.

"Will, if they ever have a draft for scorekeepers, you'll go in the first round." This proclamation was welcomed with grunts and chuckles. I don't think he meant it to be mean. Kevin wasn't that type of guy, not self-aware in that way: Even though I (and everybody else) was acutely aware he had been drafted by the Mariners (in Seattle, wherever the hell *that* was), I doubt he was even thinking of it when he said it. Truth is, I *was* a good scorekeeper. I think he meant it as a compliment. I think he was being nice. Even appreciative.

This is not how I felt about it when he said it. When I've told this story before, I've made myself into some sort of dugout Dorothy Parker. I cock an eyebrow, turn my head warily in his direction, and proclaim, "Kevin, if they ever have a draft for people who blow their talent and end up working for the city, you'll go in the first round." That story is patently false. I said nothing at the time, and it is only through hindsight that the "witticism" makes any sense at all. No one would ever say that to Kevin, not because they were afraid of him, but because no one thought Kevin would turn out to be anything other than a ten-time all-star and the guy with the "Mattoon: Home of Hall of Famer Kevin Trimble" sign welcoming visitors to town. I've made up the anecdote to pump up my own importance and make myself look like the high school outcast who always had his eye on the bigger picture; truthfully, I think that's the only time Kevin ever spoke to me.

Kevin graduated as I ended my freshman year at the University of Illinois, and, with much fanfare, he announced he would be attending the school as well, under scholarship as a rare two-sport star, playing for the Illini baseball team and coach Lou Tepper's beleaguered football program, which I was already covering for the student newspaper. I wrote an article for the *Daily Illini* about his impending arrival before the school year even started. He hadn't come to campus yet, so I spoke with coaches of both teams about where he fit in their plans. All were ecstatic about this special talent.

Kevin barely lasted a week. Classes hadn't even begun, and he had already begun to chafe under Tepper's workout regimen. At Illinois, he wasn't so important anymore; he was just another freshman grunt trying to catch the attention of his position coaches. Like any information about Kevin, all I gathered was through rumor and innuendo. I guess he missed his friends in Mattoon. He felt alone and without an anchor. He was never a student, not really, and he worried about the supposed advanced curriculum of a Big Ten school. He asked Coach Tepper for some time off, and next thing you knew, Kevin had dropped out and moved back home. He sat out a year, and then played for the Lake Land Community College baseball team. But a year without conditioning, and with the distractions and temptations that came with it, took its toll, and he was never a star again. He played two uninspired seasons, then left the school and, yes, ended up working for the city, in the parks department. (He now works as a high school coach.) He had been handed a singular ability, and he frittered it away. I looked at him with a mixture of disgust, pity, and melancholy.

Whenever I go home these days, all the Mattoon ex-pats pick one night to head to The Alamo, a steakhouse out by the Cross County Mall. When I was home one Christmas, I filed in with some old high school pals, and sure enough, over in the corner, was Kevin, with the same six people he was hanging out with years ago. Just like I was.

He hadn't gotten fat, disappointingly, or at least not any fatter than I'd gotten. I walked over to him, said hi, and after an agonizing pause, his face registered a faint trace of recognition. "Hey, Will Leitch. My man. How you doing? I didn't know you smoked cigarettes." We made about thirty seconds of small talk, and he went back to his conversation—likely a variation on the same conversation he'd been having for fifteen years—with a "uh, good to see you. Merry Christmas." He looked happy, actually; healthy and content. Years later, when he was inducted into the Mattoon Alumni Hall of Fame, he told the *Journal-Gazette:*

> "You always think back, but I also think the year I went back
> to Lake Land was when I met my wife. I have no regrets. I met
> a wonderful woman and I wouldn't have probably met her
> otherwise. I'm definitely happy working with athletes now. I
> don't think I'd have had it any other way. I'd have loved to have

been playing football on Sundays or playing baseball, but that didn't work out."

I could make some belabored argument about how Kevin has never really moved on from high school, and how that inability to move out of his own way has cost him countless opportunities of which most people can only dream. I could say that he is stuck in the past, and that this quiet obsession with what is gone and can be nevermore is tragic. But I would be wrong. Kevin is happy. Kevin has no regrets. *He's* not the one writing this and still thinking about it: I am.

JASON LARUE strikes out, and Cesar Izturis grounds weakly to short. The inning is over. No momentum has carried over. The Cubs are six outs away. Dad and I stand up at the same time, disgusted. "Like I can listen to that seventh-inning stretch bullshit after that," I tell him as we scoot past the standing Cubs fans.

"Yeah, at least put a good swing on it, Izturis," he says. "For Christ's sake."

When the Boston Red Sox fell behind 3–1 in the 2007 American League Championship Series, reporters, after the Game 4 loss, asked then Red Sox outfielder Manny Ramirez about the importance of Game 5, if the Red Sox were panicking. His answer was terrifyingly honest.

"Why should we panic? We've got a great team. If it doesn't happen, so who cares? There's always next year. It's not like it's the end of the world."

With his team on the precipice of seasonal extinction, Ramirez had committed the one sin baseball fans cannot forgive: He'd implied that he didn't care whether his team won or not.

When the media gaggle talks about the integrity of baseball and threats to the great game, the usual suspects are gambling and steroids. But the average fan has, at this point, mostly made his or her peace with those. We've been through the wringer on both issues, and whatever our thoughts on the degrees of each offense, we accept them both as mostly out of our control and just hope *our* favorite player isn't involved. We can handle that type of scandal; the last decade has opened our eyes.

Manny touched on a deeper, more sinister fear. We invest so much emotional capital in these games, hold them so close to our souls, that we imagine the players do the same, only more so. In the moment, we convince ourselves that our happiness, our very being, rests on every pitch. The people playing the games? Lord, they must have it so much worse; we care this much, and we're just sitting on our couch. Can you envision actually being out there?

But this is not the way athletes react in the real world. An athlete—the integral part of the actual enterprise—cannot grip the experience as tightly as we do. He is far more aware of the limitations his game puts on him. He understands that no matter how hard you try, sometimes you lose. And that a loss does not send the world careening off its axis; the oceans do not fill with blood, and fault lines do not crack. The vast majority of professional baseball players never are blessed with a championship, and no one wins one every year. They nevertheless find a way to push on.

It is one thing to understand this in a theoretical sense, but it is another thing to simply state, "If we lose, who cares? It's not the end of the world," when your team is one game away from elimination. It touched the third rail.

Deep down, in a place no one wants to visit, all baseball fans fear they care more about their team than the players do. At the end of every day, Red Sox fans are still Red Sox fans, and all that comes with that; the team is their release and escape from whatever less glamorous activity they fill the working hours with. But at the end of every day, Manny Ramirez is a millionaire, and Johnny Damon can sign with the hated Yankees and not so much as blink. This is terrifying.

Maybe we *do* care more. What Manny Ramirez said does not make him a bad person, or somehow less of a competitor; it makes him a human being who, whether his team wins or loses, will still go home afterward and sleep in a gorgeous house. Manny touched on an unspeakable truth.

Most of us would give away years of our lives to have the opportunity to play major-league baseball, and we would do it for free, if they would let us.

But we're wrong. It doesn't work that way. I'm glad I wasn't a very good baseball player. I think it makes me love baseball more.

VINCE VAUGHN is singing "Take Me Out to the Ballgame," and my ears are bleeding.

KNOWLEDGE YOU NOW HAVE

1. Your father is the reason you are fat and unathletic. Sorry.
2. The reason you have a third ear is because your father refused to wear a cup.
3. The minute you step onto the field for your first game, your father will forget he ever wrote this chapter.

BOTTOM OF
THE SEVENTH INNING

In which baseball media eats itself.

My son played in his Little League world series final, which was also his last game in the league. The teams were tied at one game apiece in the series. It was the bottom of the seventh, the other team leading 7–6, and my son was up with two outs, two men on. Being the good dad, I decided to take the pressure off him by telling him that if he should happen to get up that inning, the game would be on the line. I honestly thought that this would relax him; he smiled. First pitch swinging, Mike drove a long fly ball to deep right center field. I watched as the center fielder looked up, then turned and began running full tilt toward right center. It was not even close. The ball came down about twenty feet behind him, and my son was mobbed by his teammates between first and second. The best part came after the game, when several parents told me that if their team was to lose in a situation like that, they were glad that it was Mike who got the hit. I was more proud of those comments than I was of the hit itself. Mike is now twenty-seven, a UMass/Amherst grad, and a military intelligence officer in the Army National Guard, for whom he works full-time. He is scheduled to spend some time in Afghanistan next summer, the month after his wedding. He has continued to make me the proud father through his character and his actions, just like he did that day.

— MIKE BELL, Jr., Hyde Park, Massachusetts

VINCE VAUGHN IS IN THE BOOTH WITH THE FOX BROADCASTING crew. I cannot hear it right now, but I will later. I already know what he's saying anyway.

I do not dislike Vince Vaughn. In fact, I quite enjoy him: He's funny, charming, and a better dramatic actor than he's given credit for. (He's actually quite moving in *Return to Paradise,* a movie perhaps only I have seen.) He has been in episodes of *Doogie Howser, M.D., 21 Jump Street,* and *China Beach.* He graduated high school with fellow University of Illinois alum Dave Eggers. It's difficult to root against that guy.

But after hearing that rendition of "Take Me Out to the Ballgame," I want to take him and his Cubs jersey—with "Vaughn," on the back, *of freaking course*—I want to pull his shirt over his head and send him face-first through one of those Wrigley troughs. No offense, Vince. It's not just you, specifically. It's all of *you.*

No one remembers this now, but Harry Caray, before the Bud Man ads, before the Seventh Inning Stretch, before Will Ferrell earned a spot on *Saturday Night Live* with his impression of him, was originally a Cardinals broadcaster. For a long freaking time, actually: He helmed the microphone for the Birds from 1945 to 1969. The team eventually fired him because, according to decades of rumors (oh, if there had only been blogs in the sixties!), he was having an affair with the daughter-in-law of Auggie Busch, the Cardinals' owner. When he left the Cardinals, he was already fifty-five years old. His career was only beginning.

After brief stints with the Oakland A's and the Chicago White Sox—he, amusingly, tried to calm down the rioting crowd during Disco Demolition Night by singing his trademark "Take Me Out to the Ballgame" song; the image of him failing to soothe the thousands of furious bellbottomed White Sox fans from setting vinyl aflame is so delicious that it's a tragedy it was never captured on film—he joined the Chicago Cubs in 1981. Then he became *Harry Caray*. He was sixty-seven years old.

Let us not kid ourselves: Harry Caray, while sporadically entertaining (particularly when trying to pronounce the names of members of baseball's rapidly increasing foreign population), became wildly popular in Wrigleyville because he was an old man who drank like a young man. That Harry Caray lived to be eighty-three years old is a feat that would make Keith Richards proud, had Keith Richards not died in 1983. Caray, more than anyone else, established Wrigley Field as a place more to party and carouse than to watch a baseball game: *If the broadcaster isn't taking this seriously, then why should we? Weee!* Obviously, I'm hopelessly biased, but that Jack Buck, the lifelong Cardinals announcer known for gravity, irony, and stoic professionalism, had to share a booth with that idiot for nearly two decades makes me want to cry a lot more than Buck's 9/11 poem did. If we lived on a just planet, Caray would have been renounced for the sideshow huckster barker that he is, and they'd be building shrines to Jack Buck. But it's hard for Frank the Tank to do a hilarious caricature of Buck, a man who cared more about his listeners than his own brand.

When Caray died, the Cubs kept his tradition of singing at the seventh-inning stretch alive by having various celebrities, pseudo and otherwise, hawk whatever product they were foisting on the American public by screaming the song before chatting in the booth with the boys in the bottom half of the inning. (To be fair, Buck did this once too, though with appropriate distance and, mercifully, "Root Root Root for the *Cardinals*" enunciated clearly in the verse.) It has now turned the Cubs into the official franchise of casual fan B-list entertainers with something to promote. It secured Wrigley Field as a place to be seen.

These obviously aren't real Cubs fans. Exceptions can be made for Vaughn, I suppose, Bill Murray, and Jim Belushi, who I have to assume lives right next to the park, considering how often he's here. (He's here today too, of course. It's clinching day.) But the whole thing has careened out of control. Singers have included Mel Gibson (2000), Jay Leno (1998), Mickey Rooney (2001), Muhammad Ali (1999), Kenny Rogers (1999), Eddie Vedder (five freaking times, that guy), Bill O'Reilly (2001), former Illinois Governor Rod Blagojevich (twice), Dick Vitale (1998), and Ozzy Osbourne, who sounded like he was having a series of strokes. They all wear Cubs jerseys and make fools out of themselves and don't watch the game. You know, like everybody else at Wrigley Field.

BRIEF ASIDE: Eddie Vedder, in between stints of drinking Boone's Farm, throwing shoes at a picture of President Bush, and singing in a voice that every white male over thirty can do a dead-on impersonation of, wrote a song for this specific Cubs team. He's that excited. He's that certain it's the year. They were playing it in the car on the drive to Wrigley, and we had to slam on the brakes to make sure Mike didn't have an orgasm. (It didn't work.)

Here are the lyrics:

> *Don't let anyone say that it's just a game.*
> *For I've seen other teams and it's never the same.*
> *When you're born in Chicago, you're blessed and you're healed.*
> *First time* (every time!) *you walk into Wrigley Field.*

I'm not 100 percent sure that Kurt Cobain was a Cardinals fan, he may have shot himself to make certain he would never hear that song. He'd sure as hell never would have tried to rhyme "love" and "underdog."

————

IT IS POSSIBLE the fact that we are six outs away from a Cubs National League Central championship is making me cranky.

MY FIRST REAL JOB out of college was working at the *Sporting News* in St. Louis. (I'd lived for a year in Los Angeles, reviewing movies and avoiding the beach.) Like every sports fan over the age of thirty, I grew up addicted to the *Sporting News.* How could I not be? It was, truly, the bible of Baseball.

If I might shift into old crank mode for a moment: Kids today have no idea how good they have it. Today, if you want to know the score of last night's game—or the game's highlights, or the postgame comments from the managers and the players, or hear three highly paid former athletes "analyze" the game by telling stories about setting other players' feet on fire in the dugout, har har, har har, backslap—you can simply steer the ole laptop away from pornography for a few minutes and you have everything you need. Not only do you not have to wait for it, you don't even have to *look* for it. It's right there. It takes no time at all.

The *Sporting News* was a weekly gift handed to us from the heavens. It was theoretically a magazine, but it didn't really resemble a magazine: It came on newsprint, the writing was staid and straightforward, there were no double-page photographs, and it was full of statistics like you'd find in the paper. Actually, that was the point: It was full of *all* the statistics. Unless you lived on the West Coast, the newspaper was unreliable, incomplete, too focused on the smaller picture of the paper's particular beat. The *Sporting News* had everything: Team reports on *everybody,* all the box scores from the previous week's games, basically just a massive smorgasbord of anything a sports fan—particularly a *baseball* fan—could possibly want. *Sports*

Illustrated was around too, and that was fine, sure, if you wanted six thousand-word stories on yaks and mountain climbing, but that magazine, when you were young, mattered mostly if your team happened to be on the cover. (*Sports Illustrated* covers will remain important even if the magazine ever closes. They could just print the cover, and a certain section of the sports fan public would still buy it. Cheaper too.) The *Sporting News* was for the diehards.

It had been that way since the beginning of time. President Franklin Delano Roosevelt read the *Sporting News,* and his decision to keep baseball going during World War II was partly in response to a poll in the magazine. Families sent copies of the *Sporting News* to their sons fighting in the war. It featured prominently in all the old baseball movies and newsreels of the time, as in "Dizzy Dean, pride of the Cardinals, was featured in the *Sporting News,* and said, 'Hey, kids, stay in school!'" You know how ESPN is now the center of the sporting universe, the institution that drives every conversation? That's how the *Sporting News* used to be.

The *Sporting News* is not like that anymore. Technology attacked it from the inside. Believe me, I know: I'm their featured columnist. You want to know how dramatically the *Sporting News* has changed? Look no further. Three years ago, Bill James, who said his love for baseball was initially inspired by the magazine, was asked what he thought of the current incarnation of the *Sporting News.*

He shook his head and sighed. "There is no *Sporting News* anymore." And I wasn't even writing for them yet.

It should be stated that I love the *Sporting News.* (Actually, they dropped the "the" because definite articles are unhip, but I'm gonna keep calling it the *Sporting News* anyway, because it makes this chapter longer than it needs to be.) I loved it when I was a kid, I loved it when I worked there, logging agate text and copyediting online box scores at 1:30 A.M., and I love it now. It's different now, obviously: The box scores are gone, team reports have been cut down, and they do a lot of athlete-centric things, "what's on Chipper Jones's iPod," that sort of deal. It only comes out every two weeks, but I still devour each issue. They work their can off over there, and they put out a great product every two weeks, despite the odds. Because the odds want them to die.

No matter how good the *Sporting News* is, the majority of the sports fan population will be disappointed with it because It's Not What It Used To Be. The *Sporting News* is, from this view, a more useful publication than *Sports Illustrated* and a vastly more useful publication than *ESPN: The Magazine* (not that I don't enjoy Stuart Scott informing fans that it's rude to boo, and that if we're so upset, *we* should get out there and try it). But it doesn't matter. Time turned what made people love the *Sporting News* into something that didn't need to exist. The *Sporting News* changed for the times. But that's not enough. Brand names live to be denigrated now.

In one of my columns for the *Sporting News,* I made fun of the two New York baseball stadiums and invited *SN* readers to email me their pitches as to why their stadium was unappreciated. I would "reward" the best pitch by buying them and me a ticket to a game this year. I received some impassioned pitches for Detroit, Arlington, Philadelphia, Toronto, even Tampa. But the contest was kind of rigged: I really wanted to go to Pittsburgh.

This was for two reasons. First, I'd heard from numerous people that PNC Park was a gorgeous stadium where it was easy to procure great cheap seats because the Pirates play there. But mostly: I had slated May 12 as my travel day for the game, and the Cardinals happened to be in town that day. That's cheating, but hey: It's the Cardinals. I was primed to proclaim the first person to email me about PNC Park the "winner," but because the Pirates have no fans left, nobody sent me a thing. Then, the day before I had to make a decision, I received an email from some guy, whom we'll call "Robert." His note was not inspiring—"The reason that PNC Park is different is that it's the most beautiful stadium of any sport in the entire world and it's parking lot is located near our pre-Forbes stadium, Exposition Park"—but who cares? I had my Pittsburgh resident! I emailed him posthaste, told him he won, and asked if he could make it May 12. "I'll buy the tickets," I told him. "We can just meet there. My hotel will just be a few blocks away. I'll buy the booze too!"

I was on deadline, so I began to worry when I didn't hear back from Robert for a few hours. I kept needling him, saying I needed him to confirm so I could file my next column and buy the plane tickets. I kept offering him plenty of booze in Pittsburgh, assuming that, after all, nobody fails to act when booze is on the line. Still nothing. So I finally gave up. I chose Minnesota, because I wanted to see the Metrodome in its final season. (It wasn't worth it. Baseball in a forties airplane hangar: No, thank you.) I didn't think that much more about it.

Three days later, I received an email from a woman named "Barbara." She informed me that she was the mother of . . . Robert. Who was thirteen years old. Who had told her that "the man from the magazine" had invited him to "meet" him at the Pirates game, that his hotel was right by the stadium, that he would buy his ticket and buy him lots of booze.

"He was a bit overwhelmed by your kind invite," she said, and I really, really hoped she'd seen the magazine, the column, and the "contest." Because I had just invited her thirteen-year-old son to come meet a stranger with alcohol at a baseball game. With my hotel "just a quick walk away."

I'm pretty lucky that I gave up and booked the Minnesota tickets. Because if I had shown up at PNC Park and Chris Hansen had been there . . . I'm not sure explaining the facts of the situation would have gotten me out of it.

OUT OF ALL the emails I received for the contest, I'd say 60 percent of them were from the elderly and the adolescent. Those who never gave up their childhood fetish, and those who were never aware that they were supposed to be *disappointed* in the *Sporting News.*

Where do people get their baseball news now? The *Sporting News* ceded to ESPN, but only for a while, and not all the way. Now you procure all the baseball you want straight from the source, on tap.

RYAN FRANKLIN is pitching like someone programmed a bomb right underneath the pitching mound, and it could go off at any time. A year from now, Franklin will grow a massive goatee, the size, length, and texture of a stretched-out Slinky, but at this moment, he vaguely resembles a normal human being. And he is in a hurry.

Before Vince Vaughn has even had a moment to talk about his new movie, Franklin gets Ryan Theriot to ground out to first base on two pitches and Alfonso Soriano to send a towering, but weak, fly ball to right field on the first pitch. It takes three pitches, and the FOX fellers and Vince Vaughn have only had time for two awkward moments in the booth. Reason No. 34,329,281 not to attempt to become a professional entertainer: If you succeed, you will have to make senseless chitchat in a baseball broadcast booth for an interminable inning, and if your field of entertainment is comedy, you will be expected to Make Funny Happen every five seconds while each broadcaster looks at you, waiting. The only time this ever works is when the entertainer is intoxicated. Unfortunately, Vaughn isn't there yet. But when he finished his "song," he implored the crowd, "Let's close this out so we can clinch this and go out and hit the streets and party!"

My dad, when we return to our seats, asks me, "Who is that guy anyway?"

"He was in the dinosaur movie, Dad," I say. "The second one."

"Oh," he says. "Never saw it. Does he get eaten?"

———————

THIS IS HOW baseball is covered now.

In September 2009, I spent a full day and night at the MLB Network studios in Secaucus, New Jersey. I was there for a total of five hours. Because this was Secaucus, New Jersey, I didn't leave the building.

The minute I showed up at the studios, I was greeted by Harold Reynolds, a former ESPN analyst who is the type of person who is impossible to dislike. "Will! My man!" he brayed as I stepped into his office before an MLB Network staff meeting. "You're a lifesaver, man! I'm only here because of you!"

I'm fairly certain this wasn't true, but I suspect Harold Reynolds talks like this to everyone. He's got that Bill Clinton ability to make you feel as if you are the most special, amazing person in the room. He has the best job on Earth, and the man wants to hug the world.

The MLB Network hit the air on January 1, 2009, at 6 in the evening. This is not exactly prime baseball time, but that didn't matter. What mattered is that they were on at all. After launches of quality channels like the NFL Network and the Big Ten Network floundered because they greedily demanded cable companies charge premium rates for their niche stations, the MLB Network made it a goal to be on as many cable systems as possible. It was a page from the MLB. com playbook: If you just make as much of your product available to people as possible, the diehards will bathe in your content and the casual fans will hop in whenever they feel so inclined. You make your work available to everyone and trust your product. It is baffling to me why this was considered so revolutionary.

But it was, and the network was an instant hit. (I actually had the channel on throughout New Year's Day, even though it was just showing a countdown clock until the first programming began. As you might be able to tell if you've made it this far into this book, it would be fair to classify me as the ideal MLB Network customer.)

Unlike ESPN and FOX and other networks clamoring for the highest rating possible, at the expense of the growth of the game nationwide, the MLB Network wasn't all Yankees and Red Sox. The first regular program the channel showed was *30 Teams in 30 Days,* a preview of every baseball team with interviews, highlights, and analysis for a full hour. The MLB Network did complete previews of the Pittsburgh Pirates and the Florida Marlins. Local Pittsburgh and Miami television probably didn't do previews that long. It was a channel focused solely on growing the game.

One potential concern, particularly among outside journalists, was that the MLB Network would be a house organ for the league, a twenty-four-hour apology for baseball's faults, the company line. This is a consistent problem with the YES Network, the Yankees' cable channel, which has been on the air for seven years and has said nothing about the Yankees more negative than "Joba Chamberlain is struggling a bit tonight."

This worry seemed to have some merit—after all, how impartially can you cover a league that signs your checks?—until February 7. That was the day that *Sports Illustrated* reporter Selena Roberts scooped the planet with the news that Alex Rodriguez, the beleaguered Yankees third baseman, had tested positive for performance-enhancing drugs back in 2003. (Roberts's scoop was universally heralded when the story broke, but by the time her book about A-Rod came out that summer, the tentacled beast that is Yankees public relations had discredited her, to the point that she was being accused of "not understanding how men think and live" on national radio. It must be so hard to be a female sports reporter.) When the news hit, on a Saturday, a day that MLB Network would ordinarily just show old games and highlights shows, they broke in live to do all-day coverage. Jeff Heckelman, a public relations director for the network at the time, told me, "We knew we had to do something. We just called everyone we could find and threw whoever was around on air. It was all hands on deck." This was a story that could have been tremendously damaging to baseball's reputation—the drive-by sports media loves a juicy Baseball Can't Rid Itself Of Its Steroid Past! story—and the MLB Network grabbed it and made it theirs. Not in a denying, dissembling way either. The coverage, featuring Reynolds, *SI*'s Tom Verducci, Matt Vasgersian, and the newly hired Bob Costas, was gripping, tough, fair, and completely on point. Costas did an extended interview with Roberts that passed every journalistic smell test you could have given it. Any fear that the new station would try to paint the league in an exlusively positive light was eradicated. The breaking news coverage was the MLB Network's Hugh Grant on Leno moment. "People took us seriously after that," Heckelman said.

I sat in on a 2 P.M. meeting of MLB Network staffers planning out the evening's coverage. The network, during a typical weekday, goes on the air live at 6 P.M. and stays live until all the West Coast games are over. It features live look-ins of games, analysis, "Ballpark Cams" at half the stadiums (with all of them supposedly set to be ready for the 2010 season), and constant breaking news. It is the closest thing to a twenty-four-hour active news station in sports—ESPN always has some sort of product or personality to sell—and it is a massive endeavor. And they started it on the fly. That requires lots of day-of-game planning, and that requires lots of meetings. There's a producer who runs the meetings, but mostly, it's smart people, players like Reynolds and reporters like Verducci and Jon Heyman, talking baseball with the passion of those who care about it more than anything in the world. I know the feeling.

I watched the baseball men talk about picking the runner off first, about how to adjust to the breaking ball when you're looking fastball (and you should always look fastball), about the ridiculousness of pitchers claiming their struggles are because they're "tipping their pitches." (Al Leiter is particularly offended by this. "Jesus Christ, doesn't anyone just suck anymore?") At the end of the meeting, Billy Ripken, a network analyst and the younger brother of Cal

Ripken, came in and introduced himself to me. "Where you from?" he said. "You don't sound like a New Yorker."

I told him I was from a tiny town called Mattoon, Illinois, a town he might be familiar with. His brother is the figurehead of the Cal Ripken Youth Baseball League, and the league once had its national championship game in Mattoon.

As it turned out, Billy and Cal had spent a whole week in Mattoon. He had a few opinions. "Fuck me, dude, you grew up there? The only good thing about Mattoon is getting your ass OUT of there," he says. "That's one boring-ass hick town you've got there. No wonder you live here now."

Before I had a chance to tell him that, hey, I kind of like that boring-ass hick town, he was down the hall, askin' if anybody's got somethin' to FUCKIN' EAT! They clean him up when he's on air. He's quite good.

They all left the meeting and went out on the air and did the same thing for six hours, minus the *fucks* and the *ass*. They were having the time of their lives. There was a time when you absorbed your baseball news from the *Sporting News*. Then there was a time when it came from ESPN. Now the smart baseball fan watches the MLB Network. The advertisements and sponsorships, they bring in pure cash, funneled exclusively to Major League Baseball. The workers have discovered the means of production. They are merely selling the product. As always, there are millions of buyers. How could there not be?

MY DAD has never watched the MLB Network. It's channel 219 on Illinois Consolidated's cable system, and he can't ever find it. He still subscribes to the *Sporting News,* however. It's not his kind of magazine, though, not anymore. It's just that his son writes for it now, for some reason.

Franklin finishes off Ryan Theriot on three pitches and the inning is over, in a flash. Vince Vaughn goes away. "Should be quite the party tonight," he tells Tim McCarver.

I assume FOX is going to bring out Leo Hildebrand for the eighth. Because it's all about the baseball at Wrigley Field, as always.

KNOWLEDGE YOU NOW HAVE

1. That *Sporting News* story is why your father has to register with the local authorities every time we move.
2. Your father enjoys Vince Vaughn's acting but feels the same way about him that Republicans feel about Sean Penn. Just shut up and act, all right?
3. We're gonna get back to the main story now, promise.

TOP OF THE EIGHTH INNING

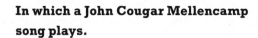

In which a John Cougar Mellencamp song plays.

As the '96 season thankfully drew to close, one in which my Tigers would finish thirty-nine games behind the Yankees, I decided to catch one last game. I thought about asking Dad to join me, but figured that he would rather not go, with the team so bad. In the third inning, I sat enjoying the sights and smells of Tiger Stadium, including the JumboTron in left field. The cameraman panned the audience and stopped on this old guy ... my dad, laughing away with two younger women at his side, neither of which was my mom, his bride of over fifty years. The camera stayed on Dad for what seemed like an eternity. They were having way too much fun! Recognizing that he was sitting in the season seats belonging to a family friend, I made my way over to his section—not sure of what I would find. What I found was Dad, who had been given six tickets, sitting next to two women whom he had met outside the stadium standing in line to buy tickets: He had given them his two extras. Sitting below him was Mom, not caught on camera. We laughed until we cried.

— TOM PIOTROWSKI, Ypsilanti, Michigan

CERTAIN CITIES IN THE UNITED STATES, EITHER BECAUSE OF GEO- graphy, history, or demographics, are safely ensconced as Baseball

Cities. It's part of the local fabric; it's ingrained in the people, in the urban planning, in the overarching psyche.

St. Louis, obviously, is one of these places. When I was living in St. Louis in 1998, logging those box scores and agate text until 2 A.M. at the *Sporting News,* the Arizona Cardinals—the team I have half-heartedly cheered for during those cold, angry months when there's no baseball—happened to be playing the St. Louis Rams at what was then the TWA Dome. The date was September 27. Both teams were 1–2 at the time, and they were both traditionally wretched. The Dome was far from full, and it was quiet and antiseptic. Domes that host bad teams are the loneliest edifices you will find.

I was ecstatic to be there, though: Growing up in Mattoon, I'd cheered for the then St. Louis Cardinals and didn't abandon them when they abandoned me for Arizona. Through years of misery, and absolutely *zero* playoff appearances, this was the first time I'd ever seen them play in person. St. Louisans who didn't stick with the team had more vitriol toward the football Cardinals—thanks to bumbling, tone-deaf owner Bill Bidwill—than they had love for the Rams . . . but all told, they had little of either. And today, they *really* weren't paying close attention.

See, that day, September 27, 1998, happened to be the last day of the St. Louis Cardinals' baseball season, just down the street at the old Busch Stadium. 1998 was no normal year for the St. Louis Cardinals and their fans: This was the Mark McGwire year. McGwire entered the game with sixty-eight home runs, just two more than Cubs rival Sammy Sosa, and their back-and-forth chase had captivated the nation and set St. Louis ablaze. Mark McGwire could have said, "You know, I'd like to turn Laclede's Landing into Caligula. From now on, everyone in the area must wear togas and have sex with the three people standing directly to their left," and the mayor would have passed an ordinance within seconds. McGwire was king in 1998. Tickets to that game at Busch were golden tickets; they were the shroud of Turin.

Meanwhile, I was down the road at the TWA Dome, able to hear a couple of fans jeering the Arizona Cardinals' coaching staff *on the opposite side of the field.* (This was before the Rams began pumping crowd noise over the loudspeakers. They do this.) The Rams-Cardinals game began at noon; first pitch of the Cardinals-Montreal Expos game (starting pitchers: Matt Morris and Mike Thurman) was at 1:15. The TWA Dome was not the cool place to be that day. There were far more noteworthy local occurrences than whether or not June Henley would lead the team in rushing yards that year. (He would, edging out the immortal Greg Hill.)

Former Illinois Fighting Illini running back Robert Holcombe scored a Rams touchdown in the first quarter, and the football Cardinals "struck back" with a Joe Nedney field goal, making the score 7–3. Then the Rams, in the second quarter, began to drive.

The Rams drove down the field, picking apart the Cardinals' defense en route to what could have been an early decisive touchdown. It was fourth down and 1, at the Cardinals' forty-yard line, and the Rams were going for it. They were trying to put their boot on the Cardinals' throat early. (Football metaphors are always so much more violent than baseball metaphors.)

Rams quarterback Tony Banks barked out the signals, hoping to draw the Cardinals' defensive line offside, and prepared to snap. Then, all of a sudden, out of nowhere, the TWA Dome exploded in a cacophony of noise. The place was silent . . . and then *WHAM,* the walls were shaking. A bomb had gone off in the Dome. It was as if someone pushed a button, and a tomb became the site of a rave.

Banks, never the calmest signal caller to begin with, freaked out: I think I saw his helmet lift up off his head and spin. He began looking around, bewildered, wondering if he'd missed something, if maybe his running back had suddenly broken into a pantless jig, if maybe a phantasm had risen from the thirty-yard line and begun dragging souls with him down to Hell. Banks pulled away from center, threw his hands up, and . . . then the whistle came. Delay of game. Five-yard penalty. No more going for it. The Rams punted. The Cardinals' throat remained blissfully unstomped.

What had happened? Mark McGwire had hit his sixty-ninth homer.

It was off Expos rookie Mike Thurman, with two outs in the bottom of the third inning. The TWA Dome fans, watching their televisions in the luxury suites and listening to their Bartman pocket radios in the rafters, were keeping far closer tabs on McGwire than they were on Banks. When McGwire's shot left Busch Stadium, they went crazy. The explosion caused Banks to lose his bearings and end up with the delay-of-game penalty. The Rams were forced to punt, and Cardinals ended up scoring fourteen straight points and securing the victory. It was a devastating loss for the Rams. The season ended up being the Cardinals' first playoff appearance in sixteen years. I couldn't have scripted it any better.

After the game, I ducked in a sports bar with a friend of mine just in time to watch McGwire hit his seventieth homer, off Carl Pavano. The place was filled with people who had just left the Rams game . . . and they were almost all wearing baseball Cardinals jerseys. And they were all cheering as if nothing bad had happened to them all day.

The baseball Cardinals and the Rams might as well play on different planets. St. Louis is a baseball town. Always has been, always will be.

THE CARDINALS clearly have their best scoring chance here in the top of the eighth, and with them still behind by only one run, one feels quietly optimistic about their hopes. It's the 2–3–4 hitters, Ryan Ludwick, Albert Pujols, and Felipe Lopez, with Big Dog Troy Glaus still lurking down there if anyone reaches base.

Unfortunately, the Cubs have brought in Carlos Marmol. Cubs manager Lou Piniella has brought in the nasty right-hander as the setup man for Kerry Wood, a pitcher who's far inferior to Marmol but is A True Cub. He once struck out twenty men in one glorious afternoon at Wrigley, still the best pitching performance I've ever seen. (And the stat folks agree with me: His Game Score, a simple sounding term that's actually quite complicated, is one of the three highest of all time. And he gave up a hit.) Since then, Wood has been the throbbing, infected heart of Cubs fandom: all broken promises, all misplaced optimism, all *woulda shoulda coulda.* The Cubs wasted three, maybe four, good years of their prime in this decade waiting for Wood and Mark Prior to finally heal from their various Dusty Baker–induced maladies. It never happened. They ultimately gave up on Prior and installed Wood as the closer, under the concept of If He Pitches Less Maybe He'll Hurt Less. He is a middling closer; Marmol's a better pitcher. But the Cubs have invested too much now. They can't let him go. Every time Kerry Wood is in the game, he's a reminder of dreams that have long since died and been replaced by the inevitable compromises of life, perfection marred by harsh light and sad truth.

This is to say: I love it when Kerry Wood is in the game.

Carlos Marmol? Not so much. Marmol is all wicked slider and nasty fastball. His Achilles' Heel, the reason the Cubs are even *bothering* with Wood in the first place, is that Marmol struggles with his control. I am not a professional baseball scout, and I only know what I've learned sitting on my arse hollering at the television screen. But it always amazes me that people who work in baseball proceed as if control—the actual process in which you throw the ball *and have some idea where it's going*—is a minor issue, something that can be ironed out, smoothed, a tiny widow's peak that just needs a dab of Botox. When a player doesn't know where the ball is going, it doesn't matter that he can throw it ninety-five miles per hour, or can horrify the gods with a ridiculous twelve-to-six curveball. If you cannot throw the ball where you want it to go, why are you pitching? Isn't that the most important part? No one seems to side with me on this. Scouts treat control like a symptom rather than an inherent attribute. It makes no sense.

I'm trying to streamline this little rant into a thirty-five-second sound bite for Dad and Mike while trying to drink a beer, the last beer of the game, as Marmol warms up and Ludwick swings in the on-deck circle. It comes out something like "Marmol's wild! Why do people not care about that? Wild is bad! Wild is thhh—[beer shoots out of my mouth as I work into a lather] Oh, shit, excuse me, sorry. Here, here's a napkin. Anyway."

Dad looks at Mike. "He's starting to look a little nervous, ain't he?" Dad is in the denial portion of mourning. He's accepted that we might lose and is trying to curry favor with Mike so that when the Cubs win the division and commence their world domination, Mike will save Dad from the salt mines and allow him to live in one of the guest houses, simply feeding Ryne Sandberg grapes while I'm forced to carry hundred-pound bags of coal up the stairs to the penthouse of Lou Piniella's luxury condo so that his furnace might have the heat necessary to run one of his fifteen Wiis. It is also possible that I'm a little delirious. It's hotter today than I thought it would be.

"He looks like he knows this is about over," Mike says, and his cockiness, his assurance, strikes me as creepy.

For three pitches, Carlos Marmol makes me look extremely smart, not that I'm saying anything anymore, lest I begin having visions of Nick Stavinoha rising above Wrigley Field like a dragon and engulfing the denizens of Harry Caray's bar in the righteous flames of Hell. (How fast did I drink that last beer, anyway?) He begins the inning by throwing three consecutive balls to Ludwick. We couldn't possibly ask for a better way to begin the top of the eighth inning than a leadoff walk to Ludwick with Pujols on deck. The rest of the Cardinals lineup is apt to swing at bad pitches from Marmol, to play right into his hands. Not Pujols. And with a runner on, Marmol won't pick around the corners either, not with a one-run lead. We just need one more ball. This whole game is ours if we can just get Ludwick to take one more ball.

Marmol takes a slight walk off the mound and takes those deep heavy-cheeked breaths all people take when they remember that they have to breathe. Tim McCarver mentions that when batters have two strikes on them against Marmol, they are 14-for-190. Good thing we're far from that. We only need one ball. Marmol hops on the rubber and does a little quick-pitch, a breaking ball (on 3–0?) that's clearly inside. Ludwick, hardly a showboat, drops his bat and jogs to first base . . . and then he is called back. The pitch is called a strike. It's a terrible call. We have gone from having our one ball to being one pitch closer to 14-for-190.

I jump up and just scream, surprising even myself. I'm a quiet baseball fan—I'm Bartman!—who mostly just sits and jots in his score book and mutters to himself and anyone unfortunate enough to be sitting next to him. But not here. I'm stunned by the call; I'm flabbergasted; I'm primed to kill whoever it takes to overcome this grievous injustice, to set the historical record straight. I'm standing up with my arms spread wide—beer in one hand, score book in the other; this will totally be my album cover, if I ever record an album— screaming as loud as I can "You've GOT to be KIDDING ME!" If you strain, you can actually hear me on the telecast.

The reason you can hear me on the telecast? I'm the only person yelling. In fact, everyone in my section, and as far as I know, everyone in the stadium, is looking at me like I just shrieked "Holy shit, you guys, BOOKS!" in the middle of a library. The game is irrelevant at this point. It is all prelude to a celebration. Am I the only one who saw this sin? This stain? This *filth*? This scalding of the great game? THAT WAS A BALL.

Dad, looking the way he does when my sister has a little too much to drink at dinner and starts getting lippy with the waiter, tugs on my Ankiel jersey sleeve.

"Easy there," he says, soothing. "Sit down."

"That was an unbelievable call," I say. "We NEEDED that pitch. That wasn't even close!"

"I know," he says, still soothing, still defusing, cutting the blue wire. "Just sit down."

I do. Two pitches later, Ludwick hits an easy loping fly ball to center field. Edmonds catches it, and there is one out. We do not have our runner. There are four outs to go. 14-for-191. Pujols walks to the batter's box, once again the only man in red on the field.

CERTAIN TOWNS are just baseball towns, and having grown up near St. Louis, I can pick them out immediately. Some towns have baseball at their center, at their core. The Patriots won multiple Super Bowls, but that was an amusing, somewhat pleasant sideshow to the Red Sox's two World Series wins, something to pay passing heed to when it's cold outside. Detroit might be crumbling as an urban epicenter, but that whole town—and of course the suburbs every white person has fled to—unites behind the Tigers like they're a talisman. San Francisco has a breathtaking stadium right on the water that attracts insular, pasty tech heads and homeless people alike. And yeah, if you're going to force me to admit it: Chicago, Bears obsession and Michael Jordan diversion aside, has baseball in the blood as well.

In other cities, baseball is a leader in exile, dormant only temporarily, biding its time until it can rise again. Team mismanagement, weak finances, and inertia have forced the game to cede the stage for a while, but when the home teams recover, as they eventually must, it will become the center of public discourse as it has so many times before. Cincinnati. Kansas City. Pittsburgh. Baltimore. Those are baseball towns. They will rise again.

And then you have New York. The Giants and Jets will always take up a sliver of the public psyche, and the Knicks will always appeal to the intelligensia envious of players' ability to stave off age and stomach weight. But this is a baseball town. This is the ultimate baseball town. The Mets, with their tortured history and colorful characters, have enough pathos and passion by themselves to take over a small planet. But the Yankees, the Yankees are the company team of a company town. They are Miller in Milwaukee, Skyline Chili in Cincinnati, General Motors in Detroit, Google in San Francisco, Warner Bros. in Los Angeles, Coca-Cola in Atlanta, Microsoft in Seattle, Coors in Denver. They are on the periphery of every conversation. Even if you don't care about baseball, even if you've never sat through a whole game, even if you hate them and love the Mets (or the Red Sox, or the Cardinals), you always know how the Yankees are doing. They're everywhere. In New York, the Yankees are smog.

When I moved to New York in January 2000, I became fascinated with the psychology of Yankees fans. They never seemed particularly concerned about losing. Like, it didn't even *occur* to them that they might lose. This makes sense, considering 2000 was the team's third consecutive World Championship, and fourth in five years. I attended the Yankees' American League pennant–clinching Game 6 victory over the Mariners at Yankee Stadium, my first trip to the Bronx, and I was struck by just how unflustered the fans were by a 4–3 seventh-inning deficit. As you might have noticed, I get a little panicky when the Cardinals are behind in a game that's ultimately meaningless to them. In a playoff game? I'm a disaster when they're *up* by five.

The postseason is so maddening, anyway. The baseball playoffs are, by nature, random occurrences. In 2007, the Boston Red Sox, the team with the best record in the game, began the season at 2–3, playing Kansas City and Texas, two of the worst teams in baseball. In April, this was hardly worthy of note, even in Boston. But a 2–3 stretch in the playoffs would be considered an epic collapse. A postseason series loss does not mean that Boston is a bad team, or even worse than Anaheim. It will just mean they lost three out of five games. It happens all the time.

If you put the Washington Nationals in the playoffs, no matter how bad they are, they'd have a legitimate chance to win the World Series, because lots of goofiness can happen in three weeks, for no specific reason other than chance. This can be dispiriting to those obsessed with the notion that the postseason is supposed to reveal the mettle of a champion; we want our winners to be winners, not random victims of circumstance. That's not how it works. Because of baseball's fickle, micro nature, every postseason game is an upset, a statistical anomaly. This fits the game itself; statistically speaking, every single base hit is against the laws of probability. That the game's ultimate prize is settled by a mad dash is in the spirit of the game we love, not against it. In the postseason, everything is bigger, and I'm not just saying that because we're subjected to extreme close-ups of pitchers' nose hair for a fortnight and a half. This expansion of importance only elevates the game. In the interminable regular season, instances of mental error and pressure-induced paralysis are forgotten and swept away by the daily tide.

In the postseason, though, it all matters desperately. It is as if the intense microscope of the playoffs expands the game to its natural size, the size it was all along. The playoffs require us to focus on each game's small moments, the tidbits that slip past us the first six months of the season but obsess us now. A championship can be decided by the game's greatest slugger stepping up on the biggest stage, or it can be decided by the tiny man who dinks a 0–2 slider in front of the charging left fielder who slips because it rained that afternoon. We have no idea and no control. We never do; October baseball reminds us of this, every night.

That's how you're *supposed* to respond to the playoffs, anyway. But not in New York. At that Mariners game, Yankees fans just smirked; their team was coming back, obviously. And they did: David Justice's three-run homer in the seventh sparked a six-run rally, and not even an eighth-inning home run by an up-and-coming short-stop named Alex Rodriguez could bring the Mariners back. The fans around me treated the victory like an honors student who had aced a test. When you're as smart as we are and you study up, of course you're going to get an A.

That was, until 2009, the last time the Yankees won the World Series. Those nine years of "failure" didn't do much to change the general mind-set. Yankees fans have to be the only fans left in sport who believe victories are some sort of birthright, a logical result rather than a pleasant happenstance result of talent, dedication, circumstance, and plain luck. If the Yankees don't win, it's not because the breaks didn't fall their way, or because their opponents might have their own talent, dedication, circumstance, and luck; it's because the Yankees failed. Part of me feels bad for Yankees fans. They can never experience that sublime joy of the underdog, the feeling that you are breaking through some unknown barrier and the elation at what might come next. One of the problems with the Yankees during the dog days of the mid aughts was that they always seemed confused that the other team refused to cede to the ghost of Mickey Mantle's liver. *Didn't they know they were playing the Yankees?*

Then they won the World Series in 2009, and all was normal in Gotham. The Yankees represent the civic character of New York, imperialism, exceptionalism, the idea that this is the only city on earth that matters, the old line that those people who don't live in New York must just be kidding around. These days, after the economic collapse, terrorism, and rampant unemployment have taken their toll, New Yorkers are all gripped by a collective fear that the good times have come and gone, and might never come back. But the New York Yankees do not operate this way. The interlocking NY stands, perhaps alone, as the last symbol of New York's self-evident, world-sanctioned superiority. The Yankees expect to be the best, period. It's tough to find anything else left in New York that holds that kind of power.

So while the rest of us tighten our belts and brace for the worst, the Yankees open a state-of-the-art, $1.6 billion stadium. While the executives at AIG are held out as venal masters of destruction and shamed into giving up their bonuses, the Yankees spend $423.5 million on three players. While the housing market tanks and nobody will buy so much as a pair of socks unless they're 75 percent off, the Yankees dish out two-and-a-half times more money in one off-season than the rest of the American League combined.

In Yankee Land, it is always 1927, and 1961, and 1998. It is not enough merely to win: The Yankees must dominate. That is the brand. If the Yankees aren't world conquerors, lording their financial and cultural superiority over the penny-pinching peons that make up the rest of baseball, then who are they? That's the New York way. It's why I both love and hate it here. It's why we all do.

MY FRIENDS here in New York all have ambitious travel traditions. Jesse spends a week every summer with his parents in Hawaii. Aileen goes to see distant relatives in Ireland. James and his kin go skiing in Aspen.

Me? Kansas City. Philadelphia. Houston. Growing up in Central Illinois, we never went to Disneyland. The Cardinals never played there.

When the Cardinals schedule came out when I was a kid, my dad would sit with a Magic Marker and circle one three-game road series. Then, come summer, my parents, sister, and I would pack into the Buick Skylark and schlep to the most storied destinations. Pittsburgh. Cincinnati. Milwaukee. Wherever the Cardinals were playing. (We'd take one road trip a season.) My mother and sister would drag us to some local curiosity during the day—the William Howard Taft Museum in Cincinnati is even duller than you'd think—and then Dad and I would drag them to the stadium at night. The deal worked out all right. Your childhood travel memories might involve staring up at the faces of Mount Rushmore or feeling the mist of Niagara Falls. Mine are in the upper deck of Riverfront Stadium, eating hot dogs while a tubby man wearing face paint screamed obscenities. Or Dad learning to hate Dave Parker in a Cincinnati hotel bar.

My parents come to visit me in New York City once a year: When the Cardinals are in town to play the Mets. I wouldn't expect them to come any other time. A trip to Citi Field is an excuse for them to come out here. They don't like New York, but they do like seeing their son. A three-game series with the Cardinals in town—that's what secures them coming out here in the first place. They can handle baseball, and New York's love of baseball is the one aspect of the city that spans the chasm between life in New York and life in Mattoon.

I live 878 miles from my parents. It's a $300 flight, round trip, to St. Louis or Indianapolis (the closest airports to Mattoon), and because the terrorists ruined everything about travel, it takes roughly seven hours door-to-door. We all have our own lives, and it's just hard. Family life is confusing as you grow older. Your parents understand your life less, and you theirs. My parents have friends and worries and hopes and troubles and daily mundane activities that I will never know or comprehend. I can't explain to them my fears about my career, about my work, and they can't explain to me whatever it is they're going through on a daily basis. (I assume it mostly involves back pain and hot flashes.) The entry fee for a deep, meaningful conversation becomes steeper every year. It's just hard.

So we have the Cardinals. They can always visit New York. I live very far away. But Citi Field is right there. And so is Busch Stadium. I can be there in seven hours. They are excuses to visit. They make us feel closer. Someday we won't be able to do that. Someday I won't be able to get there. But I can get there now.

CINCINNATI HAS taken a 3–2 lead on the Brewers, so the Cubs will need to win this game. Carlos Marmol has found his control. On a wicked 1–2 slider, he forces the great Pujols to pop out to the second baseman. Then Felipe Lopez grounds out to Derrek Lee at first base. Marmol is *nasty.* And he's in absolute control. We're three outs away. The crowd roars.

Dad says something I've been dreading he would say all day. "Well, looks like we picked a *perfect* day to get out here."

He's kidding, and he's not. And no matter what happens: He's here, and so am I. It is kind of perfect. We're in a baseball town, after all.

KNOWLEDGE YOU NOW HAVE

1. This is why you do not live in Boise or any other town more than a two-hour drive from a baseball stadium.

2. This is why when your mother made me take her to Paris, your father brought his computer with him to watch the Cardinals-Dodgers game at four-thirty in the morning.

3. Holy shit, you guys, BOOKS!

BOTTOM OF THE EIGHTH INNING

In which there is a Brooklyn roof.

All my friends were afraid of my father because he was a big guy, and my friends never heard him say a word unless he was yelling at me. I was fourteen or fifteen and my Babe Ruth team was up to the plate. I was sitting on the bench, and because there was no dugout, you could see the stands, houses, and parking lot. My father was standing leaning up against the bleachers when a teammate hit a high foul ball. The crowd on the bleachers scurried away and my father just stood there. The ball hit the top of his head: It sounded like a sledgehammer striking a concrete basement floor. The ball bounced off his head, went almost as high as it was hit, and landed in the parking lot. My father did not turn red, cry out, or rub his head. My junior year I was a catcher for my high school and broke my left finger in practice. I played the rest of the year with a painful broken finger because I wanted to be tough like my father. Dad later admitted it hurt like hell.

— PAUL SAVARD Jr., Waterford, Vermont

2009. I AM SITTING ON THE ROOF OF MY APARTMENT IN BROOK-lyn, high enough that I can overlook downtown Manhattan, the Statue of Liberty, the Verrazano Bridge, and the Brooklyn Bridge, drinking a beer with my father. It's the summer of 2009, nine months after the game at Wrigley. The Cardinals lost at Citi Field to a dreadful Mets team earlier that night, and my mother and my girlfriend are asleep downstairs. It's past midnight. I have to go to work the next day. But we're up there, drinking. It's one of those perfect summer nights that feel like fall, a slight breeze coming from the East River, and airplanes, thanks to a recent change in the LaGuardia Airport flight routes, are floating to their landing just about a thousand feet over our heads. We can watch their entire process, no longer scary, not eight years later, as they come in from the south, over Staten Island and Bay Ridge and on to Queens. I find myself staring at one plane in particular, flashing a red light on one wing and, oddly, a blue one on the other, as it glides in, seemingly motionless, until it's right on top of me. I'm lying on the ledge of our Cobble Hill apartment building, a wide enough ledge that I'm not worried about falling off, smoking a cigarette, and staring upward. Dad's sitting on the ledge next to me. Dad doesn't like that I smoke—no father would, or should—but he recognizes, as a former addict himself, that lecturing me about it isn't going to stop me from doing it. (My mother does not recognize this.) Plus, I suspect he secretly likes it. He always lets me know it's OK to smoke around him, in a way that makes me think he misses the smell, that former smokers never really overcome the desire to be at least *around* cigarettes. When my father talks about how poor he and my mother were during the early years of their marriage, he tells the story of digging through old ashtrays looking for cigarette butts that might have just a smidgen of tobacco left in them. "You could usually find one," he'll say. "Enough to get you through the next hour, anyway."

I've been living with my girlfriend for about three months, and we've been dating for about two years. I'm thirty-three years old. There aren't that many shopping days till Christmas. I've been engaged twice in my life, but never married. (One was my decision, one wasn't.) My father knows this. Which is why I'm telling him I'm going to ask my girlfriend to marry me before I'm telling anyone else. Because he won't make a big deal about it. Because it'll be the middle part of a conversation about how frustrating it was to watch Kyle Lohse pitch today, about how awful Rick Ankiel's strike zone discipline is, about how we desperately need some lineup protection for Albert Pujols, about how lucky we are the Cubs haven't gotten their act together this season, not yet.

That I'm telling him this while staring up into the sky watching planes pass over, drinking a Budweiser Select, and smoking a Marlboro Light, rather than, you know, sitting and looking him in the eye, is of course the point. Plus, it's late.

"Well, she's a great girl," he says, and she is, and he knows that, and I know that, which is why he says it. It's easy and simple and will segue into the next topic. "Congratulations." He clinks my Budweiser Select with his. I don't really like Budweiser Select. The whole thing feels like a marketing gimmick. What does "Select" mean, anyway?

I'm about to ask Dad who's pitching tomorrow—I know who it is, I always do, but it gets us talking—when he pipes up.

"You know, the thing with your generation is," he says, "you guys are a helluva lot better at marriage than you are at kids."

I perk up and lose the flight path of the blue- and red-lighted plane. I pull myself up and let my legs dangle over the ledge, facing away from the street, toward my dad. "How do you mean?" I ask, a little taken aback. This isn't about tomorrow's starting pitcher at all.

"Well, if we're gonna get into this, I'm gonna need another beer," he says. "Actually, you got any whiskey?" It's past midnight.

AFTER THAT LAST 1–2–3 inning, with the Cardinals' best three hitters awkwardly flipping their bats at the weird ninety-five-mile-per-hour Wiffle balls Carlos Marmol was whizzing in their direction, the grandstands at Wrigley Field are starting to wave in undeniable anticipation. They know this is happening. You can tell. They haven't exactly been as devoted to the action on the field as one might expect of a team trying to clinch its division—and now they've taken it to the next level. They're singing.

It is to their credit that they're not attempting to sing the tuneless Eddie Vedder ditty, though I suppose if they just started warbling and oohing inane non-syllables, it would sound somewhat similar. No, they've got an easy song to croon. They're singing "Go Cubs Go."

It is the sound of glaciers shifting, the sound of death rap-rap-rapping at your door. It is unquestionably catchy: It stores itself in the part of your brain that won't let you forget the first time a girl told you she didn't love you anymore, the time you took the live drive to the groin, the time your beloved family dog passed away. It is evil, this song: It is fucking evil.

"Jesus, what the hell is this?" Dad says.

"It's 'Go Cubs Go,'" Mike says, a smile taking over his face, his skull, his entire upper torso. "Catchy, isn't it?"

Here is "Go Cubs Go."

> *Baseball season's under way*
> *Well you better get ready for a brand-new day*
> *Hey, Chicago, what do you say*
> *The Cubs are gonna win today.*

> *They're singing . . .*
> *Go, Cubs, go*
> *Go, Cubs, go*
> *Hey, Chicago, what do you say*
> *The Cubs are gonna win today*
> *Go, Cubs, go*
> *Go, Cubs, go*
> *Hey, Chicago, what do you say*
> *The Cubs are gonna win today.*

You know the song "City of New Orleans"? You like that song, right? I like that song. Arlo Guthrie made it famous, but it was written by a man named Steve Goodman. (He also wrote the mock country song "You Never Even Call Me By My Name.") He was a bit of an underground folk hero and, as luck would have it, a die-hard Cubs fan. Goodman, who also wrote a song called "My Old Man" about his father, was born in 1948, three years after the Cubs' last World Series appearance. He died of leukemia at the age of thirty-six, in 1984, four days before the Cubs clinched the National League East to secure their first postseason appearance since that World Series. Four years later his ashes were spread at Wrigley Field. In 2007, last season, the Cubs started playing "Go Cubs Go" after every win. Steve Goodman wrote that song.

He would enjoy that. He would enjoy knowing that his fun little song, with an advertising shout-out to WGN-TV, was screamed by forty thousand people on the day they clinched the National League Central Division. *Before* they clinched it, actually. That would tickle him pink, I'm sure.

Of course, he's dead. So he never got to hear any of that, or know what he inspired. Poor guy. He should have seen it coming, though. He was a Cubs fan, after all.

The song really is catchy. It's impossible not to hum along with it. Dad appears to have the same problem. I hear him humming it next to me, and I know, because I'm in tune with him. And there's still three outs left to go. The erratic Kerry Wood is coming in. There's still a chance. But I still can't stop humming. *Hey, Chicago, whaddya say?*

I snap to when Derrek Lee hits a line drive right over our head half-way down the first-base line. We look up to see if anyone was killed.

"That get anybody?" Dad asks.

"Nope," Mike replies. "Just missed that kid in the Soriano jersey."

"Dammit."

IN 1998, I lived in Los Angeles but flew into St. Louis to do an interview for the *Sporting News*. It was the weekend that Mike Piazza had been traded to the Florida Marlins from the Dodgers, and the Cardinals were to play the Marlins that night. Dad picked me up from the airport, where he gawked at a confused-looking Mr. Piazza himself ("I play for the Marlins?") and headed to the ballpark, for beers and batting practice. It was the first time I'd actually seen Mark McGwire in a Cardinals jersey. I'd never seen anyone hit a baseball like that before, just moon shots, blasting into and through the ether. We drank and marveled. They used to run McGwire's batting practice live on local cable newscasts. 1998 was a crazy time.

We spent the evening drinking, drinking, drinking, downing $5 beers, one after another. I was twenty-two. This was exciting; I hadn't seen my father since Christmas. The conversation veered in odd directions. We talked about women he'd dated before Mom, about how weird one of my uncles was, about how Dad always thought that one girl, what was her name, the older one I dated, was pretty damned attractive, why didn't I stay with her? I never knew Dad had noticed anyone I dated.

McGwire stepped to the plate. He was facing Livan Hernandez, one of the lone survivors of the Marlins' binge-and-purge of their World Series champions from the season before. I think Dad and I were talking about how you have to double down when you've got eleven and the dealer's showing sixteen, when McGwire hit a fly ball to center field.

We leapt up to see if the ball could sneak over the center-field fence. Dad started yelling, "Get! Get! Get!"—he stole that line from Cardinals broadcaster Mike Shannon, who drunkenly wails that every pop-up, when a ball looks like it might make it over the fence but he isn't sure. The ball landed in the grass area just beyond the wall, and we cheered. "Whew, that one just barely made it!" I exclaimed. "Yeah, that was close," Dad replied.

We had just ordered another beer when a graphic flashed on the JumboTron. "MARK MCGWIRE'S HOME RUN WAS MEASURED AT 545 FEET, THE LONGEST OF HIS CAREER." It was true. The ball hadn't just slipped over the wall; it had bashed against the *St. Louis Post-Dispatch* sign that hung under the upper deck, then fallen into the grass below. You might have heard of this home run; the Cardinals immortalized it by placing an enormous Band-Aid over the sign to make it clear just how far the ball had traveled. McGwire later said, "I don't think I can hit one any better than that."

My father and I had seen one of the longest home runs in the history of baseball; we were just too drunk to notice. It happens.

I COME BACK up to the roof with two Captain Morgan and Diet Cokes, one for each of us. Rum mixed with a carbonated beverage seems like the right call here, rather than whiskey. Anything that hard will knock us both off the roof, and, frankly, we could use the caffeine.

"Sorry, I don't have any limes," I say as I hand Dad the drink. "So . . . what were you saying?"

Dad takes a big swig. He only started drinking hard alcohol in the last few years, probably because my mother, after her cancer went into remission, caught a health kick and is now in better shape than any other member of the family has ever been in their entire lives. Mom has taken to showing off her six-pack abs. This is disturbing to me, and I can't imagine that Dad, with his hard-earned, rock-solid beer gut, is enraptured by it either. Sometimes you just hit the point where you say, "You know, fuck it, I'm getting fat, I have the right." Mom has deprived him of this right. Hard alcohol keeps the gut in check and allows you to go to bed earlier. Theoretically, anyway. It's approaching 1 A.M., and Dad's belly button is still arriving to appointments twenty minutes before he does.

"You know, your mom only agreed to marry me because I had a nice bike and looked nice in my uniform."

One bitter cold February 1970 evening in Mattoon, Illinois, young Sally Dooley, eighteen, was beckoned from her quiet room by Kathy, her roommate and best friend. "That asshole Bryan isn't here yet. He's an hour late. I'm sick of waiting on him. He's probably drunk again."

Sally, a somewhat sheepish yet wild-if-provoked bookworm, rarely went out on dates. She'd met a few guys in Moweaqua, her home-town, a village of two thousand just outside Decatur and about an hour from Mattoon, but they were pretty much going nowhere, happy just to cruise around, drink beer, and try to get in girls' pants, and all three recklessly. It was a time of displacement for Sally; living with her brother Ron and Kathy, geographically too far removed from hippie rebellion, she simply wanted to go to college, studying whatever— today's choice was physical education—and find some sense of order in everything. As for guys, well, all she really knew was that she wanted to date a guy with a nice bike. That was key. But she was in no hurry.

Kathy was still screaming in her ear. "Goddamn him, Sally! He thinks he's so tough, with his motorcycle, but I'm sick of it. To hell with this. I'm going out. If he ends up showing up, tell him to buzz off and not to come by anymore. I don't like riding on that bike anyway. It just messes up my hair."

And so Kathy bolted, and Bryan showed up about a half hour later, can of Busch at his side, stoic atop his Triumph cycle, and Sally was waiting there, steeling herself to deliver the bad news. And thus was love born.

In my parents' old scrapbook, full of wedding photos and ran-dom candid shots from their courtship, there is a clipping from the *Mattoon Journal-Gazette*. It's in the Notices section, presumably copied down straight from the police report.

ARRESTED

Sylvia K. Dooley, 19, Mattoon, illegal transportation of
alcohol, underage consumption. William B. Leitch, 21,
Mattoon, illegal transportation of alcohol.

Bryan and Sally hit it off splendidly, drinking together and finding that their backgrounds were more similar than they had anticipated. Bryan was the roughneck, the guy always with his head stuck under the hood of a '57 Chevy, sneaking smokes and skipping out on every class except shop. Sally had been the smart one, enjoying only the occasional flirtation with The Other Half. But both had come from large families and both wanted to have fun while they could, before adulthood reared its nasty head.

The main difference: Bryan was going to escape Mattoon soon. With a few of his buddies from shop, he had enlisted in the air force. He was facing boot camp in about three months. This was during the Vietnam War, of course, and even though the big cities had been suffering through those dreadful protestors for a couple of years now, Mattoon had the same mind-set it had through all the other wars. You signed up and served your country, the way that you were supposed to, the way your father and his father and his father had. In the Leitch family household, the first thing Bryan saw when he woke up in the morning was the picture of his father in uniform, strong, firm, proud. For a guy with no designs on college and no real problems with the war, nothing he could tell so far anyway, waiting around for your draft card was not even a possibility. You enlisted, because that was what you did.

Boot camp approached. It had only been three months; was that enough time? To figure out if this was your life mate? Sure, they had fun together, and she sure was funny after a few cans of Pabst, but who knew what would happen in the service? What if he ended up going to Vietnam? Could he handle having her back in Mattoon, studying at Lake Land College, while he looked real life right in the face? She had come along at the wrong time. Maybe he would not have enlisted—his draft card number had indeed been low—had he known she would show up. But she had. So three months into their budding relationship, a week before he headed to Lackland Air Force Base in Texas, before life started getting weird, Bryan broke up with Sally. She handled the news well enough; it would be easier anyway, with him halfway across the country, perhaps someday halfway across the world. As nice a guy as he seemed to be, as sharp as he looked in his uniform, as bitchin' a motorcycle as he might have, he was hardly the safest horse to bet on. So they parted ways.

Sally received the first letter about two weeks after he was gone. As always, Bryan was reserved in his words. The letter was bland in form, mainly just a here's-what's-going-on, my-hair's-a-lot-shorter, have-an-asshole-drill-sergeant type of thing. It was the end of the letter that caught Sally's attention. In Bryan's scrawled, broken English was the sentence *Sally, when I get back, I think we should talk.*

For whatever reason—perhaps the close quarters with a bunch of men—Bryan couldn't get Sally off his mind. The letters started coming weekly after that, through the six weeks of boot camp and the sixteen weeks following in Wichita Falls, Texas, for basic training. By way of his expertise in mechanics, Bryan was dispatched to flight maintenance and would not be going to Vietnam. He was needed here, working on planes, an under-the-hood troubleshooter. During the sixteen weeks in Wichita Falls—when I asked him about the training, my father instinctively recited, "43151C, Flight Maintenance," like he had done so many times before, though likely not for about thirty years— the letters became more and more frequent. By now, Bryan and Sally were talking on the phone whenever they had the opportunity.

After maintenance training, he was to be stationed in Hampton, Virginia, at an air force base there, and the idea hit Bryan in a flash. As luck would have it, a fellow private at Hampton lived in Effingham, a city about twenty miles from Illinois. In March 1971, about three months after he'd arrived there, he propositioned the pal. "Hey, whaddya doing this weekend? Wanna go home for a few hours?" The drive was about fourteen hours. They would have a total of about ten hours in Mattoon, not alloting for sleep. He surprised Sally, waking her, and handed her an engagement ring. It was the same ring his mother had received from his father. Sally said yes. I do not want to know what they did with the other eight hours. They planned a wedding date in June, a mere two months after the engagement and after spending a total of two weeks together since they had broken up a year earlier. Bryan siphoned off a couple weeks of leave from the base, and they came back to Mattoon and were married. For their honeymoon, they headed to Effingham and spent a night at the Best Western Inn. Then it was off to Virginia. Mom was twenty years old. Dad was twenty-two.

"All I was was a crew cut and a uniform," Dad says, finishing the rest of his Captain Morgan and Diet Coke. Time for another one. "I didn't even have the bike anymore."

IN MATTOON, there are six houses built by my grandfather and two built by my father. (There's another one Dad and his brothers built in Moweaqua.) I remember being four years old, while Mom was pregnant with my sister, and sitting in a folding chair on the newly poured foundation, watching a tiny black-and-white television while my father hammered and sawed his way to the home where I'd spend the next fourteen years of my life. By 2000, when I'd moved to Los Angeles and my sister was heading off to college, Dad decided to build another one, this one just for him and Mom. It would have a massive kitchen, four bathrooms, two garages, and a basement with a huge television, a bar, a jukebox, a pinball machine, and endless Cardinals paraphernalia. It was Dad's last major project. "I figure I'll die in that house," he said when he was building it, and four years later, his mother-in-law, my grandmother, did. Like the other houses, like the ones my grandfather built, like that house he built while I picked my nose and chased moths in my underwear (the house just two houses down from the second one he built), it'll last forever. There's a house there that didn't exist until my dad built it. He drew up the plans, picked the materials, dug the foundation, poured the concrete, hammered the nails, laid the carpeting, installed the wiring, put in the plumbing, insulated the walls. There's a house that stands because my dad constructed it for his family. In fact, there are two of them.

MIKE SPENDS MOST of Aramis Ramirez's six-pitch at bat screaming into his phone.

"They're WINNING! Yes, they're AHEAD! The CUBS!" Everyone around him is hollering; the buzz isn't just overpowering, it's futzing with his phone. The bad connection and loco vibes are turning a simple phone call into something impossible. And that's *before* Mike tries to talk to his three-year-old.

"The CUBBIES! Yes, Jackson, the CUBBIES! That's right, the blue team. We're winning. We're gonna win the division. Daddy will be home a little later, because we'll be celebrating. The blue team won. The CUBBIES, Jackson, the CUBBIES!" I finally tire of Mike's impossible task and grab the phone from him.

"Hey, Jackson!" I yell. "The happy chickens are dancing! There's a folder with a butterfly and thirty-six daffodils. My left patella has been eaten by a Turkish fifty-cent coin. CUBBIES!" I then hang up.

"Thanks," Mike says. "I have no idea why Joan put me on the phone with him."

I wonder, if the Cubs never do anything again, if this game, this National League Central Division Championship, turns out to be the lone highlight of young Jackson's Cubs fandom, if he has a Steve Goodman life, the one season of mirth happening too young for him to understand, 2008 being the one year everyone hangs onto as they go through decades in the wilderness, the story Mike tells his son as the Cubs finish in last place every year, *Honest, Jackson, one year they won the division by beating the Cardinals and I was there with Uncle Will and his dad*, and little Jackson Cetera can't believe it, because the Cubs are always so *awful,* Go Cubs Go, Go Cubs Go, hey, Chicago, whaddya say . . .

Aramis Ramirez strikes out, and Ryan Franklin has set down five in a row. This isn't over yet. It isn't. *It isn't.*

ANOTHER DRINK. Nearly 2 A.M. Fewer planes now. Dad speaks.

You see, your mom didn't know me at all. She was just lucky. I could have been a terrible person. I could have gone to Vietnam and come back all fucked up. I could have not given a shit about being a husband, or a father. I could have been molested as a kid. I could have been a secret serial killer. I could have been one of those guys who cheated on her forever. I could have not realized I was a fag. I could have been anything. She had no idea. She just liked the car and the uniform. She was twenty years old. She didn't know me at all.

She was just lucky, you see. And so was I. We got married so young because that's what you were supposed to do, that's what my parents did, that's what everyone else did. Sure, we loved each other, as much as we could possibly understand what that was. But we had no idea. We had no idea what thirty-five years of marriage would be like, what kind of parents we'd be, what the real world was like. I turned out to be a hardworking guy, the type of guy who worked his ass off no matter what, someone who didn't have much more of a desire to do much other than raise a family and be a good husband. You wanted to write, you wanted to see the world, you wanted to go do whatever it is that you do, and that's great, you had to go, you had to do that. I didn't want to do that. I just wanted a house and some kids and a wife. But your mom didn't know that. As far as she knew, I was gonna bail in five years the first time I saw some lady in a low-cut dress or a crotch-high skirt. Maybe I wanted to go find myself. Maybe I wanted to do something other than raise a family. I didn't. That was enough for me. But when I was twenty-two, and your mom was twenty, she didn't know any of that. And neither did I.

All your friends, all those ones whose parents are divorced, like your girl's, they were just like us. They didn't know the other person for shit. That's why that happened. They didn't take the time to figure out what was gonna happen, with either one of them. They just got married because that's what you were supposed to do. Which is fine: Ain't nothing wrong with marriage. But people realized early on that, damn, this marriage shit is hard. *You gotta be in the right mind-set for that. You gotta know what you're doing. You gotta know that this is* exactly *what you want, that you've looked around and thought and experienced and bled and shit and fucked and everything else, and this is the place you were eventually going, this is what you want, this is what you were looking for all that time. You have to know that. Because marriage is the start of something, sure, but for a lot of people, they see it as the end. They don't think they see it that way, but they do, they absolutely do, and sometimes that's a good thing and sometimes it ain't. If you've never done nothin' with your life, and you go into a marriage thinking it's the end of something, then you start thinking that you ended up doing nothing at all, that you're trapped, that it's all over, that you went and got yourself stuck in something before you realized what was going on. That's what people did. That's why they all got divorced. They got married before they knew anything about the other person, but most important, they got married before they knew anything about themselves. For God's sake, I was an idiot at twenty-two. So were you. So's everybody. What business do we have making decisions at twenty-two that affect the rest of our lives? We don't. We don't know a goddamned thing. So people like your friends' parents, they hit the reset button, they started over, they quit. Maybe they ended up happy, and maybe they didn't. But they tried to make a smarter decision, a more mature decision. They probably didn't pull that off very often. But they tried.*

They thought they knew themselves better. They thought they could get it right this time.

Me and your mom, we were just so goddamned lucky. Sure, she wants to stab me in the eye half the time, and sometimes I want to wrap her head in duct tape just so she'll shut up for a goddamned second. But we wanted the same things. We wanted to be good people with good kids, and we both valued work and family and didn't think that we were some special snowflake. We thought if something hurt or sucked, you could rub some dirt on it, walk it off, move on with your life. Your mom and me, if we'd have known what each other would be like when we were fifty-five, back when we were twenty-two, we, man, we would have been scared shitless. We didn't know anything back then. We would have been so wrong. We didn't know what we wanted. We were just lucky.

But we had you guys, you and your sister. We didn't always agree on the best way to raise you. You were easier, you were quieter, it wasn't so hard to push you around and make you do what the hell we wanted you to; your sister's more hardheaded, she's louder, she's a goddamned steamroller, 'swhat she is. We didn't realize that for a while. But we figured it out. We did some stupid shit, we made some mistakes, but we loved you guys and understood that no matter what happened with us, no matter whether everything turned out the way we thought it was going to, we had you guys, we had these two amazing kids, these two other human beings, that we created, *and you're so different from us and so exactly the fucking same, and just being able to watch you grow up, being able to be there for it, to be able to sit up here and get shitfaced with you, it's an honor, it's a goddamned honor. You'll remember this. You won't remember that girl who screwed you over, you won't remember that girl you screwed over, you won't remember your first job or your first piece in a newspaper or the first time you got stoned. But you'll remember this. This is what matters. We get to do this.*

And see, Will, this is what you should be worried about. This is the downside to the way you, and the rest of your generation, does it. You took your time. You figured your shit out. You gave yourself time to fuck up, to let yourself struggle in your career, to be an asshole to women and let them be an asshole to you, to write for no money, to answer phones, to make minimum wage, to try shit out and devote yourself to what you do, to understand what kind of person you are, what you want, what you don't want, what matters to you, what don't mean shit. You took your time. That was smart. That woman down there, that woman you're going to marry, you'd have never gotten her when you were twenty-two. You would have fumbled it, or she would, or both of you would have. Each of you now knows the other, and yourselves, well enough to understand what matters, what each of you wants, just how lucky you are to have found each other. You value it. I guarantee you there are going to be fewer divorces now because people are taking so much time. You're doing it right. You did it right. You found the right girl, and she found the right guy.

But I don't know if you're going to be able to do this. By the time you have a kid, you're gonna be thirty-five, thirty-six, thirty-seven years old. When your son or daughter is the age you are now, thirty-three, you're going to be nearly seventy years old. I can tell you this: There ain't no goddamned way I'm gonna be up here drinking rum and Cokes with you til two in the morning when I'm seventy years old. I won't even live that long. Getting married so young, even if I had no idea what I was doing, allowed this to happen. It gave me the opportunity to watch you and your sister not only grow up, but turn into actual adults. And to live with you the way that you live. I don't understand New York, or what the hell she's doing out in San Francisco, but I can get glimpses of it, I can see that it makes you happy, I can drink with you and go to ball games and stay up late and talk about all of it. We weren't doing this fifteen years ago. We're doing it now. We're lucky. We're fucking lucky. We're all so fucking lucky.

But I don't know if you can do this. I think this is your trade-off.
This is what I'm saying. You guys are getting marriage right. But we
got kids right. You guys are sticking test tubes in your ass and taking
goat genes so you can have babies when you're forty, and you end
up with messed up Octomom shit. You made the right decisions for
you. But there ain't much time left. And someday you're gonna be tak-
ing your walker across the street, or your motorized Segway or your
rocket packs or whatever the hell you'll have then, and you'll look at
your thirty-three-year-old kid and you'll wish that you were able to
do this. I'm not saying there's anything wrong with it. There isn't.
Which is more important? Which matters more? I think you're going
to be a hell of a dad . . . but I have ten years on you, at least. That we
get to do this while you're an adult, that we can sit up here and drink
and second-guess La Russa and watch planes, that's a direct result
of me and your mom being lucky idiots when we were twenty years
old. You made your own luck. That's great. But I fear you'll pay for it
down the line. Life's just too short, that's all it is. You only have so
much time. You can't fit it all in. You just have to be as lucky as me
and your mom. I'm blessed to have you and your sister and your
mom, and I can't believe it, I musta been a goddamned nun in a
former life or something. Every dad wants his kid to have a better life
than he did. And I fear you won't. I fear you won't. And you deserve
one. And so does your kid. If you ever have one.

And you better have one. Because I ain't gonna be here forever.
I'd like to meet him. Or her. Clock's tickin', bucko.

OK, it's about bedtime for Bonzo. Big game tomorrow. Wain-
wright's pitching.

I drain my glass. This is not exactly how the conversation went.

JIM EDMONDS grounds out to Felipe Lopez at second base, and hey,
Ryan Franklin looked pretty solid out there today. Not that anyone

cares right now. Three outs to go. Kerry Wood coming in. Troy Glaus, Adam Kennedy, and Skip Schumaker coming to the plate. The crowd is roaring. Mike is bobbing up and down again. Dad stands up and watches Albert Pujols jog into the dugout.

"You know, this really is a nice ballpark," he says.

Three more outs. One last chance. One last chance to get this right.

THE NEXT MORNING, hungover and blurry, Dad and I walked to the hardware store just down the street in Brooklyn. I'd bought a new television, coinciding with my parents' visit, so Dad could help me install it. And by that, I mean "Dad does the work and I hand him tools." It's always been like that. It doesn't bother either of us, not anymore.

Dad needed a ratchet, or a socket, or something, I don't know. As we walked into the Ace store, I saw a picture of a middle-aged Puerto Rican man wearing a Mets ball cap, sitting at a workbench, surprised by the person taking the photo, not smiling but not annoyed, just in the middle of something. *Hi honey, you know I don't like having my picture taken but OK, go ahead, how's your mom, is dinner ready?* Beneath the picture was a caption: "PAPA 1932–2001."

Behind the desk was a man, maybe forty-five or something, who spoke no English and looked an awful lot like the Papa in the photo. Dad walked up to him and said, "Ratchet?" The guy nodded and walked to the back of the store, with Dad in tow. I didn't follow. I just watched them back there, picking up tools, showing them to each other, nodding more, smiling, communicating in that Dad language that only those who have spent a lifetime doing manual labor, building things, fixing things, can understand. We paid the man and Dad shook his hand. *"Gracias,"* my dad said, and I damned near lost it right there.

TOP OF THE NINTH INNING

In which the game comes to an end.

My favorite baseball memory actually comes from my early twenties. I played on a recreational baseball (not slo-pitch) team in a fairly competitive league, and one season we traveled to a tournament in Bracebridge, Ontario. It happened to fall on the weekend of my undergraduate convocation, so my family decided to come up to the tournament with me after the ceremony. On the first day I hit and fielded well, but my team was blown out three times. All my dad could say was "Good games out there." The next day we were hanging around before the final game watching one of my teammates make disgusting remarks about women sitting within earshot. The women were clearly upset and moved further away. My dad looked at me with a wry smile and said, "Interesting people you play with." The final game was yet another blowout loss, our only run coming when I doubled, stole third, then stole home by leaping over the catcher as I wasn't fast enough to beat the pitch. I was pretty disheartened after two days of abysmal team baseball. Why was I playing on such a lousy team? Why was I paying to be part of a team that couldn't win a game? Could I personally have done more? As I left the field, my dad looked at me and asked, "Did you have fun out there today?" I stopped for a second and thought about it. My team was terrible, but I still loved baseball. After so many

years of playing, my dad reminded me that baseball is about
escaping the seriousness of life and having fun for a couple of
hours in the sun. I answered "Yes."

— PETER SNOW, Hamilton, Ontario

THERE IS NOT A SINGLE PERSON AT WRIGLEY FIELD SITTING
down. I assume that this has always been the case, people standing
up and rejoicing when their team is about to achieve something historic and lasting, but the actual notion of getting up from your seat
and roaring in anticipation of a pitch is a relatively new phenome-
non. In 2009, while attending an American League Division Series
game between the New York Yankees and the Minnesota Twins, I
was sitting next to Steve Wulf, editor of *ESPN: The Magazine,* one of
the inventors of Rotisserie Baseball, and one of the smartest baseball people I have ever known. (In junior high, I read his book, with
Daniel Okrent, *Baseball Anecdotes,* which is just a compendium of
old baseball stories, about eighty-five times in a week.)

Wulf told me that people never used to value open discourse at
baseball games, the standing up and whooping during a third strike,
until the days of Dwight Gooden.

"People didn't care about the strikeout," he said. "When Gooden
took baseball by storm in the mid-eighties, it suddenly became more
dominant, more imposing, more impressive to strike a guy out. So
people began yelling for strikeouts and making those 'Ks' on the
scoreboard. Gooden started that. Now everybody does it." Considering at the time he said this, Brian Bruney had two strikes on Jason
Kubel, an immortal batter-pitcher matchup if I've ever seen one,
I have no doubt he is right. I hate the strikeout. The Cardinals never
have big strikeout pitchers. They're three double plays, pitch to contact, and a cloud of dust.

We don't even have three strikes right now. Kerry Wood is
merely throwing his warm-up pitches, and everyone is up and en-

gorged. They applauded when Jim Edmonds made the last out of the eighth and never took their seat again. This leads to a vexing situation for my father and me. If we were at Busch Stadium, and the Cardinals were down by one run heading into their last at bat, we'd be up too, trying to fire ourselves up, optimistic and fevered about a late-inning rally we would intellectually know probably wasn't going to happen but visualize nevertheless. But here, we should be sitting. Here, we're just the sad souls on the wrong side of history. We stand anyway. "My legs are gettin' tight," Dad says, as an excuse, though I'm sure they are. That man has worked on his feet for forty years. The fact that I sit and type for my profession has never quite made sense to him. I don't think he considers it Work. I am loath to disagree with him.

Mike is having no such issue. I'm not sure he even notices we are here.

Standing next to us is the man with the Cubs T-shirt and a (blue) Cardinals hat. I have been trying to ignore him for hours. Dad is too damn friendly, and the man strains to make eye contact with him. Dad finally sighs and acquiesces.

"This is exciting, isn't it? It's really something to see, you know?" he snivels, the sniveling little sniveler. "You don't get to see this every day, you know? To be here at a big moment like this? It's exciting. It really is. Even you guys have to appreciate it, right? How could you not?"

"Sure," Dad says. "Sure we do." He then turns and hand-mimes masturbation. "*Pffffft!*" he says, his face hilariously distorted. *This fuckin' guy.*

ON MY TWENTY-FIRST BIRTHDAY, October 10, 1996, I watched Cardinals third baseman Gary Gaetti hit a grand slam off Braves pitcher Greg Maddux in Game 5 of the National League Championship Series. My friends from the *Daily Illini* (including Mike) and I had just shown up at the bar, and there were already six shots in front of me. Two of them were Prairie Fires (a mixture of tequila and Tabasco sauce), two of them were something called a Three Wise Men (one-third Jack Daniel's, one-third Jose Cuervo, one-third Johnnie Walker), and the last was a thin test tube of Southern Comfort. Mike called that one my "chaser."

When Gaetti hit the grand slam, I leapt up and knocked all six of them over, to the groans of my colleagues, most of whom were from the Chicago suburbs and thus pretending to be Cubs fans. With the win—a win they ultimately achieved—the Cards would go up 3–1 in the NLCS, a seemingly insurmountable lead. But the homer by Gaetti, an alumnus of Mattoon's own Lake Land College, a man with a mullet (which I'd had two years earlier) and beer gut who was the most popular professional athlete fifty miles south of Champaign on I-57, sent me to the pay phone of the White Horse, the bar right across the street from the college newspaper's office. We didn't have cellphones back then. But I had to call Dad. Collect, of course. I *was* in college.

Dad accepted the charges. "Holy shit!" he said. "They may win this damned thing!" (The Cardinals were heavy underdogs to the Braves, who ultimately went on to lose the 1996 World Series to the Yankees and rookie Derek Jeter.)

"It's unbelievable," I said. "Gaetti! Lake Land!"

"Hey, happy birthday, by the way," Dad said. Dad notoriously forgets my birthday. So unpredictable, so indulgent, those birthdays. "Where are you at, anyway?"

I paused. Even though I'd drunk with my father a few times by this point, I wasn't particularly eager to tell him that about fifteen evil-minded college journalists were lining up to pour poison down my throat. "Uh . . ."

"Oh, you're at the bar, right?" he said. "Well, don't do anything stupid." Now he paused. "Hell, do something stupid. Cardinals are gonna win on your birthday. Go crazy, folks, go crazy." He cackled.

A friend beckoned me back to the bar. I heard Mom in the background of the phone line. *Bryan, is he drinking? Here, give me the phone. I take care of college kids at the hospital all the time and we have to pump their stomachs. Here, lemme talk to him.*

"Have a good time," Dad said. "Go Birds." *Click.*

I don't remember anything after that. I'm told I did twenty-one-and-a-half shots in two hours. That last half shot, according to Mike, was one of the spilled ones I sucked off the table.

At 8 the next morning, my college apartment's phone rang. It was my mom. She started to say something, something I would have never heard through the jackhammers, but Dad took the phone. "I got tickets to the World Series, if we make it," he said. "You don't have class that day, do you? Sally, dammit, get out of here."

That World Series never did happen. Well, it did, but not for another decade. There were fewer shots that time. It was a lot more fun, though.

THE 2006 Cardinals World Series might have put me on a terrorist watch list.

After Brandon Inge struck out on yet another Adam Wainwright Bugs Bunny curveball—it was the same curveball that nailed Carlos Beltran in the NLCS, a pitch so debilitating that it inspired a commenter of Deadspin to say, "Beltran didn't realize he was hitting. He just thought he was trying to avoid detection by a *Tyrannosaurus rex*"—after we screamed and screamed and danced and screamed, after the mystery man took the picture of my parents and me, after I randomly started chest-bumping people I ran into in the Busch Stadium concourse, we finally, around the time security realized it was time for these red-clad lunatics to leave the park at last, left the park.

The scene around Busch Stadium was what it would look like after a zombie apocalypse if all the zombies were actually puppies who exhaled nitrous. It was unabashed chaos, the landscape littered with googly-eyed Midwesterners running into walls, lying around the ground kicking their feet in the air, climbing the Stan Musial statue outside, taking off their shirts and waving them in the air, as if beckoning for a rescue they hoped never actually came. For some reason, I keep thinking of this kid:

That's something you would only do to your child only if you were in the midst of gleefully idiotic revelry, the ecstasy of brainlessness. I'm not even sure what that paper there is made of. Do they still have carbon paper? Was that bobblehead packaging? *The Cardinals just won the World Series! Holy shit! Here, give me something to write it down on, so we can assure the fact that it happened. And let's make it into a hat! Here you go, Joey! It's a hat! Look at Joey, dear! He has a hat! Waaaaaahhhhhhhhh!!!!!!!*

At one point, I looked over at my mom, who has spent enough years tolerating my father's and my obsession with the Cardinals that she has made it her own. She started laughing, giggling, really, and said, with a lopsided, schoolgirl smile, "Let's race!" We started running, nowhere in particular, not even parallel to one another, just *somewhere.* Everyone felt like running.

The three of us—Dad had been awfully quiet, just a big dumb doofy grin on his face, the look of a fourteen-year-old who has just seen his first pair of live breasts—were high-fiving everyone we could find. The whole crowd looked dangerously close to a spontaneous mass orgy. A big happy bomb had gone off. I glanced back to the Stan Musial statue, where a St. Louis police officer was gently, affably coaxing down five gentlemen hanging off various The Man appendages. One dove down and landed in the cop's arms. The cop picked him up and spun him around, and then they hugged. There was no law. It was a glee riot.

Once we calmed down enough to be able to speak in complete sentences, Dad, in his first words since Inge struck out, said, "Beer. Let's go grab a beer. I need to sit down." This was not going to be a simple endeavor. Those who weren't able to secure a ticket had been in various downtown bars since the beginning of the game, and they seemed to be running laps around all those exiting the stadium and then heading back to their safe home table bases. Every bar was packed with hollering people, and they weren't going anywhere. And then word began to circulate among the crowd. All the bars in the area, Paddy-O's, Hrabosky's, they'd all, every single one of them, run out of beer. This would have been thought impossible. St. Louis? Home of Budweiser? With a stadium named after Busch? *Out of beer?* This was like learning that Los Angeles had run out of convertibles, or that San Francisco had run out of people handing you pamphlets. The city of St. Louis had become dry. And no one even cared. No one was even mad.

We flittered around, doing our own zombie walk now, two hours after the game, exhausted and freezing but shuffling about hypnotized anyway, barely even talking anymore, just limply raising our hands when yet another fan went to slap them. (My hands were actually beet red the next morning, and I'd been wearing gloves.) Where to go next? All the hotels downtown had been booked up by out-of-town media, and my parents had rented a hotel in Collinsville, Illinois, about half an hour's drive away, not counting the traffic clusterphooey awaiting anyone who dared try to make it over any of the Mississippi River bridges. We needed someplace to sit down.

Then we ran into my friend Brian, his wife, and an old mutual friend of ours. They hadn't been at the game, but when it became clear that the Cardinals might just do this tonight, they drove down to the ballpark to be a part of it all. I like Brian, but I've never had the urge to hug him, but I think I darned near buggered him right then and there. Brian and I used to work together in St. Louis, and he's one of those friends whose company you don't realize you enjoy all that much until he's not around. He said he knew a bar down the street that was quiet and unheralded. We could all duck in and drink until we figured out our next move. For now, our next move would be drinking.

The bar was sparsely populated, but it certainly wasn't quiet. And they had beer. The six of us sat and talked about every inning of the game, the key moments, Chris Duncan's crazy errors in right field, how terrified we were when Sean Casey homered for the Tigers, how the ninth inning was tighter than it probably seemed to people at home. At home, they were putting on their jackets and readying to hit the streets.

My parents are in their sixties now, and the clock neared 2 A.M. It was time for them to head home. I'd been staying with them all week, for the whole World Series, but now it was time to go back to New York, go back to my life. I'd bought a one-way plane ticket home, not knowing when the series would end. Mom was yawning. Even Dad was starting to waver. It was time to go home. Dad came over and just put his hands in the air and unleashed a "Heeeeeyyyyyyy!" and Mom even nodded weakly. We'd found the beer. We'd won the World Series. Time to go home.

Brian and the rest of us ended up at a Steak 'n Shake at four-thirty, drunkenly wolfing down the world's greatest cheeseburgers as Cardinals fans streamed in and out, dropping by the table, people we didn't know and would never meet again, one big Cardinals orgy that lasted all night. It was the loudest fast-food restaurant outside of Times Square. At 6 A.M., everyone went back to Brian's, and, with a Captain Morgan and Diet Coke in my left hand—knowing I'd need the caffeine—I bought a ticket back to New York that left at eight-thirty in the morning. I had purchased one-way airfare into New York City, with no bags, for a flight that left in two-and-a-half hours. I called a car service and headed to Lambert International Airport. Time's a-wasting. Get out while the getting's good.

At the airport, the woman at the American Airlines counter eyed me suspiciously, probably because I reeked of alcohol and obviously had not slept. Before she gave me my ticket, she wrote "SSSS" on it and directed me to a special security line. I thought little of it.

When I went through the X-ray scanner, the man with the fancy badge and card hanging around his neck looked at me askew and directed me to a back room. "Could you come with me for a moment, sir?" I obliged. He could have told me to stand on my hands and I would have done it. I might have been already, now that I think about it.

In the back room, he opened up my carry-on bag and asked me to take off my shirt and pants. I'm glad he worked there.

"Just doing my job, sir," he said.

I did not care. I didn't mind a damned bit. The Cardinals had just won the World Series, and nothing was going to upset that. The man, named Charles, even noted my giddiness. I looked at him the entire time with the dopey grin of the gleefully narcotized.

"Usually people get a lot more annoyed about this," he said.

"Cardinals, man," I said. "Cardinals."

"Weaver really was amazing, wasn't he?" he said, as he handed me back my pants.

TROY GLAUS is the leadoff hitter, and we're hopeful, with his keen batting eye and Wood's penchant for walks, he can at least reach base, and maybe even pounce on a mistake, like he did with Lilly. The crowd is silent through two balls, then roars for a strike. Another pitch up and in—Wood has been struggling all month—and then . . . outside! Ball four! The Cardinals have the potential winning run at the plate. Lou Piniella, who had warned Cubs fans not to "count their chickens" before the game does his wobbly, tubby, probably-shouldn't-be-wearing-a-baseball-uniform-anymore pace through the dugout. Tony La Russa puts in shortstop Brendan Ryan to pitch run for Glaus. A year later, Ryan will grow an epic handlebar mustache, which, through the power of the mustache, will turn him into one of the best-fielding shortstops in baseball. Right now, though, he just has a depressing soul patch. I hope it makes him faster.

Adam Kennedy is at the plate. When he was announced, Dad—who can never, ever remember the batting order—audibly groaned. I look at Mike, who still doesn't look the slightest bit nervous, or aware of anything around him. Kennedy, even though Wood is always wild and *just walked a guy on five pitches,* swings at the first pitch and bounces weakly to second. Ryan is forced out at second, and Kennedy barely beats the throw to first. Adam Kennedy is just the worst.

The man who will ultimately replace him at second base, Skip Schumaker, comes in to pinch-hit. FOX's broadcast reminds us that the Cubs are on the verge of heading to the postseason two consecutive seasons for the first time in one hundred years. A helpful reminder. "It is a beautiful evening for an outdoor party," he tells us.

"Seventy-four degrees, and these fans are ready." My father and I are focused on Skip Schumaker. Love Skip Schumaker. Guys like Skip Schumaker exist so uncoordinated, untalented white people can convince themselves that they could have played baseball, if only they'd been given the chance, if only someone would have named them "Skip." Of course, Skip Schumaker is an elite athlete; he wouldn't be here if he weren't. But we all hang onto the "Skip."

On a 1–1 pitch, the Cubs/Cards guy next to us answers his cellphone and starts talking about some business deal. Even Mike hates him now.

A ball outside ("You don't want the party to turn into a grilling," McCarver tells us.) and one, two, three foul balls. That's what guys like Skip Schumaker give you. They give you foul balls. Finally, after five fastballs, Wood whips a breaking ball right over the outside corner of the plate. Schumaker is fooled, and he's walking toward the dugout before the home plate umpire even calls strike three. Wrigley explodes. There's one more explosion left to go.

I turn to Dad. "You want to leave?"

He snorts. He knows I'm kidding. The only act worse than watching the Cubs clinch the division over the Cardinals in his first visit to Wrigley Field is leaving a baseball game early. Dad and I once waited out a four-hour rain delay with the Cardinals down 11–1. The world has certain rules, certain laws that keep Earth from spinning out of its orbit and careening into chaos, and you just don't break them. Dad smiles. My dad has a nice smile.

AARON MILES is in to pinch-hit as the last chance. Aaron Miles hits a home run every three or four years. He takes a ball high. And then.

"A high fly ball to center . . . [crowd inhales at once] . . . [Jim Edmonds glides lazily under it] . . . and for the first time in a century . . . BACK-TO-BACK POSTSEASONS FOR THE CUBS!"

I think that's kind of a lame call, myself.

———

"**GO CUBS GO** . . . GO CUBS GO!! . . . Hey, Chicago, whaddya say . . . Cubs are gonna win today . . ."

They're already playing the song, and everyone in Wrigley is singing it in unison, like some cursed, perverted, mutant *kumbaya*. Mike isn't, though. He's just looking down and grasping his hands together, bobbing back and forth. I'm almost proud of him. I look at Dad, and he's mouthing the words to that damn song. (A week later, he will call me, anguished. "It's still in my brain! Goddammit, it's still in my brain!") The Cubs pile in a heap on the mound, hugging one another, dancing around, reveling in the glory of thousands of drunken, wild-eyed blue-clad Northsiders, and Lou Piniella, for the first time all season, appears not on the verge of keeling over. The Cardinals, surely on orders from Tony La Russa, stand on the dug-out's edge and applaud the victorious Cubs. Sometimes La Russa's relentless obsession with sportsmanship drives me up the damned wall. The idiot to Dad's right is hopping up and down like a child not being allowed to pee.

After the song has played six or seven times, the Wrigley PA system plays that Eddie Vedder song. The alternative music revolution of the early nineties has not completely overtaken Wrigleyville— I imagine they listen to Bush, or Sugar Ray, or Snow, or Gerardo, something evil and insidious and wrong—and the crowd quiets, not sure what to sing along with or what to do. It's the first time I've seen Mike look depressed all day.

The Cubs go in the dugout, and that seems to be it. And then . . . they emerge back onto the field with champagne bottles. Each of them appears to have at least two. (Carlos Zambrano is carrying six, I think. It's likely he had them with him all game, or even that he started out with eleven and these are the only six he has left.) They commence a big lap around the field, shaking the bottles up and spraying the bubbly into the crowd, showering the fans that have been lifting them up all season. This is a classy, almost touching move, and Dad can't help himself.

"That's nice," he says. "That's the right way to do that."

"Bah, I hope they knock out some fan's eye with the cork and the Cubs end up getting sued," I say, but I don't really mean it.

AFTER ABOUT half an hour of this, after politely hanging around for Mike's benefit, I suggest that we leave. Mike turns to me. "How many times have we gone to a movie together and you've made me stay through the end credits to 'show respect' for the people who worked on the film?" he says. I do this a lot. It's annoying, I confess. "Lemme stay for the credits, OK?"

We stay for the credits. The song keeps playing. Another fifteen minutes pass. Dad and I stand there, hands in our pockets, stuck behind a slow person in the checkout line. Mike takes his eyes away from the Cubs dugout, where the team has finally headed toward their cramped clubhouse for more drunken revelry, and beams. "All right, I'm ready for a beer. Several." He then looks at Dad and me. "Oh, you Cardinals fans, you're so cute. I gotta get a picture of this."

And he takes this photo:

Dad's the one on the left.

THE STREETS around Wrigley are packed with revelers, and I wonder if they were out there all day or if they just streamed out of their overpriced dingy apartments when they realized a party was about to start.

It doesn't take me long to learn the answer. As we walk out onto Sheffield Avenue, we're greeted with a seemingly boarded-up apartment building, with wooden planks in the windows and what appears to be a padlock on the front door. I must be seeing it wrong, though, because, out of nowhere, people start streaming out of the building through a gap in the second-floor windows. Look, I have proof:

I have no idea who that woman is, but Mike insisted that we pose with her.

It is that familiar glee riot. There's even a man like me at the airport, pantsless and shirtless, running around in a block-long circle, hugging everyone in site. To be fair, my face was not painted blue at the time. His is.

We navigate our way through the masses and find a spot at the Cubby Bear. We take our seats and order a pitcher.

Today, in Chicago, there is no rivalry. As we sit at the back of the bar, Mike trying to boost our spirits by talking about people we used to go to college with and Illinois Fighting Illini basketball, we are not the Cubs' friendly rivals, the sunny contrast to the nasty Yankees–Red Sox death match out east. We are not the hated Cardinals today. We are the Washington Generals. They are the Globetrotters. And they're tossing confetti and juggling basketballs everywhere.

It's for the best, I suspect. When Dad returns from a restroom sojourn—how he made his way through the nine hundred people in this bar, I have no idea—he's got some dude with him, a Cubs fan who got to talking with Dad while waiting in line for the bathroom and now *just can't wait to buy this guy a beer.*

His name is Paul. He has two beers with us. We're there for four hours. We talk about baseball and the Cubs in the postseason and my sister and my girlfriend and Mattoon and college and that time I was on HBO and blogs and journalism and girls and kids and armpits and passing gas in cars and how I have no sense of smell and how crazy this place is gonna be for the playoff games and what would happen if the Cubs actually won the World Series and athlete's foot and that girl I used to date what's her name and the military and the election and is Obama gonna really win and the world's obviously changed 'cause in my day some redneck assholes would have made sure his African father who tried to leave his pregnant white mother never made it to the airport and wow we've come a long way and Hillary's probably still pissed and John McCain's a good man and Mike can grow facial hair but I can't and Dad could grow a beard by forty but he was a helluva lot closer at thirty-two than I am and should the Cardinals go after a pitcher this off-season and we should think about going to Spring Training in Florida next year and how long after the game can we leave our car in the lot and they're probably stingy about that.

Then it's dark, and Dad wants to catch the train back to Mattoon that night, and I have a flight back to New York the next day. "Might as well go now," he says. "I'll be back by midnight." Dad pays the tab. Dad always ends up paying the tab.

AT THE TRAIN STATION, Dad shakes Mike's hand as he gets out of the car, and I walk him to the platform. It always feels like something dramatic should happen on a train platform. Nothing ever does, though, not anymore. I wish more people took trains.

We sit in the plastic Amtrak chairs at the gate, waiting for the *City of New Orleans* back down to Memphis to be called.

"So, I should be home for Christmas," I say.

"Make it back for the Illinois-Missouri game, and we'll sit in the basement. Your girl can come too. You make her a Cardinals fan yet?"

"Well, she's from Georgia, but she has to hang around me, so yeah, pretty much."

We sit in silence. I'll see him again over Christmas. And then next year during the Cardinals trip to New York. And then during my own trip back to St. Louis. And then again at Christmas. And then the same thing the next year, and the next year, until there aren't any more years, until traveling ain't so easy anymore.

I'm not sure parents age. My dad's hair is grayer, and his stomach is larger, and he puts on glasses when he reads the menu at Del Sol for Wednesday night margarita night. But he's the exact same guy he was in that photo with Tito Landrum, and me, and Mom, and Jill. So are they. He'll always be older than I ever will be.

They call for Dad's train. He gets up from his chair—slow, slow, creakier than I'd like—and shakes my hand. "Good game," he says. "Let's do it again next year."

He starts to walk away, and turns back.

"Have a safe trip back to New York," he says. "I'll call you after the game Tuesday. I'll be at Busch. Keep your phone on."

I did. The Cardinals won that one, 5–3 over the Arizona Diamondbacks. They'd been officially eliminated from playoff contention earlier that afternoon, but Ryan Ludwick hit a three-run homer and Kyle Lohse set a career-high with his fifteenth win. Dad still has the ticket stub to that one. He keeps all of them.

"Hey, it's pretty loud here," he yelled that night, just after Ludwick's homer. He kept being distracted by someone sitting next to him.

"Who is that?"

"Oh, that's Joel, some guy I met before the game," Dad said. "I told him about our game at Wrigley, and he bought me a beer. I had an extra ticket. I told him about your Web site. He says he's gonna check it—hey, base hit!"

The crowd roared, and we lost the connection. I can always call him back. I can always be sure he'll answer.

ACKNOWLEDGMENTS

I have no idea why anyone writes books. I've yet to find someone who didn't go slightly insane in the process of putting one together. I wouldn't have survived the process without these people.

My agent, David Gernert, is a stronger believer in me than just about anyone else. I'm not sure where that comes from, but I'm honored and touched by it. At Hyperion, Will Balliett was more enthusiastic about this project at the beginning than I was, and provided the desperately needed "you're doing fine, keep going" prods at every appropriate interval. Sarah Landis was a smart, encouraging presence to shepherd this book to completion; meeting her during the writing process was one of the highlights of the experience. The reason this book makes sense at all is thanks to Hyperion's editing staff, and the reason you're holding it in your hands is thanks to Hyperion's marketing staff. Frankly, I wonder if their names should be on the cover instead of mine. And David Hirshey, who edited my last book, is an ongoing unofficial consultant . . . and, in the process, has become a lifelong friend.

It's not easy to write a book while still working full-time at a magazine, but the following people at *New York* magazine made it possible: Sam Anderson, Eric Benson, Kera Bolonik, Ira Boudway, Lane Brown, Nick Catucci, Jessica Coen, Megan Creydt, Joe DeLessio, Jed Egan, Jon Gluck, Mark Graham, Logan Hill, Hugo Lindgren, Ben

Mathis-Lilley, Adam Moss, Emily Nussbaum, Jessica Pressler, Mary Schilling, Jen Senior, Chris Smith, Adam Sternbergh, Carl Swanson, Ben Williams, and Jada Yuan. Special shoutout to Geoff Gray, who was my one-week writing buddy during a critical time in this book's production.

No one would let me write books if it hadn't been for Gawker Media and Deadspin, where I got my "start," at least in the public arena. (Before that, I suspect the only person who ever read anything I wrote was me. And usually not even that.) So thanks to Dashiell Bennett, Tommy Craggs, Rick Chandler, Gaby Darbyshire, Nick Denton, Jack Kogod, and Lockhart Steele. Drew Magary awes me with his talent and productivity, and I owe him specifically for this book's title, which he came up with. Most of all, thanks to A.J. Daulerio, who has not only kept the site alive, but taken it to places I never could have dreamed. In spite of all that, he'll still be the best man at my wedding. While we're at it: I wouldn't be a writer in the first place if it weren't for Tim Grierson, and I wouldn't have stayed one if it weren't for Aileen Gallagher and Greg Lindsay.

Here's the big list of people who must be included, either because of their inspiration, assistance or their astounding ability to remain my friend. Kimberly Keniley-Ashbrook, Jami Attenberg, Alex Balk, Buzz Bissinger, Amy Blair, Mike Bruno, John Carney, Jim Cooke, Dave Cullen, Jeff D'Alessio, Denny Dooley, Mike Dooley, Matt Dorfman, Mike Dupree, Nathaniel Friedman, Jason Fry, Julia Furay, Eric Gillin, Christopher Goodman, Derrick Goold, Jeff Heckelman, Bob Hille, Matthew Hiltzik, Sally Jenkins, Chuck Klosterman, Dan Kois, Andy Kuhns, Matthew Leach, Josh Levin, Chris Bergeron Linton, Mark Lisanti, Bernie Miklasz, Rob Neyer, Dave Oaks, Kristen Pettit, Matt Pitzer, Whitney Pastorek, Lindsay Robertson, Mike Ryan, Michael Schur, Dan Shanoff, Joe Sheehan, Bill Simmons, Michael David Smith, Wynne Stevenson, Jonathan Supranowitz, Spencer Turkin, and Jason Zillo.

I can't believe Mike Cetera and his wife (and my friend), Joan, let me use their stories in this book, but I thank them for it. We're gonna make young Jackson a Cardinals fan yet.

This book is about family, and mine is the reason for everything I do. So, to my mother, Sally, my sister, Jill, and, of course, the life-force that is Bryan Leitch . . . thank you for being the best mother, sister, and father any human could conceivably ask for.

Lastly, about a month after this book hits stores, I will be marrying Alexa Stevenson, the most amazing person I have ever met. Not only did she help me choose the father-son stories that begin every chapter, she put up with me throughout this entire process. I have no idea how she does it and remains literally the favorite person of every single person I know. I am truly honored to get to spend the rest of my life with her.